D1534858

MOSCOW REHEARSALS

MOTHER by Gorki, at the Realistic Theatre, Moscow

MOSCOW REHEARSALS

AN ACCOUNT OF METHODS OF PRODUCTION IN THE SOVIET THEATRE *by Norris Houghton*

WITH AN INTRODUCTION BY LEE SIMONSON

WITH A NEW FOREWORD BY THE AUTHOR

OCTAGON BOOKS

A DIVISION OF FARRAR, STRAUS AND GIROUX

New York   1975

Reprinted 1975
by special arrangement with Norris Houghton

OCTAGON BOOKS

A DIVISION OF FARRAR, STRAUS & GIROUX, INC.
19 Union Square West
New York, N. Y. 10003

Library of Congress Cataloging in Publication Data

Houghton, Norris.
    Moscow rehearsals.

    Reprint of the ed. published by Harcourt, Brace, New York.
    Includes index.

    1. Theater—Moscow.   2. Theater—Production and direction.
    I. Title.
PN2726.M6H6   1975   792'.0947'31   75-14010
ISBN 0-374-93981-0

Manufactured by Braun-Brumfield, Inc.
Ann Arbor, Michigan

Printed in the United States of America

TO

CHARLES CRANE LEATHERBEE

IN MEMORIAM

FOREWORD TO THE 1975 EDITION

Forty years have passed since I first set foot in Moscow, forty years since I sat down to record my impressions of the Soviet theatre. I was a young man then and the Soviet theatre was even younger than I—by seven years. We were both full of enthusiasm and as I reread this volume I think that some of my own enthusiasm carried onto its pages.

In forty years we have both changed. Since this volume is not an autobiography, my own changes need not be dwelt upon. But the Russians' should be noted. Certainly much of the fervor of revolutionary excitement about which I then wrote has subsided. The intervening years have not been kind to the Soviet theatre and I have been saddened by the visits to Moscow I have made in intervening years—in 1937, in 1960, 1962, 1970, 1973—largely because in forty years I have seen no signs that true freedom of expression, the right of the artist to say what he pleases as he pleases, has made any progress toward realization. I thought surely by this time the Soviet Union would have acquired sufficient self-confidence to allow for artistic freedom, but apparently not.

Nonetheless, rehearsals in Moscow are still exciting experiences, the artists of the theatre are still dedicated and vastly knowledgeable of their craft, and performances in Moscow are still worth travelling 6,000 miles to see. Because I believe, however, that what happened there in the mid-1930's may never since have been duplicated in Russia or anywhere else, I am persuaded that this account can be read today both for its historical value and for the insights it can perhaps provide into the contemporary theatrical scene in Moscow.

NORRIS HOUGHTON

New York
1975

Preface

B OOKS in English about the Soviet theatre have been written for the most part by critics and historians of the stage who have criticized and chronicled. Being neither critic nor historian, I have attempted to make a record of the Soviet theatre not externally from the standpoint of an observer and recorder of effects, but internally through the eyes of a participating craftsman. No one who spends even half a year in Soviet Russia can expect to come out unaffected in one way or another. I went in expecting to concern myself only with the technical processes of an art. I came out six months later filled with all sorts of ideas (and confusions, too, I admit) about that art and about the Soviet experiment-which-is-no-longer-an-experiment and about the relationship between the two. The technical processes are recorded herein and some few of the ideas and impressions besides. These latter have become for me the significant part of the whole study.

I really have no right to call this an account of the Soviet theatre, for it is concerned only with the theatres of Moscow. Six months was not a long enough time for me to study with any thoroughness the dramatic work in other parts of the Union, so it seemed wiser to concentrate my attention within the capital. But I am aware, and wish to point out emphatically, that excellent work is being done in Leningrad, in Tiflis, and in other places to which I make no reference.

Since my study has been confined to Moscow, the theatrical center of Russia, New York, the theatrical center of the United States, has seemed the appropriate city of

America to compare with it when comparisons have offered themselves as a means of pointing the meaning to various things I have seen. I hope that the frequency of allusions to the New York theatre will be accepted with this understanding by readers in other parts of the country.

The reader who discovers that I have not touched upon the Soviet ballet, opera, or cinema must not conclude that I do not consider them worthy of report. Again the limitation of time has restricted my field to the dramatic stage, and it is just because I consider these other branches of the theatre to be so important that I have preferred not to do them the injustice of a cursory study.

In the rendering of Russian proper names, always a difficult problem, I have generally followed the scholars' international system of transliteration which, while rendering such familiar names as Tschaikowsky unfamiliarly as Chaikovski, yet seems to me the closest and most accurate method to employ.

I have been frequently asked since I left the Soviet Union whether I was allowed to see the things I wanted to see, whether I had freedom to come and go and to talk to people as I pleased. I should like to record the fact that every effort was made by everyone with whom I came into contact to open up to me all the work of the Soviet theatre which I wished to observe. To P. I. Novitski, head of the Theatre Section of the People's Commissariat of Education, I am particularly indebted, as much for the information derived from personal conversations with him and from public addresses of his, as for his courtesy in officially introducing me to all the theatres of the R.S.F.S.R. To all the theatre directors, actors, régisseurs, designers, playwrights, technicians, trade union and government officials with whom I was associated in my work, and whose name is legion, I am equally obliged for generous co-operation.

My first acknowledgment, however, must be to the Guggenheim Foundation whose appointment of me to a Fellowship made this study and the writing of this book possible. My thanks also go to Professor Henry Wadsworth Longfellow Dana, who helped me to break the Moscow ice; to Lee Simonson for valuable assistance in the pursuit of my study and its publication; and to Elizabeth Reynolds Hapgood for assistance in translating the material in the appendix to this book.

NORRIS HOUGHTON

Introduction

FOR the artist all roads once led to Rome; yesterday to Paris. Today, for the artist in the theatre, whether actor, director, or designer, the road leads to Moscow and the theatres of the U.S.S.R. Like the successive schools of modern painting in France during the last half of the last century, they formulate with gusto and precision aesthetic problems that are hazily conceived elsewhere and produce astounding solutions that become patterns of experiment for the rest of the world. But unlike so many of the experiments of modern painting, the productions of the Soviet theatre are never purely technical *tours de force*, are rarely esoteric, and are not addressed to coteries of specialists. They have been understood and greeted with enthusiasm by huge audiences that continue to pack every theatre to the doors. The exponents of the art of the theatre in the Soviet Union have accomplished what the doctrinaire leaders of every other form of modern art have failed to do: they have been daring and original; they have not compromised for an instant with what, in every other country, the public is supposed to want, and have nevertheless created an art that is fundamentally popular, evokes mass enthusiasm from the Caspian to the Baltic, and is integrally a part of national life.

Neither famine, pestilence, nor the fear of sudden death impeded this theatre's growth in the early days of the Revolution when our first American observer, Oliver Sayler, dodged street fighting on his way to the doors of the playhouses where Stanislavski, Tairov, and Meierhold imperturbably carried forward their programs. In spite of the successive economic crises of the Nepmen period, and the Five Year Plan, the Soviet theatre has grown to an amazingly fecund and vital national art. Under an absolutist political régime it has remained free to accomplish what most of the presumably free theatres of Europe and the United States still fumble for. Every variety of method is practiced simultaneously and is pushed to a maximum of expressiveness, every degree of realism and stylization in acting, direction, and stage setting. In contrast, the programs and the pretensions of our "art theatres," dedicated to the cult of a romantic freedom of expression, seem uniform and even stereotyped. Often the same play, acted and staged in diametrically different ways, can be seen in the same season at rival playhouses. Every kind and variety of playwrighting holds the boards simultaneously: the classics of Europe such as Shakespeare and Schiller and the classics of bourgeois Russia such as Tolstoy, Chekhov, and Ostrovski; romantic plays such as "Camille," the romantic operas of Wagner and Bizet as well as the romantic operas of Chaikovski and Moussorgski and in addition operas, plays, and ballets, proletarian in their ideology or vehicles for revolutionary propaganda. Eugene O'Neill's "Anna Christie," "The Hairy Ape," "Desire Under the Elms," and "All God's Chillun" have been successfully staged. There are as well comic operas, satirical revues, theatres for children, puppet plays, and the folk plays of the Jewish, Ukrainian, and Georgian theatres. I visited Moscow twice, for a week in 1926 and for another in 1932. Had I been able to stay for three I would undoubtedly have written a friend what Norris Houghton wrote me last winter: "I have been in Moscow twenty-one days. I have been to the theatre twenty-one nights, and I have not seen the same play twice." I ended each visit by seeing two plays a night, and climbed into

my sleeping-car berth and stayed there twelve hours to re-
cuperate, each time, from the most exciting week of theatre-going I had ever known.

The Soviet theatre has been analyzed and described in
illustrated books and illustrated lectures. I have read most
of these books and given some of these lectures. But none
of them, I think, has sufficiently centered attention on the
questions which most interest any student of the modern
stage: What is the source of the Soviet theatre's amazing
and inexhaustible vitality? How and why does it so consistently renew its energies? The Soviet theatre is of course
heavily subsidized. But a subsidy in itself has never saved
a theatre from routine dullness; witness the Comédie
Française, the Odéon, or most of the royal theatres and
opera houses of pre-war Germany. Our experimental theatres rarely survive a decade and if one does it ceases to
be experimental. Most of our younger generation can
graduate from college courses on playwrighting and play-
making only into the little theatres that never grow up.
The perennial complaint about most of our talented actors
is that so few of them mature as artists. Why do the ideas
of our innovators so rarely get beyond the pages of illustrated monographs, why does so little of the creative imagination they might give the theatre get through the stage
door? What in contrast is the especial gift of the Russians
which enables them to fuse and integrate their talents
into a dynamic theatre, that cannot be stamped into a
single mold even by the iron hand of revolution, that has
survived half a dozen aesthetic revolutions of its own, that
continues to foment them and yet remains an integrated
whole?

This book is, I think, one of the first, if not the first, to
analyze in adequate detail the aesthetic organization of
the Soviet theatre in an attempt to understand the tech-

nique of its creative efforts, to study not only the product but the process, to explain how and why the work of the Soviet theatre is done so completely and effectively that the eventual performance is almost invariably dramatically expressive and emotionally exciting. Although Mr. Houghton spent every night in the theatre, he was wise enough to spend his days in the rehearsal room, wise enough, before he started out, to acquire a working knowledge of the Russian language so that he could understand what he heard there. Knowing at first-hand the methods of American theatre production he is equipped as well to give us a first-hand picture which reveals how complete the aesthetic organization of theatrical resources can be, how fundamental the training of the actor, whatever his method, how deeply a director's imagination, whatever his theory, can permeate every moment of a performance. We begin to understand not only why the rehearsal of a play can take six months or more, but why the final performance is an expressive whole and not a mass of over-elaborated detail. Mr. Houghton gives us fresh, sharpened, and concrete analysis of the incessant interplay of theory and experiment, emotion and idea, the patient integration of body and voice, inflection and meaning, movement and environment, picture and action, which finally brings a script to life.

The road to Rome, Paris, or Moscow is a dangerous road if too piously trod. Salvation cannot be imported. An excessive admiration of the greatest models breeds the academy. Mr. Houghton, as his final chapters show, is well aware of this; he makes no pretense to have discovered a secret or brought home a formula. But even the casual reader of these pages will become aware of the kind of intelligent, coherent, and concerted organization that is needed in our theatres if the giving of plays is to remain for us a vital form of contemporary art; and every worker in the American theatre, after sitting in at these Moscow rehearsals, should get a fresh sense of the kind of creative effort that lies before us if our own theatre is to fulfill its present promise.

LEE SIMONSON

Contents

List of Illustrations

Mother,   *frontis.*

Following page 140

Intervention
Pickwick Club
The Iron Flood
Aristocrats
Dead Souls
Woe from Wisdom
La Dame aux Camelias
Masse-Mensch
The Optimistic Tragedy
Egyptian Nights
Eugene Onegin
Prince Igor
The Storm
Intervention
The Human Comedy
Love and Intrigue
Eugene Onegin
The Spanish Curate
Twelfth Night

MOSCOW REHEARSALS

CHAPTER ONE

Moscow Scenes

SEPTEMBER first is called International Youth Day in Soviet Russia. It was on that day that I arrived in Moscow to begin my six months' study of the theatre. Moscow is, on days of big celebrations like this Youth Day, a vast theatre in itself, and I arrived in the midst of preparations for one of its frequent spectacles. In the late afternoon I was taken on my first drive through its streets. The choruses were assembling in the outlying factory districts, ready to march with banners and songs to the great Red Square, the stage of this demonstration, where against the towering whitewashed brick walls of the Kremlin, their audience—including Joseph Stalin—would witness the performance and greet the participants. It is astonishing to eyes used to parti-colored displays to discover the exciting effect of great masses of solid color. Everywhere was red, only red—flags of red, streamers of red, buildings draped in red. Against the background of such decorated streets, the slowly advancing lines moved toward the Square.

The performance was to begin at seven o'clock. Its routine consisted in the youth of Moscow marching past their leaders, several hundred thousand strong, in their massing afterward within earshot of the giant loudspeakers which would amplify the staccato phrases of Comrade Stalin speaking from the rampart of Lenin's tomb. Seven o'clock found me on the way to the Opera, to the first perform-

3

ance of the International Theatre Festival which I was using as a kind of quick introduction to Moscow's theatres. The car had to be abandoned halfway to the theatre because many streets were closed to traffic that evening. As I threaded my way through the lines of young people waiting to move to the Red Square, I felt that there, all about me, was *real* theatre. In one street the crowd was singing in lusty unison; at a corner three boys were dancing a peasant dance while the group around clapped hands to keep time for them. "The Russian is infected with a passion for spectacles," wrote Stanislavski. He was talking of the stage, but there in the streets, before I had entered a single theatre, I felt that passion. I should have liked to stay on with the crowd, to march with them to the Red Square and watch them stage their mighty show, but I had come to see the other kind of spectacle, so I went on to the Opera.

The faraway music of the bands and the tramping of distant feet echoed through the classic portico as I entered what is one of the handsomest grand opera houses of Europe. Inside, the elegance of Russia's Empire style remains untouched—the white and gold rococo decorations, the crimson satin damask hangings, the crimson velvet chairs of the orchestra floor, all are still there. But there is a new curtain hanging in the vast proscenium and its all-over pattern of hammers and sickles and revolutionary dates reminds one that this is no longer the imperial opera —now it belongs to the proletariat.

The full orchestra played the rousing Internationale in stately tempo, the audience resumed its seats, the curtains parted, and the opening scene of "Prince Igor" was revealed. What a surprise! Here were colorful settings very much in the conventional operatic tradition but given a new vividness and warmth by this Moscow artist; here were gorgeous costumes and trappings, huge choruses which filled the sixty-foot stage; the whirling Polovtsian dances I had nowhere seen more lavishly staged. The opera of the proletariat was a match in magnificence for any royal or plutocratic opera anywhere in the world! Outside the house, water-stained old Muscovite palaces and cathedrals might be crumbling in desuetude or striving to keep face through utilitarian service to the cause which had destroyed their creators, but within the theatre the splendor of barbaric Russia's castles and churches, princes and slaves filled the eye with romance, pomp, and glitter.

It was the theatre, however, rather than the opera, which I had come these six thousand miles to see, and the next night was my introduction to it. The play was "Intervention" by a Soviet writer named Slavin and the theatre was the Vakhtangov Theatre. Plays begin in Moscow at seven-thirty and one must be prompt, for late-comers are not admitted to the auditorium until the first intermission. I had arrived in ample time and so had opportunity to study my surroundings. This was one of the most important theatres in Moscow, I had been told, but what a strange-looking place it was—no gilt, no cherubs, no rococo details here; no velvet curtain, no upholstered seats, no carpets, no crystal chandeliers. Plain plastered tan walls were without relieving ornamentation of any sort. A mouse-colored heavy flannel curtain hung in the proscenium; a row of spotlights on a bar hung from the ceiling a few feet in front of the curtain without masking of any kind. The seats had no cushion padding, no upholstery. Like undertaker's folding chairs, their wooden backs were set at the most uncomfortable angle possible. The thought that I must sit thus bolt upright for the four hours which I had been told Russian plays lasted, was disconcerting. "Certainly the theatre offers little to charm its audience here," I reflected. I mistily thought of the red plush of the old Empire Theatre in New York and of

the blue velvet of the theatre in Indianapolis where I saw
plays during my childhood. That was what theatres should
look like. They should have glamour, they should take one
away from humdrum life into some enchanting place
where splendid things might happen. This theatre was
matter-of-fact, hard, real. It could become at once a huge
hospital ward or a laboratory if its chairs were exchanged
for the proper fittings.

Having thus taken startled stock of my material surroundings, I surveyed my fellow spectators. They, too,
were quite matter-of-fact looking. Most of them appeared
to have come straight from their work—no jewels, no
soft satins, no smooth shirt fronts. I admitted that such
costumes would have looked amiss in the coldly utilitarian
auditorium, but they would have helped me to feel a little
less strange. It seemed to me that every tenth person in
the theatre was a soldier. I tried to remember when on
Broadway I had seen privates or "gobs" in a legitimate
theatre, but I could not. And how many boys and girls!
The New York theatre is on the whole an adult theatre.
Save at Christmas holiday times, our audiences are middle-
aged audiences. Nightly in Moscow half the crowd seems
to be under twenty-five. A bell rang twice through the
foyers. There was a final surge of people entering. I looked
about and scanned the balcony and the orchestra. Not a
single empty seat! I was to go to the theatre ninety times
in Russia, and not more than a dozen times was I to see a
vacant chair.

The lights dimmed and the play began. Its story was set
in the days of Allied Intervention during the Russian
Revolution. Odessa, Black Sea port in the south of Russia,
was busy with Bolshevik and counter-revolutionary intrigue during the hot summer days and nights of 1920.
The opening scene, in a little park overlooking the quai,
was electric with tension. In the harbor below were a few

Allied battleships, from the interior news of Red advances kept coming. The Russian theatre has a way of throwing you at once into the heart of its excitement, no slow build-up; we are in two seconds thrust into the midst of it all. The stage floor slopes upward away from the audience at almost a thirty degree angle. A strange effect that gives —the spectators seem to be hurled straight up into the action and the actors seem to be projected out into the audience. The effect is much as it is in a nightmare when the earth seems to rise up to meet you and then is suspended halfway. Against a deep dark blue sky the sharp scarlet, corn yellow, emerald green, and white of the park's formal flower bed stand out in hard sunny relief. The sun scorches down on the populace scurrying nervously about, stopping one another to ask for latest news, scanning the sea's horizon. What a populace! This is no theatrical mob scene. In fact, it is no mob scene at all. There are only a dozen people moving. Each one is a vivid personality—soldiers in white uniforms, shop girls, grand ladies with stupid escorts, young students, each one a definite individual. None of them seems to look like an ordinary person, yet all seem to be very real. Again one is reminded of a nightmare. Men with long noses have *very* long noses, women with large hats have *very* large hats, thin men are *very* thin, fat ladies are *very* fat. They are a little like characters of a Peter Arno album come to life. They are all real types but exaggerated and caricatured to become something more than single individuals. They speak with sharp, biting rapidity; everyone is obviously living at high nervous tension—but that was the kind of days they were.

The opening scene is short. It stops with a jerk. The curtains close. But there is no pause. From entrances beside the proscenium the characters enter onto a forestage and continue the action. Perhaps it is a street, it does not matter. The point is to keep things moving. No time to draw a breath. Now another full stage scene. The plot begins to unfold. There are a group of Reds carrying on undercover work in this seaport town. The hero—if there is a single hero, which there isn't; there are half a dozen of them—seems to be tutor of the son of a rich bourgeoise. She is conniving with the Allied generals. The son, a good-for-nothing, tries to sell information to whomever will pay a good price. Eventually he betrays his tutor into the hands of the Whites.

The action continues in short staccato scenes jumping about through Odessa: to the docks, to the headquarters of the White army, to the tutor's study, to the park again, to the warehouses of the merchant woman, to the laundry shop where in a back room the Commissars meet their agents while ironing girls in the front shop sing two songs —one to warn of strangers' approach, one to tell of the arrival of friends. Never in the theatre have I heard music used to create such excitement and suspense as do those two monotonous little themes. Music, incidentally, carries through much of the performance and always it increases the tension. Most excitingly staged is the scene in an out-door café where the tutor is tracked down by White sol-diers and caught as he sits at a little table. There are a dozen such tables on a terrace which seems to hang at the edge of space—there is only the deep night sky be-yond. The quiet crowd of seaport folk at the tables watches exhibition dancing on the little stage at one end of the terrace. But the audience cannot watch the dance; it can only keep its eyes fixed on the little table in the corner where the tutor sits behind a newspaper. It feels the im-minent danger, the most remarkable communication of intangible fear I have ever seen in the theatre. I try to force my eyes to wander over the scene and take in the moving couples and figures, to watch the waiters come and go, but I can only sit transfixed, waiting for the end. It comes.

The play moves on to the prison cell where the tutor and two other captured Red companions are confined; then on to a drug store where the traitorous pupil is shot as he runs out into a thunderstorm; on to the side of an Allied transport ship where all the populace assembles to seek escape from the advancing Reds; on to the final scene where three of the Interventionist soldiers, forsaking their comrades, are shown ascending the great steps of Odessa to join the Bolsheviks and replace, in number at least, the three comrades who had been executed—the tutor and his two friends.

With three pauses for breath, which is all the intermissions seem to be, the play has swept through to its end. The auditorium's bleakness has been forgotten because the stage has been so alive. A decorated, soft interior would have hurt the atmosphere of this kind of drama. This is living stuff. We have all, the Russians and I, forgotten the hardness of the wooden chairs, forgotten the stiff backs. We have been sitting only on the very edges of our seats for four hours. Now that the performance is over, the enthusiasm of the crowd is unleashed. They stamp and cheer. The play has been in the repertory for a year, I am told, but the ovation is like an opening night's. Every performance in the theatre in Russia seems like a "first night." There is the same electric excitement in the air time after time.

When I went home that evening, although still hot with excitement, I tried to think soberly about the performance and to catalogue my impressions. First of all, I was sure that this was one of the theatres about which I wished to know more. The Vakhtangov Theatre's bright, vivid style attracted me tremendously. Here was the substance of reality but with an added outward form which made it more than a mirror of life. There was nothing abstract about these people and this action, and yet there was a theatricality which made everything seem intensified to a point where it became almost unreal. Certainly I had never seen theatre like this. I must discover what they were driving at and how they accomplished these startling effects.

Then I considered the play. It was not a very well written play, I was sure of that, although my Russian was still pretty sketchy. There was far too much complication and confusion in its development. There was also a great deal of hokum and melodrama, I knew, and there was a great deal of what we should call the elements of propaganda. All these things I had been brought up to disapprove of in the theatre. Why was it that their presence here did not offend me, that instead it excited me? I decided that the melodrama was so good because it was *real*, that the propaganda did not seem to be such because it was simply the portrayal of actual history.

Two days later I entered for the first time the Moscow Art Theatre, a spot sacred and awesome to the man of the theatre, for it is the home of the greatest dramatic organization of this century. It is a quiet and distinguished place. The audience seems to talk in lower tones here; their hair is combed more carefully. Their shirts are cleaner than in other theatres. They seem to share the foreigner's respect for the ground they tread. There is carpeting on the floors here and softer lights. The walls are a dull gray green and the woodwork is dark oak. There is little decoration save in the promenade foyer where photographs of their great men and scenes hang on the walls in dignified array. The seats are unupholstered here, too, but after the experience at the Vakhtangov Theatre, I am prepared to forget their existence altogether. The curtain with its famous sea-gull, the device of the Art Theatre, taken from Chekhov's play, "The Sea-Gull," parts, and the play, "The Days of the Turbins," begins.

This is a play dealing with the same period and events as "Intervention," but what a difference! The performance begins quietly in a gentle drawing room with violet-tinted walls and white woodwork. It is evening and the curtains are drawn in the windows. The lovely pieces of Russian Empire mahogany glow softly. There are quiet and intimacy. The Turbin family, two brothers in the White Russian army, and their sister, are gathered for an evening at home. A country cousin, an amusing gawky lummox, and another White Guard officer, the sister's lover, join the group. There is a supper, cheerful talk, some drinking and an argument. The scene which began so quietly mounts naturally to an exciting end, though how, it would be hard to describe, for there is nothing apparent about it. It seems to flow from within itself without a break. Actors talk to one another in the tones of normal conversation. Their entrances and exits are not stage "business"; they are simple comings and goings. When they sing the old Russian national anthem, grouped around the piano, it seems the most obvious and natural thing to do, nothing "stagey" at all. On this stage no actor is better than any other; there is complete give and take. One finds oneself interested in the family, in the whole group of people, not in each character separately.

The story of the play is complicated, particularly to a foreigner not conversant with the intricacies of the counter-revolution of the 1920's. That two wings of the White army opposed each other while both were opposing the Reds is confusing, but it is the activities of these two White forces that form the plot of the central part of the play. There is a scene in the general army headquarters of the Ukraine which shows the desertion of the White commander into the protecting arms of the Germans when the Reds press close; there is a scene in a trench hut where the ragged, hairy, common troops campaign in cold, dreary bitterness—a striking contrast to the red and gold elegance of headquarters.

There is a magnificent scene in the huge stair hall of a deserted schoolhouse where the White soldiers, told of the treachery of their general, are ordered to disband by their colonel, eldest of the Turbin brothers. They refuse, and demand that they be allowed to continue to fight for their tsar—a striking situation to find in a Bolshevik play. At the top of a long sweeping staircase, rising directly away from the audience, Alexei Turbin stands with drawn revolver facing the angry young cadets, thirty or forty of them filling the stair and the hall below. All we see of them are the backs of their long dark blue coats and an occasional head turned in profile, but we feel their surging movement up the stairs, their check, irresolution, change of mind, their renewed determination, their final defeat, all visible in the backs of their heads and the set of their shoulders as they listen to Alexei's sharp incisive phrases while he paces the landing above their heads. This scene is highly dramatic, it is of the essence of the theatre, and yet one feels that it is not theatrical. The excitement is real. One is oneself standing on the stairs. The cannonade that announces the arrival of the Red army in the city seems no stage effect, and when a detachment of Reds enters the hall and Alexei is shot as he stands alone on the stairs, one is overcome by that helpless feeling that one should be doing something to assist and cannot.

The play ends in the quiet key in which it began. The younger brother, wounded too, but not fatally, is carried home unconscious. The tragic news of Alexei's death is told in a simple and profoundly moving scene. There is no stage grief, the sorrow here is real. These are no actors

playing a scene; the people in this violet room have lost a
dear companion. On the play moves to a final scene. It is
Christmas Eve and enough months have passed for the
room and its inhabitants to have taken on their usual appearances again. While the country cousin helps Elena to
decorate the simple Christmas tree, the Red army advances
into the town. Its approach is merely felt within this room.
When at the end of the play the bands of the victorious
invading troops are heard playing in the distant street,
and the Turbins stand quietly at the window listening to
the strains of music that heralds a new order and a new
day, we know that life for them is over and it seems a hard
thing.

When this play was first produced about eight years
ago, it was promptly banned, for, as one can appreciate, its
picture of the hated White Russians was a little too sympathetic to please hardened Red hearts. But after five or
six years it was allowed to reappear and has ever since been
one of the most popular plays in Moscow. The reader may
draw his own conclusions as to the meaning of this change
of attitude.

This performance at the Moscow Art Theatre was not
the shock to me that the Vakhtangov's had been, because
I was more prepared for it and more accustomed to the
style which is the basis of most of our own. Except for the
big scene on the stairs, there was little that was highly
spectacular in the production. Its greatness lay in the con-
summately artistic use of the material offered by the playwright and by the actors; in the elevation of the very non-
spectacular to the highest reaches of drama; above all, in
the living, breathing reality which was so completely re-
created. All the things that I had expected of the theatre of
Stanislavski were there. But in the next performance
which I saw at the Art Theatre and in still another one

later, things I had not expected were exhibited and I was
given new revelation of this great theatre's work.

Three days after I saw "The Days of the Turbins," I
returned to see "The Marriage of Figaro." Here was
theatre of a completely different order. Here was fantasy,
lightness, music, dancing. The settings of Golovin established at once the spirit of the performance. His major
color scheme was bright orange and cerise. Visualize that
combination of colors and you know what the production
was like. I call to mind enchanting rococo swirls and
curves, little gilt chairs, vividly striped walls, high pow-
dered coiffures decked with bright feathers, little swinging
iron-railinged stairways up and down which scampered
hoop-skirted chambermaids pursued by amorous peri-
wigged valets, and a final scene in a fabulous garden with
at least a dozen little rococo summerhouses, and everywhere boxwood hedging, in and out of which popped the
cerise and orange and emerald-green figures, moonlight
over all, tiny Chinese lanterns strung all about through
the hedges, and a finale in which the entire stage started to
go round and round in time to tinkling music.

This was indeed a revelation. A theatre that could play
with such simple dignity the moving story of the last days
of White Russia on one night and on the next serve up
such delectable fantasy which seemed to have no connection with the temper or the manner of the theatre of real
life, must be studied. Although the style was so different,
there were things that carried through from the other Art
Theatre production I had seen: the ensemble acting was
the same—all characters seemed to be equally important,
equally interesting and equally well-played. The fantasy
seemed to be *real* fantasy, if that paradox conveys something. What that connection was I determined to find out.

My determination was strengthened by their "Pickwick
Club," a dramatization of the Dickens book. I went to

the theatre a little skeptical. How could a Russian theatre, especially one as intensely Russian as the Moscow Art itself, bring to life characters as intensely English as Dickens'? I need have had no qualms. This theatre became for those few hours nineteenth century England. The Mr. Pickwick was the Mr. Pickwick one has always imagined. Sam Weller and all the others were made completely, vividly alive. They were not story-book characters, they were people with the most astonishing set of idiosyncrasies imaginable, wearing the most startling pink waistcoats and striped trousers, but still quite real. The settings were vividly alive too—real and yet highly theatrical, a great surprise in the Moscow Art Theatre. The first scene consisted simply of a backdrop, in the center of which was painted a huge mirror and in the painted mirror was the painted reflection of all the rest of the room—the other walls, the window, the sunlight pouring in, the tables and chairs. None of this scenery was actually on the stage. All of it was shown to us in this mirror. In a later scene when Mr. Pickwick was in jail, the scenery suggested a Thomas Benton mural. Again there was but a painted backdrop, the great barred entrance, beside it a stairs and above it a gallery, and then—what was remarkable—the place was peopled with figures, painted on the stairs, on the gallery, all over the place! All the rest of the world has been saying for twenty years that you should not combine two-dimensional scenery and three-dimensional actors, is still saying it. It was a lesson which the world learned partly from this Art Theatre itself, and here in 1934 was that same Art Theatre, sanctum of realism, painting tables and chairs on its drops and mixing up painted figures and flesh and blood people on the same stage!

These three plays were not, of course, the only plays I saw at the Moscow Art Theatre. There was the unforgettable performance of Gorki's "The Lower Depths," after seeing which I felt certain that the soul of the theatre is words and acting. These actors, Kachalov, Tarkhanov, and the rest might have played their play in an empty barn and I would, I am sure, have been just as moved to laughter and to tears. Lights, scenery, and costumes passed unnoticed beside the power of these people who could make you laugh one minute and cry the next by the simple movement of a hand or the tone of a voice. There was "The Cherry Orchard" which I saw twice, the second time at the gala performance on the seventy-fifth anniversary of Chekhov's birth, when Knipper-Chekhova, the playwright's widow, played Madame Ranevskaya, and as many of the other actors as still remain played their original rôles. There were a dozen other plays which I saw at the Art Theatre, all of them memorable performances.

The reader must realize that the Art Theatre, like all the other theatres in Moscow, performs according to the repertory system. That means that each theatre has anywhere from four to fifteen different plays which it is prepared to perform in rotation, a new play each evening. In America we know this system only through its application in the grand opera and in a few Shakespearean companies, Eva Le Gallienne's Civic Repertory Theatre a few years ago, and in one or two other isolated professional and semi-professional theatres. To the artists, this system is of great value, for it keeps them from ever getting into that rut into which constant performance of the same play night after night for months forces our actors. They approach each performance fresh and alert. The theatre keeps itself flexible and the public has much more to choose from. For the foreign theatre student it is a grand system, for it enables him to see for himself how the style of each theatre has evolved. I could see, for instance, "The Lower Depths" as it was played in 1902, "The Marriage of Figaro," created in 1927, and "Pickwick Club" just finished.

It is as though the Theatre Guild were to continue to play from time to time "The Goat Song," "Caesar and Cleopatra," "The Doctor's Dilemma," "Reunion in Vienna," "R.U.R.," and "Strange Interlude," for instance, side by side with their new "Taming of the Shrew" and "Porgy and Bess." To do this, of course, they would have to have a permanent acting company and an exceedingly flexible acting company, and that is what each Moscow theatre has.

There are some forty professional theatres in Moscow and by that I mean much more than forty playhouses. I mean forty groups of actors and actresses, directors, technical, literary, and administrative staffs who work together not only from play to play, not only for a season, but for years. That is why I felt some hidden connection between a performance of "The Days of the Turbins" and "The Cherry Orchard" produced more than twenty years before. That is why after seeing "Intervention" at the Vakhtangov, I was prepared for the brightness and theatricality of "Princess Turandot" or "Love and Intrigue" at the same theatre. Each theatre seemed to have a language especially its own. Every production was played in that language and all its actors seemed to know it and speak it. They could do this only because they had been talking it together for a long time.

From that week of the International Theatre Festival another evening stands out. It was the evening of my first visit to the Meierhold Theatre. Meierhold, I had always been told, was the leader of the Revolutionary Theatre. His name was coupled with the photographs I had seen of strange constructivist scenery—the stage filled with ladders and platforms, ramps and slides and bare scaffoldings. I was curious to see what was meant by this, for when I had seen it tried in America, I had felt that neither audience

nor many of the artists had had any idea what it meant.
I was not, however, to find out that evening, for the play
which Meierhold had elected to present to the Theatre
Festival was his latest, "La Dame aux Camélias." While it
was certainly a different sort of theatrical experience from
any of the others I had had in Moscow, it was far from
being the revolutionary revelation I had expected.

I entered a theatre which looked at first glance like any
other in Moscow until I turned to the stage. Then I saw
that there was no curtain hanging in the proscenium and
the unlighted set was standing in place. Unmasked spotlights stood on platforms in various parts of the auditorium. Suddenly there was a crash on a huge gong and
the lights flashed out—another crash and the stage lights
snapped up and the play began. The shock with which
the performance got under way was so different from the
gentle easing into action which I was used to, slowly dim-
ming lights, if any sound that of fake church bells or
dinner chimes, that I was at once startled into attention.
That was the intended effect, I suppose. But where was the
constructivist scenery? To my untutored eye this looked
like an unfinished high school production. Across half the
stage hung a pale blue flannel curtain on a wire; it
stretched diagonally from the lower right hand corner
where the proscenium should have begun and did not.
This curtain was about twelve feet high and above and
behind it were visible the tops of other pieces of scenery
and the railing of a staircase. On the opposite side of the
stage was a piece of solid wall with a French window in it.
It stood in space; that is to say, it had no connecting wall
on either side of it, there was no ceiling above it. Instead of
the ramps and scaffolds, there was a huge grand piano,
Louis XV and XVI chairs, rugs, gilt candelabra, fine stuffs
strewn about the stage. As I made this examination the
performance was proceeding. The cast was dressed in fine

stuffs as well; there were many jewels. Music played intermittently. All this was far from creating a realistic illusion—there could be no doubt that this was complete theatricality—but the surprise at finding Meierhold using actual things, actual windows and doors and fireplaces at all, was so great that I failed to appreciate just what he was doing with them.

I need not tell the familiar story of Camille. All I need to remark upon is that the whole thing was played in a sharp staccato key, which is the one way, I am sure, it should not be done. Characters jumped and bounced about the stage with disconcerting vigor. Actors kept making entrances from the side doors of the auditorium whence they climbed up on to the stage. When the act was ended there was a blackout, then the house lights came up. Those who did not go out to promenade saw the crew come out on to the set, sweep the stage, rearrange the properties, prepare for the next scene. Never for a moment either before, during or between and after the action was one allowed to forget that he was in the theatre. There was no effort made to re-create an illusion. Meierhold is unalterably opposed to that. That is one reason, I believe, why "La Dame aux Camélias" was an unfortunate choice for his theatre. There were, however, many superb moments in the production, effects of startling beauty. These were chiefly based on compositional arrangements of movement and pose. It would be a far cry, perhaps, to liken the gambling scene to an Italian fresco, but the same flowing rhythm locking the figures together and carrying the eye in swinging movement up to the stairs and back again, is apparent in the Meierhold staging. Movement was the challenging thing in this theatre, and it was to find out how this movement was created that I was anxious to make further study of Meierhold's work.

Before I did so, however, I returned to see other performances of his. Cromelynck's comedy, "The Magnificent Cuckold," was more the sort of production I had expected of Meierhold. Again, when I entered the theatre it was to find no curtain. But the stage presented a different picture this time. The brick back wall of the stage formed the background. In front of it on the bare stage was an arrangement of platforms whose scaffoldings were completely unmasked. The bare boards and cross bracings were all visible to the audience. There were ladders and slides and three wheels of different sizes hanging above the highest platform which were later to revolve, apparently at will. There was no furniture on the stage, nothing that looked like anything! It appeared to be a structural representation of the thriller equipment of Coney Island stripped of its painted externals. There was a fairly large cast; everyone in it was dressed alike in blue jumpers. It looked as though a group of airplane mechanics or gas station attendants had gathered together to put on a play. The plot is the old triangle situation, a man, his wife and her lover, given by Meierhold what they call in Russia "social meaning." This is apparently accomplished by the introduction of acrobatics. The cast races and tumbles about the stage, turns somersaults and cartwheels—and all for a purpose. I can suggest this purpose by describing the entrance of the lover. At another theatre there would be a knock at the door, the man would enter, see the object of his affection, move toward her with eager steps, smile and take her in his arms. They would both "register" joy at the meeting. Meierhold places the lady at the foot of a tin slide, the lover climbs up a ladder to the top of the slide, zooms down it, feet first, knocks the lady off onto the floor, and shouts something that sounds like Russian for "Whee!" Thus does Meierhold express the effect of an eager lover meeting his mistress. The spirit of the scene is established directly by this completely abstract action. Of course, Meierhold knows that lovers don't enter down slides in real life, but he believes—or did twelve years ago when he produced this—that the emotion of abandonment and joy with which the man is filled can much more accurately be revealed if he slides down a ten-foot S curve to meet his lady than if he follows the dictates of natural movement. When this is understood, there is some meaning to Meierhold's work. When other things are understood, there is still more meaning to it. I decided that apart from the fact of the historical importance of the Meierhold Theatre as the mainspring of the revolutionary stage in Russia, I wanted to study his work in order to appreciate better his finished productions which I would see.

It was after the Theatre Festival was over that the Realistic Theatre opened its season. I went to its opening night to see a play called "The Iron Flood." The Realistic Theatre is also called the Krasnaya Presnaya Theatre in Moscow, named for the district of the city in which it is situated. It is a young theatre, it is experimental, its style is not yet definitely set, it is a theatre for a predominately worker audience, there is nothing like it in Moscow. All this I was told before I went. It sounded as though it would make a good fourth theatre in which to concentrate my study, for I wanted one to represent the young revolutionary studios. (I had already decided to study the methods of the Moscow Art Theatre, Meierhold's and the Vakhtangov theatres.)

That night was one of the most exciting I spent in Moscow. When I arrived in the little building which houses Okhlopkov and his company, I found the doors of the auditorium not yet open. The audience was standing in the foyer. I assumed that since this was the opening night, something had gone wrong within the theatre. Finally, when all the audience had arrived and was restlessly moving about in the foyer, we were startled by a couple of people who burst open a door of the auditorium from within with a shout, dashed out through the crowd and disappeared. At the same time the other doors were flung open and the audience entered the auditorium. But was it the auditorium or was it the stage? There was no curtain, no proscenium, no stage at all. Opposite the entrance doors a long mound stretched. From behind it a blue dome of sky rose, swept overhead and down behind where I stood near the doorway. One end of this raised hillside was screened with bushes; the other end sloped down with rocky incline toward the door from which the two people had emerged into the lobby. Along two sides of the mound were chairs and into them the bewildered audience found its way.

The hillside was filled with people making preparations for a camp fire. The two who had run through the crowd had been off with a jug to get water. The whole place was in the half-light that precedes night. It was impossible to read a program in such light, but there was no desire to, for I was too busy accustoming myself to the situation. Was I sitting on the stage with these actors, or were they in the auditorium with me? The half-light became less around me, the light on the hillside increased, the action, which had already been going on, became coherent and the play itself began. There was little to it. This, it seemed, was an advance detachment of the Red army which we had joined, an army of men, women and children, engaged in the Bolshevik Civil War. They were cut off from the rest of the Reds and were about to face a wing of the Whites. Their preparations for camp, for attack and defense, the battle and their final victory, snatched from impending defeat with the aid of the regular Red troops who arrived at the crucial moment, were the stuff out of which the play was made, nothing more. That

evening we spent four hours with the Red army in the
field—that was all; but what an experience! Imagine
coming in off a quiet street and finding oneself in a
pitched battle. The harrowing excitement of the film "All
Quiet on the Western Front" had this to relieve it, that
the audience was looking on from seats a hundred feet
away from the screen on which the action was pictured;
one could look from it to the reassuring red twinkle of the
exit lights and remember that one was really in a building
on Broadway. But here the action was all around you.
The wounded dragged themselves across your feet, the
people were cheering each other on beside you, the relieving troops you could hear coming behind you and sweeping over you, above your head the night sky hung. A
racking experience that, and one I do not recommend to
theatre-goers who want only to be amused. I came out
trembling on the surface and profoundly moved within.
Here was theatre that was life. And if it was to me, how
much more so to the rest of the audience, to men and
women who had themselves slept on a rocky slope with one
arm under a loved one's head and the other clutching a
machine gun, to people who had themselves gone through
the agony of those days.

That night I understood what the Marxists had been
driving at in their "interpretation of art." This was an
exaggerated example, no doubt, but it made their point
more real. Art, they had said, must be part of life, it must
reflect the struggle that is going on in life, a struggle based
on class aligned against class. Art cannot exist for its own
sake; art as escape is impossible; ivory towers are impossible. The individual artist cannot look upon his creation
as the expression of his own individual emotions; he cannot become absorbed in his personal relationship to a dish
of grapes or a plate of dead fish. He must use his art to
convey some meaning to the beholder. His music, his paint-

ing, his verse, his theatre, must have meaning for the people, must concern itself with them and their problems. In Russia the people are everything. "Art must belong to the people," said Lenin. It does.

The excitement of these half dozen performances which I have described I experienced often again both in these four theatres and in many others. I remember, for instance, the first production which I saw at the Kamerny Theatre of Tairov. It was of a Soviet play called "The Optimistic Tragedy" by Vishnevski. The inside of the Kamerny Peter Fleming has described as looking like the inside of the turret of a battleship. With its flat unrelieved gray walls, its two upper boxes which look like observation posts, its proscenium which curves concavely away from the audience and in which a gray steel fire-curtain opens heavily sideways to reveal another gray flannel curtain hanging within, that is exactly what it does resemble. It made an ideal setting for "The Optimistic Tragedy," a play about the conversion of the Russian navy to the side of the Bolsheviks in 1918. Two sailors flanking the proscenium addressed the audience directly in excited tones before the play and in the intervals between scenes. They were a sort of combined commentator and exhorter. The stage was set in a stylized abstraction of an arena of battle. Low architectonic forms in gray were massed against a dark gray-blue sky across which at times scudded darker gray clouds, against which at other times was the silhouette of barbed wire pickets. Without much change it was now the deck of a cruiser, now a battlefield. Soldiers in dark blue lined themselves against each other, some supporting, some opposing the single woman Commissar who commanded the field. Superb lighting and staging and movement of masses of people were the things that gripped me in this performance—all of these aesthetic reactions, you note. The acting was not great and I was little moved beyond the sensuous satisfaction derived from a well-mounted production. That continued to be my reaction to this theatre after I had seen other plays—its surface technique was excellent, beneath that there was little.

I could fill this volume with descriptions of play after play which I saw in Moscow. I could tell about the rollicking but exquisite performance of "Twelfth Night" at the Second Moscow Art Theatre, done against a sepia drop of an Italian hill town, among a forest of slender gold Renaissance columns and arcades; about plays done in Yiddish at the Jewish Theatre, or in Gypsy at the Gypsy Theatre. I have described mostly Revolutionary history plays, but there are many other kinds, and I could describe farces like "Strange Child" at the Satire Theatre, or plays about problems of contemporary Soviet life like "My Friend" at the Theatre of the Revolution, or old Russian classics, Ostrovski at the Maly Theatre, Chekhov, Tolstoy at the Moscow Art, classics which continue to draw great crowds. I could make this book a series of descriptions of exciting evenings in Moscow theatres, but that is not what I want to do, for I myself was really more interested in what went on by day in these theatres, how these various breath-taking effects were being conceived, how these artists were working at creation. I wanted to find out what it was like to work under almost ideal conditions, in a place where there was no commercialism in the theatre, where the state was supporting all losses, where the stage was free to set the standards of culture as well as to reflect them. Here the stage could lift the people to it, not sink to them, for it need keep no eye on its box office. Here it had an audience which flocked to its doors—it seemed almost as though the theatre were to the Russian people what sport is to America.

With performances by night of plays like these I have

described, and operas, ballets, cinema; with rehearsals by
day in half a dozen theatres watching something created
out of nothing; with conversations with great artists explaining why they were doing the things I saw them do,
the six months were filled. They swept by like a single
week and scarcely before I had time to draw a long breath,
I found myself on a ship looking back over the Black Sea
at the receding coast of Russia. I am a theatre craftsman,
not a dramatic critic. I am interested in means quite as
much as in ends, and the methods of the Russian stage are
as exciting as its results. In Moscow people in the theatre
are not working through trial and error, by intuition.
They *know* what they are trying to do. They seek consciously to perfect their art. That is why study of their
processes of work is so envisioning, why it becomes the
key to an understanding of the finished products as well
as of the greatness of the theatre itself. There are other
keys. They will come afterwards. First, let us examine the
way these theatres work.

CHAPTER TWO

Preparation for Work

THE DEMAND for actors and theatre workers exceeds
the supply."

I was sitting in a large handsomely furnished room in
what was no doubt once a merchant prince's mansion on
a quiet side street in Moscow. In its merchant prince days,
however, the room probably had no large flat-topped
mahogany desk such as the one across which I was facing
Tovarishch Furminova; it certainly had no Tovarishch
Furminova. She is the director of the Technicum of the
Central Theatre Combinate, a large and powerful woman
with a gentle smile and a grace of manner which belies
the severity of her black dress and her sizeable desk. She
is a famous figure aside from her position in the school, for
she is the widow of Commissar Furminov who worked with
and has recorded the career of Chapayev, both of them
heroes of the early days of the Revolution. It was she who
made this significant statement.

"The demand for actors and theatre workers exceeds
the supply." Surprising news that is to one coming from
the New York theatre of today. In America young people
are urged to enter any profession other than the theatre,
which they are told has room for no one unless he is outstandingly able; even then he may have to walk the streets
and the casting offices for several years before he is allowed
to prove that he is. For three years I myself tried to be
allowed to show New York that I could design scenery,

27

but the union which controls that branch of art refused
me admittance simply because the supply exceeded the
demand. And now Furminova was saying, "The demand
exceeds the supply." If I do not use that statement as the
text of a book (and I very well could, for in those words
is summarized one of the great forces affecting the theatre
in Russia today—there is a *demand* for it), I can at least
use it as the text of this chapter. It is the way in which
the theatre meets this demand for more actors and artists
about which I wish to talk—the way it makes more actors.

An American man of the theatre one day remarked to
me, "I go to Moscow after three or four years' absence
and find scores of young actors who were not in the theatre
before, but who play with a maturity which suggests that
they've been acting for at least ten years. See if you can
find out when you are in Moscow where they come from
and how they are trained so rapidly."

The Russians are famous for their training of dancers.
The praises of the ballet schools of Moscow and St. Petersburg have been sung for years and everyone knows that
the Russians take their future "prima ballerina assoluta" at
the tender age of seven or eight, subject her to the most
rigorous training and give her the most meticulous care
for a good ten years before they consider her ready to toe
her way into the spotlight. It would be surprising if equal
attention were not paid to the training of artists for the
dramatic theatre, since it also occupies such a distinguished
position among the arts of Russia. The attention is comparable but its methods are less spectacular, for the emphasis is placed not on the small child but on the older
young person, as it must be, the training being not so much
physical as intellectual.

The preparation of actors and other craftsmen and
artists of the stage is effected in Moscow through two formal channels and in one rather indirect fashion. First,

there are the schools, or "technicums," as they are called, which are associated directly with individual theatres. There were about eight of these in 1934. Each theatre controls and administers its own, absorbs the graduates into its permanent company, and is thus able to extend its work because of the increased number of members at its disposal. The Maly, Kamerny, Vakhtangov, Meierhold, Second Moscow Art, Gypsy, Jewish and Revolutionary theatres all had technicums in operation while I was in Moscow. Secondly, there are the schools of the theatre organized and administered under the direct supervision of the People's Commissariat of Education. In Moscow only one such existed in 1934 and it was the Central Theatre Combinate, an amalgamation, as the name implies, of two schools, the State Theatre Technicum and the State Theatre Institute. The third training field, a feeding ground to some extent for the other two, is the theatrical collectives within the factories and collective farms. All of these latter are amateur and none of them exist for the direct purpose of helping the professional theatre create new actors as do the technicums and the Combinate, but it happens that the regular theatre schools draw many of their students from these collectives.

2

The widespread desire to participate in the theatre, either as a spectator or as, in almost any humble way, a performer, which is testimony to the Russian's talent for and his love of the theatre, accounts, I suppose, for the fact that almost every large factory and farm has its dramatic circle with a regular program of work.

It was during the first year of the First Five Year Plan that the "Agit Brigades," as they were then called, came into being. "Agit" is an abbreviation for "agitational" and their purpose during this early period in the drive for rehabilitation was to present through various means criticism of current problems and to engender enthusiasm for the tasks at hand. It was really a two-fold purpose which they had: dramatic expression and propaganda, and of the two I suspect that the latter was uppermost in the minds of the participants. Their material was crude and topical, more animated posters than anything else, and little attention was paid to form. One factory group produced twelve plays in a single year. Under such circumstances they had very little connection with the art of the theatre except as an expression of the primitive urge to present ideas more clearly through dramatic representation.

In 1932 an Olympiad of these "agitational" groups was held. After it, a decree was issued by the government demanding that they give more attention to artistic principles. It is interesting that this came at the same time that the professional theatres were being told by the government that they might exercise more self-determination, and a general lessening of the propaganda element in art was being felt. Out of the "Agit Brigades" developed dramatic circles which paid more attention to their actor members than to the dramatization of social slogans. Instead of a dozen plays, only four or five, but of better quality, were produced a year. Emphasis was placed upon technique of speech, movement, study of the history of the theatre, and upon raising the cultural level of these groups. To assist in this work came instructors who were actors in the various theatres, the Moscow Art, the Vakhtangov, and the others. Factory laborers in Moscow were, and are, being made familiar with the working ideas of the great theatres. Imagine the union of locomotive engineers in this country organizing a dramatic club where the members in their spare time discuss the methods of the Theatre Guild as opposed to the Group Theatre!

Not every laborer, of course, participates in this work as a performer. Probably not more than six per cent of the workers in a factory are active in its dramatic circle, and most of them are younger workers. They work in the factory until three-thirty or four o'clock, then in the evenings they go to their club where the dramatic circle has its own room or, in some cases, even a stage. Here about twenty evenings are spent in rehearsals under the direction of a professional actor. If the production is particularly good, it is given in one of the larger clubs and at several performances, even perhaps going on a little tour through the districts of Moscow.

In 1934 a second Olympiad was held and a number of the "agitational" groups represented showed marked improvement. Until this last year the repertoires of these groups were chiefly composed of club plays, written for amateur consumption, and they probably did not get very far from a rather infantile projection of social propaganda. But now these groups are producing many of the same plays as the big theatres, and classical dramas find a place along with Soviet ones. Molière seems to be popular with these amateur groups who are not, I am relieved to report, encouraged to tackle Shakespeare. Two modern plays and one classic in each year's program is the repertoire of the average "agitational" dramatic group.

I can best illustrate the tie between these collectives and the professional theatre by telling of a young man who was a member of the dramatic group in the great automobile factory at the edge of Moscow named after Stalin. He was very much interested in acting, and showed such capability that he was allowed to play the leading rôle in one of the group's plays. The manager of the factory happened to attend—it may have been his custom, I don't know—and he was tremendously impressed by the talent of the young mechanic-actor. The next day he telephoned to the First Art Theatre. "I have here," he said, "a boy whose acting I think quite good. I wish you would send out someone from the Theatre to the next performance of the circle and see what you think of him. If you consider that he has real ability, I should like to have you take him as an apprentice to the Art Theatre. The factory will pay his expenses." The Art Theatre sent one of its régisseurs who agreed with the factory manager and the boy was accepted as an apprentice.

I like this story because it illustrates a situation so different from the one existing in America, and because it helps to answer the question which is so frequently asked: "But"—the question always begins with "but"—"but is there any chance for a person who shows talent? Don't they all become standardized and mechanized and have to work in factories?" At every point the story shows how different is the approach to the theatre in Russia and America. First, how many factories in the United States have good dramatic clubs for their manual laborers (not the white-collar employees)? Second, if such clubs existed, how much interest would the average business executive take in its activities and with how much critical judgment could he witness its work? Third, granting a good club and an artistically sensitive director, what theatre exists in New York which would be sympathetic to his suggestion that it send out a representative to Paterson or Hackensack, let us say, to consider a talented mechanic as a possible apprentice; in the fourth place, how many theatres in New York have permanent apprentice groups in which the young artist could become enrolled to learn more about his art? It is more common for casting directors to send young men back to factories (without offering to pay their expenses thereto), than it is to imagine the reverse procedure taking place in the United States.

3

To get an idea of the training work which the large theatres of Moscow are doing, let us follow this young mechanic of ours through his career of the next four years. The Moscow Art Theatre, at which he has been accepted, has, at the present time, no formal technicum. It has preferred in recent years to accept three or four exceptionally promising young people into its organization each year, not to go through a regular course, but rather to come, through an assimilative process, to a knowledge of the Stanislavski system in theory and practice. These youngsters are thus thrown much more closely into contact with the actual production work of the theatre; all of them play from the outset at least walk-ons in three or four plays; they attend rehearsals and the practice classes which the members of the theatre company themselves continue to hold. Their training is as rigorous as that received in the larger and more organized schools of the other theatres, perhaps more so because, in view of the small number of apprentices, the work is more personally supervised. There is no set point in the Art Theatre's plan at which the apprentice ceases to be one, and becomes a full-fledged member—no graduation exercises. The customary time of apprenticeship is from three to four years, but less talented young people may serve a longer period of trial before doing any real acting; a very able one may get a nice little part or two while still only a cub.

We should get a much better idea of Moscow theatre training if our mechanic had been sent to the Kamerny Theatre Technicum. This Technicum is the oldest in Moscow affiliated with an individual theatre. It has existed for eleven years and in the season of 1934-35 it had sixty-nine students. Our young worker, to have been admitted there, would have had to submit to the entrance requirements of the Technicum along with the other one hundred and fifty or so who annually apply for admission. He would have to have received an elementary school training, and then he would have taken an examination in reading—dramatic reading, the early stages of it held as a sort of group contest. As the weeding-out process advanced, he would arrive at last at the point where his work would be judged by Tairov himself, and if the director of the theatre approved of him, he would be accepted. If it was in 1934 that he entered, he would have been one of the twenty-eight students who, accepted from the one hundred and fifty applicants, formed the first-year class. The ages of all of them were about eighteen.

His first year he spends only part of his day at the Technicum. Since he had been living in Moscow while working at the Stalin automobile plant, he doubtless already has a room and so would not be eligible for the dormitory which is provided to house the students who come from the collective farms or are accepted from cities or towns outside Moscow. He will probably continue, as a matter of fact, to do his work at the factory by day, for the work for first-year students is only part-time.

The early autumnal Russian twilight will find him on his way to the theatre, for at five o'clock his classes begin. Entering through the side door he climbs the stairs to the second floor above Tairov's large "cabinet." Here at the top of the theatre there are three or four bare white-washed rooms, an office, some showerbaths. His first class this afternoon—the schedule varies each day—is dancing (ballet, not ballroom, of course), so donning his practice costume, a pair of trunks, he enters the practice room. For thirty minutes there will be work at the bar, then half an hour devoted to some elementary *pas* and *tours*. He works at this with such diligence that the casual visitor dropping into the room to see what goes on might well think that he had entered a regular ballet school. Just as the Russian *maîtres de ballet* believe that their pupils should have a little dramatic training, so the directors of the theatre Technicum think it best for their actors to have a grounding in the ballet. Of course, the student cannot get very far in his ballet work (as a ballet master would be quick to assure him), since he only began it at eighteen, but a few hours a week at it should, after four years, give him flexibility of body and balance. A visit to a fourth-year dancing class and a comparison of its work with the "freshmen's" proves that.

Our mechanic-turning-actor continues in classes each of an hour's duration until about eleven o'clock, having had time-out in the early evening for supper which he would be given free in the theatre's dining room. His class in dancing would not be his only exercise. He would have an hour (not these same courses every day) of what the curriculum lists as "gymnastics: rhythmics," an hour of acrobatics and an hour of fencing. At the Kamerny Theatre probably a larger amount of time is spent in fitting the body for the stage than at most of the technicums, for Tairov's system is synthetic and his actors must be able to execute whatever patterns of movement are the basis of the production. They must be able to dance and pantomime, if it is light opera which Tairov is next to mount. His famous musical show, "Giroflé-Girofla," requires the cast to perform enough circus antics to justify their course in acrobatics.

At the beginning of his second year, the student must give up his job as mechanic, for now the business of becoming an actor is going to occupy his entire day. He will now receive the small stipend which is granted to all students after their first year by the *Narkompros* (abbreviated title in Russian for the People's Commissariat of Education, which I shall use hereafter to designate that department of the Soviet government). His work will have to improve as he continues in the Technicum, for there is a weeding-out during the four years, and by the time he enters the third year his class will be about half the size it was at entrance. In this third year he will be appearing in mob scenes in the larger productions, perhaps even in his second year he was drafted for this; in his fourth year he will understudy and play a few "bits." Therefore much of the time in these last two years will be spent in actual rehearsal on the big stage.

During his four years he will have studied a great variety of subjects. *Narkompros* has made certain minimum requirements which all theatre technicums must meet, so that for the most part when we study the curriculum of the Kamerny Technicum we are also considering the curricula of all the other schools. The government places a great responsibility on its artists and it wishes them to be as well and as broadly educated as possible. The courses include Political Economy, History of Western Theatre, History of the Russian Theatre, the Russian Language, Russian Literature, Western Literature, Psychology, History of Art, History of the Methodology of the Kamerny Theatre; Voice Production, Choral Singing, Solo Singing; also Make-up, Stagecraft, all the Gymnastic-rhythmic-dancing-acrobatic training I have described, and most important, of course, Mastery of Acting. The courses in history, literature, politics, economics and art are required by *Narkompros,* the relative attention paid to music and physical culture varies with each technicum, and the Mastery of Acting each theatre teaches in terms of its own system and the ideas of its creative leader. From the beginning every potential member of the company receives a grounding in the idiom and the style in which he will later create. It is this which helps to give each theatre its own internal common-ground of understanding of terminology and of aim.

For a clearer idea of this key course in Mastery of Acting, let us go to the Technicum of the Maly Theatre. Since mastery of acting is the basis of the Maly's fame, we should learn more from this particular course there than elsewhere.

During the first year of the course not a word is spoken —all is in pantomime. This is one of the elements of the Stanislavski preparation. In fact, the Stanislavski system is the basis of training for the students at the Maly, as it is for most of the Moscow theatre technicums. In the second year, when the control of movement has been learned and the necessity for speech can no longer be restrained, but has developed directly and simply as a consequence of the movement, words are added. Almost at once the second-year student is plunged into Shakespeare and Molière. He is not expected to grasp the subtleties of the rôles, it is simply felt that when the time comes to use words, they might as well be grand ones, and the director of the Technicum believes that the characters of Shakespeare and Molière are more sharply drawn and clearly defined than characters in the Russian classics. Therefore, study of Ostrovski is postponed until the third year when the student works also with Ibsen and Hauptmann; then concentration on the psychology of the rôle is begun. In the fourth year the students work on two studio productions: one Russian and one foreign classic. Now they go back to Shakespeare, to Molière or to another classic, and this time try to "incarnate" the rôle. In other words, whereas in their earlier study they had only occupied themselves with the words of the play and the external shape of the characters, now they delve into the meaning of the drama and try to give psychological reality to the people of the play.[1]

This seems to be pretty advanced work for young actors between the ages of seventeen and twenty-five, twenty per cent of whom have been enrolled from collective farms where they have had only the sketchiest literary education—many of them almost illiterate. But it shows how Russia's great classical theatre tackles the problem of preserving the classic tradition for the future generation and of creating actors who can work directly and intelligently with classic material. It also serves to show how the emphasis varies in different theatres. At the Maly it is mastery of the "mighty line" and familiarity with Shakespeare at the tenderest age possible, while at the Kamerny it is complete control and flexibility of the body.

If we go to the school of the Meierhold Theatre we shall see the same attention paid to physical development. It is not called a technicum there, for it does not offer the full curriculum required of an official technicum; it is more a large and organized group of apprentices. A great deal of the student's time from his very first day is spent in actual rehearsals conducted by Meierhold personally. For reasons which I shall subsequently point out, this is particularly essential at the Meierhold Theatre. Every morning there is a class in "bio-mechanics." This is the basic principle of Meierhold's revolutionary work. The official definition of bio-mechanics formulated by one of Meierhold's chief régisseurs, Korenyev, and approved by him, suggests that the term may be applied in connection with the preparation of the actor.

"Bio-mechanics," writes Korenyev, "is the name given by Meierhold to a method of training actors elaborated

[1] The further explanation of this, which is part of the Stanislavski system of acting, appears in the succeeding chapter.

by Meierhold himself. The actor must acquire the neces-
sary skill for his profession through a study of movements
of people and animals.

"The subject of bio-mechanics is an attempt to find
active laws for the actor's movements within the frame of
the stage. With this purpose in mind, Meierhold made
experiments in drawing schemes for the movement and
style of acting, its exact definition and regulation, taking
into consideration all possible needs of the actor.

"The trained body, the well-functioning nervous sys-
tem, correct reflexes, vivacity and exactness of reaction,
the control of one's body—in other words, the general
feeling for space and time, and coördination of move-
ments with each other—such are the results of the appli-
cation of bio-mechanics. Such is, at the same time, the basic
approach, which, together with a certain talent for music
and a certain amount of intelligence, Meierhold asks from
his actors."

I spent an hour one morning watching the Meierhold
apprentices at work. There are no classrooms in his theatre,
for at this time he is occupying a renovated moving picture
house until his own new building is finished, and space is
at a premium. All classes are held in the lobby of the
theatre where, behind a few screens, the twenty-five young
men and women of the group were practicing. It was an
exercise to music based on the movements of a boxing
match, and the give and take, thrust and guard, had been
carefully observed and set down in a formalized annota-
tion. "The actor must acquire the necessary skill for his
profession through a study of movements of people and
animals." When this exercise was completed after many
repetitions, mattresses were brought out and the boys of the
group practiced tumbling for another half-hour.

In addition to their work with bio-mechanics, I was in-

terested to learn that the students are required to study the
Stanislavski system of acting. This, I think, is a surprise
to people who know how bluntly Meierhold opposes the
art of the Art Theatre, but it shows forcefully how
fundamental all Russian theatre people consider Stanislavski's training methods to be. I should say that everyone
in the Moscow theatre world has a knowledge of the essen-
tials of that system even though he may devote all his day
to a refutation of them.

4

I have left Tovarishch Furminova sitting behind her flat-
topped desk for a most discourteous length of time. It
is high time we returned.

Every book about the Soviet Union must contain a few
statistics and since Furminova furnished me with the only
interesting ones relating to my field, I feel that this is the
appropriate spot to unburden myself of them, although by
the time the reader gets to them, the statistics will undoubtedly be no longer applicable! It seems, according to
Furminova, who was one of a Commission appointed by
Narkompros to assemble the figures, that before the Revolution in all of Russia there were 250 theatres; now there
are 560. Before the Revolution there were a paltry 8,000
actors, 1,000 of whom were chronically unemployed; now
there are nearly 25,000, none of whom are unemployed.
There are, in addition to the 25,000 actors, 1,500 régisseurs to direct them, and 5,000 other theatre specialists—
managers, directors, literary advisers, etc., to assist, supervise and interpret them.

Furminova offers us other statistics more directly concerned with the subject of this chapter. There are now
throughout the Union 4,687 clubs which are either
dramatic or have theatre groups active within them. These
include the clubs in factories and collective farms which I

have previously described. There are now 168 theatrical schools, whereas before 1917 there were but 30 in the whole country. Today these 168 schools are teaching 26,000 students.

St. John Ervine, in his review of Markov's recently published book, *The Soviet Theatre*, condemned the author harshly for his emphasis on statistics, particularly concerning the number of playhouses newly built or about to be built throughout the Union. He announced very positively that we must not forget that quantity does not mean quality, and in this I heartily concur. The Bolsheviks, like the Americans whom they admire, are very apt to place too much faith in figures; at the same time Mr. Ervine's native theatre has neither quantity nor quality of actors and artists comparable to the Soviet, a statement which I trust he will not try to refute until he can speak from personal observation.

The demand-exceeding-the-supply situation exists not only in Moscow but throughout the Soviet Union. If anything, there is a greater demand for actors, for theatres, in the provinces than in the already well-supplied capital. The entire country, made familiar with the dramatic supremacy of Moscow through years of hearing of it, looks to that city to furnish it with its artistic mentors. It is to supply this demand that the Central Theatre Combinate is chiefly concerned. Its Technicum is unique among the 168 dramatic schools in that it is the only one which does not prepare individual actors only, but is devoted to the preparation of a whole collective theatre. Its Technicum prepares the company, its Institute trains its commanding or leading staff. To make clear the difference between them, I shall consider them separately, the Technicum, being the more elementary school, first.

As the Combinate has for its aim the supplying of theatres to the country, so it goes to the country for the material out of which to organize them. The majority of its students come from outside Moscow. Each year a traveling staff of twenty makes a huge tour of the U.S.S.R., visiting the clubs and factory circles of the provinces. They even penetrate into remote parts of northern Siberia and central Asia. Wherever talent appears to them, they bring it back to Moscow. In 1934 there were 2,000 applicants for the Technicum's three sections: drama, music-drama, and theatres for the national minorities. Into the first section sixty were accepted, into the second thirty; the national minorities came as groups, there being now four of them. The choice from among the applicants is made on the basis of an examination which they undergo when they get to Moscow; the unsuccessful ones are sent back to their provinces, the successful ones are given dormitory rooms, provisions are made for their food, and a small stipend, varying with the individual's ability, is given. For all this *Narkompros* pays and it is now supporting five hundred students in the Technicum.

The students of the drama section are divided into groups, the nuclei of future collective theatres. These groups retain their identity throughout the four-year course. They are trained collectively and they go out together to form a theatre. There are about thirty young men and women in each group. This creation of a whole theatre seems to me one of the most interesting of the many experiments in collectivization in the U.S.S.R. It is also exceedingly valuable from the standpoint of preserving, for the rest of the Union and for the future, the Russian tradition of the perfectly integrated acting ensemble in the theatre.

Perhaps the quickest way to outline the curriculum of the Technicum would be to present in the following table form the courses required during the four years. There are no electives. By an examination of the number of hours devoted to each and the place in the four years where the work comes, you can see for yourself the way in which the young actor's training develops and where the emphases lie.

Course	Hours First Yr.	Hours Second Yr.	Hours Third Yr.	Hours Fourth Yr.
History	130			
History of Communist Party		60		
Political Economy		60		
Economic Politics		60	40	
Dialectic Materialism		90	70	
Russian Language	90			
Russian Literature (19th century)	90			
Literature		90		
Military Affairs	45	70		
Psychology			70	
History of ancient theatre	90			
History of modern theatre		90	90	
History of Art			50	
History of Literature			40	
Gymnastics	65			
Rhythmics	90	90		
Dancing	90	90	65	80
Physical Culture		45	45	
Acrobatics		45	45	
Fencing			90	
Diction	180	165	135	40
Mastery of Acting	390	410	590	850
Music Appreciation	90	90	70	
Make-up		90	60	
Playwriting				90
Directing				90
Stagecraft				90

The most important course is obviously, and quite naturally, the Mastery of Acting. It is in this key course that the group asserts its unity. An instructor is chosen for the group from one of the important theatres—an actor, for in the Technicum prominent actors teach actors, régisseurs teach régisseurs. Most of the instructors come from the Moscow Art Theatre, for since the Stanislavski system is the basis of all teaching of acting here, it seems wise to have the teaching come directly out of his own theatre. There are, however, instructors from the Meierhold Theatre and from the Kamerny Theatre as well. The instructor who takes over the group teaches it, in any case, the principles of his own theatre, whichever it be, for the four years. This gives the group artistic cohesion and a common style which, after four years' study, it has come to understand. The first years are the significant ones, for that is the formative period. Most of the students have arrived young and fairly inexperienced, at least unformed in style. (They are eligible from the age of sixteen.) After the grounding in the system which will characterize the group, the students study as part of the Mastery of Acting course in their fourth year "modern theatrical trends." This study gives them a knowledge of other systems of acting than the one which they are making their own. It broadens them but does not really affect their previous three years' preparation.

I remember particularly, from among classes which I attended, one in Mastery of Acting. It was my first visit and when I arrived the work was already in progress. The instructor was a young actor of the Art Theatre, but at the moment he did not appear to be instructing. In fact the entire room was in silence. It was a lesson in pantomime. One after another the students rose, performed the complicated piece of pantomime through which each tried to tell a story. When the pantomime was over the student explained the story and the instructor pointed out at what points it failed to carry to its audience. When the class was dismissed, a dozen or so of them came to my corner to have a talk with their American visitor. We were all about the same age and they were as interested in my reactions as I was in theirs. Adroitly they became the interviewers instead of the interviewed, and the young Soviet Russians have a way of asking direct and often embarrassing questions. Which Moscow theatre did I like best? Were American designers better than Russian designers? What system of acting was practiced most widely in America? What did Americans think of the Russian theatre? Who paid for the cost of production in American theatres?

The music-drama department of the Technicum is divided into four groups. These groups are not collectives like the drama sections, for to send out a complete opera theatre would require ballet and orchestra as well, and the Technicum is not prepared to train them. In music-drama work the methods of the Stanislavski and Nemirovich-Danchenko Musical Studios are being followed. In fact, a number of the members of those Studios are trained here. An examination of their curriculum reveals that the Mastery of Acting courses occupy the largest number of hours in the first two years but are not taught thereafter. Among the background courses, foreign languages appear—a noticeable omission from the preparation of drama students. The courses pertaining to music naturally predominate, although potential prima donnas are required to study physical culture, dancing and make-up as well.

The department devoted to the creation of theatres to send to the national minorities is an exceedingly interesting one. With more than half of its territory lying in Asia, the U.S.S.R. contains within its boundaries many peoples whose civilizations and cultures are both picturesque and backward. Recognizing the value which the theatre has

been to it in propagandizing European Russia, the Communist Party wishes to utilize it to carry its message to
the faraway reaches of the land. Above and beyond that
purpose, which is for the Communists a utilitarian one,
there is a desire to build up for its own sake whatever
artistic form exists in the primitive dances and dramas
which these people have and also to bring to them some
Western culture.

There are four groups which have come from these
minorities to the Central Theatre Combinate. There are
the Ossetians who come from a remote part of the Cau-
casus, the Yakuts from the extreme northern part of
Siberia, the Kazaks who inhabit the part of central Asia
which includes Turkestan, and the Kara-Kalpaks from the
southern part of central Asia. Each of these groups has its
own language, and it is in that language that most of its
work is carried on, although all these minority groups in
the Technicum are learning Russian.

I shall always remember a class of Yakuts which I
visited. From their home well within the Arctic Circle, it
takes them two months of traveling to reach Moscow.
When their summer vacation arrives, they have just time
to get home, spend three days with their people and start
back again! They were dressed in that pathetic approximation of western clothing which ill becomes so many of
the Bolsheviks and ill fits all of them. Their faces were
strongly Mongoloid, there was an Eskimo quality about
their appearance which shirt and trousers or cotton dress
could not eradicate. They were rehearsing in their own
Yakutian language a translation of Molière's "Le Bourgeois Gentilhomme"! To see these tiny black-haired
yellow-skinned young men trying to assume the airs and
manners of the French seventeenth century was amusing
and a little touching. They worked very hard and they
showed a nice sense of humor. The rest of the class who

looked on while the half-dozen performers went through their scene was very eager and enthusiastic. They were all obviously anxious that I should like it too. I did.

In the State Theatre Institute which forms the other half of the Combinate are one hundred and twenty students between the ages of eighteen and thirty or thirty-five. There are four departments in the Institute. The first is devoted to the training of régisseurs [1] for drama and opera. The second is for scholars and scientific specialists in the history of the theatre. The third is confined to the preparation of managers of art sections. The fourth trains young people to become the managing directors of theatres.

Seventy per cent of the first course for the training of régisseurs is Mastership of Acting. Without exception every person in Russia with whom I talked about directing plays stated it as his belief that a régisseur could direct capably only when he knew as much about the art of acting as could be learned from being an actor himself. How different this is from the situation in New York where directors have served apprenticeship as either playwrights, stage managers, designers, or at schools where in courses on the "art of directing" they have only read about actors. In Moscow the great directors frequently—some of them regularly—appear with their companies, they perform side by side with them. When, if ever, has New York seen Guthrie McClintic, Philip Moeller, Gilbert Miller, Rouben Mamoulian, Elmer Rice, Robert Edmond Jones, Norman-Bel Geddes, Worthington Miner, any of our better-known directors, appear on their own stages? I do not say that they should, any more than I say that Stanislavski and the

[1] Clarification of terminology seems necessary before proceeding further. Throughout this study I use the word "régisseur" as synonymous with the American director of a play. The foreign Theatre Director, as referred to later in this paragraph, is the equivalent of what would be an American *super*-theatre manager.

other Russians should not. I merely wish to emphasize this difference in the point of departure in direction.

This attitude toward directing explains why the Institute requires its students of directing to learn as much about the mastery of acting as it requires its students of acting to learn. In this first course a play is taken up and everyone works on it as actors and régisseurs. In the second and third years a certain amount of time is spent in observation of production methods at the better theatres in Moscow. At Vakhtangov Theatre rehearsals I used regularly to meet a boy and a girl from the Theatre Institute who were watching rehearsals, and at the rehearsals of Gorki's "Enemies" at the Moscow Art Theatre, two young men from the Institute were present, like myself, to study directors' methods. They were, in fact, supposed to understudy a small part apiece, and to play it in rehearsal when the regular member of the cast was absent.

In the vacation interval between the second and third years, the students of the régisseur course work as assistant régisseurs for four months. During their fourth year they are sent out to the place where after graduation they will be working. Here they do a production on their own, which is reviewed by a Commission, and at the end of the year they come back to Moscow to take state examinations which will qualify them to become practicing régisseurs.

Of the other courses offered at the Institute, the most interesting and significant is, in my opinion, the course for directors of theatres. It is an altogether unique and remarkable work. The director of a state theatre in any city in the Soviet Union is in a position of responsibility and prominence in that community which is appropriate to the dignity of the position of the theatre in the Russian Bolshevist society. The person to occupy this post must be one familiar with the cultural background of everything connected with the theatre. He must come out of the proletariat, since there are nothing but proletarians to choose from. But there are few of them at this time in Russia already possessed of the breadth of culture as well as the specialized capabilities necessary, so the Soviet Union must create its cultural leaders out of whole cloth. That is what this particular course in the Theatre Combinate is trying to do.

There are thirty young men and women preparing themselves to become theatre directors; they are among the older students in the Institute. They study the history of the theatre, of the fine arts, music, applied art, scenic design, stage direction, and something which is called the "planning of theatrical economy" which was defined to me as "the art of being able to organize a theatre." One phase of it includes a knowledge of bookkeeping.

I know of no dramatic school, academy or institute anywhere which can match the scale on which the Central Theatre Combinate is contributing to the world of the theatre. There are many edifices in the U.S.S.R. which are called by the elegant and very Soviet title of "Palace of Culture." There are few which have such right to the title as does, in its own way, the old merchant prince's mansion on the quiet side street of Moscow.

Before closing this section on theatre preparation directly administered by *Narkompros*, I feel that I should make brief mention of one other project, not yet accomplished but nobly conceived. I heard of it first when, the week before leaving Moscow, I went to pay my final respects to the First Teacher of the Soviet theatre—Stanislavski. It is his own project. He has offered his services to the government to found special courses for régisseurs who will work directly and personally with him for six months and then start two studios for drama and for opera which will continue thereafter under his general supervision as long as he shall live. The plans had not yet been worked out when I left Moscow in February, 1935, and the project may never materialize, but it was a gracious and generous offer from one who is neither young nor strong, and what Stanislavski offers no one in Moscow would be apt to refuse.

CHAPTER THREE

Actors at Work

THERE has been long discussion in the theatre, brought to a head in recent times by the writings of Gordon Craig, about the relative importance of the actor and the director: whose contribution is the essential one? In looking about the Moscow field in an effort to find some sort of basis for dividing it, I was reminded of the two points of view, for there the theatres obviously fall into three groups: those which exist for and are created by the actor, those which exist for and through the director, and those which exist for the actor but are created by the director in closest association with the actor. On this basis, it seemed to me, was the satisfactory way for me to divide my theatre study. The division into Left, Center and Right theatres which Huntly Carter and others use has an ideological and historical basis and I was seeking a working one. I shall try to explain what I mean by the divisions and why I consider them the logical ones in a consideration of method.

The Moscow Art Theatre is one of the chief supporters of the idea of a theatre of the actor, by the actor and for the actor. One of its principal tenets has been the supremacy of the ensemble at the expense of all individual creative exhibitionism (in its best sense), including *régie*. Its director, Stanislavski, was first and foremost an actor himself. The system which he worked on for so many years was a system of acting for actors. The reputation which the Art Theatre, through its foreign appearances, made for the Russian stage abroad was one based on the supremacy of acting.

I do not wish to imply that the Art Theatre does not have able directors; Stanislavski is one of the greatest living directors today, and some of his assistants, the younger men and women who now actively direct at the MXAT,[1] are excellent. But their position in the picture is rather that of a combination wet-nurse and doctor. Their presence and assistance at the birth of the play is essential, but the play is actually given birth to by the actor; the pangs are his—or hers!

In 1897 Constantin Stanislavski and Vladimir Nemirovich-Danchenko met to lay the plans for a theatre which would attempt to satisfy the need which both felt for a new kind of art in the theatre and a new approach to its functioning. Their meeting in a Moscow restaurant where they spent the whole day and most of the night (a typically Russian procedure) discussing their beliefs and outlining their plans, is a famous incident in theatrical history. Both were dissatisfied with the existing theatre which had become commercialized and vulgarized during the latter days of the nineteenth century. It seemed to them to have become what they called a "theatre of performances." By that they meant a theatre devoted to representation of outward form, one in which the artists studied the period of the play, its history, conditions, modes of life, in order to reproduce its appearance correctly, but solely from the standpoint of onlookers.

Both Stanislavski and Nemirovich wanted a theatre in which truth would supplant the artificialities which had

---

[1] MXAT are the initials used commonly in Moscow to identify the Art Theatre: Moskovski Khudozhestvenny Akademicheski Teatr. The X is the character used in Russian to indicate the kh sound which does not exist in English. I shall use MXAT often hereafter as an abbreviation for "Moscow Artistic Academic Theatre."

grown up in the stage of that day, in which perfection of the ensemble would replace the uneven and unpredictable intuitive genius of a few stars and the conventional hokum of the time, in which beauty would be achieved through simplicity. In their theatre the actor must put himself in the place of the hero. They called theirs the "theatre of inner feeling." In the theatre of performances the director could do a good measure of the actor's work for him, could describe to him the elements he was to reproduce; in the new theatre he could not. Here it was the actor who must place himself in the position of the character, the actor who must experience the inner feeling and he alone. The director could only help him to discover the character and urge him on to experience the inner feeling. Stanislavski and Nemirovich immediately began the foundation of a permanent company, a step significant in itself, for at that time the theatres formed their casts from season to season by that general hit-or-miss bargaining process which New York enjoys today.

A strong influence upon Stanislavski, who directed the productional side of the new theatre while Nemirovich controlled the literary, was that of the Players of the Duke of Meiningen whose work became known to Stanislavski when they visited Moscow. They emphasized attention to revealing the meaning of the text of the play, to reproducing historical details with exactitude, and the importance of ensemble acting. The first production of the Art Theatre was Alexei Tolstoy's "Tsar Fyodor" which took place in October, 1898, after some seventy rehearsals— quite a contrast to the half-dozen rehearsals which the Maly, with modern stock company speed, was then devoting to its new light Frenchy fare. In this production Stanislavski showed the effects of the Meiningen influence and began to lay the foundations of the theatre's style: simplicity of speech and action, use of actual things to surround the actor, the truthful and exact portrayal of emotions. His idea, he said, was "to chase the theatre from the theatre."

The second production of importance was Chekhov's "The Sea-Gull," and with its performance the theatre began an artistic alliance with Chekhov which was as important for the development of its character as was the alliance of the Maly Theatre with Ostrovski. "The Sea-Gull" was a play in which the action and dialogue were of secondary importance—the thought of the dramatist was in the underlying meaning. In all the subsequent plays of Chekhov the Art Theatre continued to be occupied with revealing the play that lay beneath the text. It was in this way that it came to its emphasis upon the study of man's inner experiences and feelings.

In the repertoire of the Moscow Art Theatre several other trends were manifested. There were plays of history and manners; there were plays in the spirit of the fantastic, revealing the poetic side of the theatre. The line of symbolism and impressionism was early present in the theatre in the works of Ibsen (excepting "The Enemy of the People"), Maeterlinck, Hamsun, and later, Andreyev. Into the field of social and political drama also, the Art Theatre entered with its production of Gorki's plays, "The Enemy of the People," and Tolstoy's "The Power of Darkness."

It was along that other line, "the intuition of feelings" as Stanislavski calls it, that the theatre was most successful. All the plays of Chekhov, most of Hauptmann, Turgenyev, Dostoyevski, and Griboyedov's classic, "Woe from Wisdom," were plays in which the outward form cloaked an inner and far deeper meaning which the artists of the Moscow Art Theatre seemed able to catch and bring to life. In many of these plays that inner problem was, for the Russian intellectual of the first days of the twentieth century, his own. Therefore with such a repertoire, including also the Gorki plays, the Art Theatre became the theatre of the advanced intellectuals; it was the revolutionary theatre.

Not only intellectually but artistically the theatre devoted itself to all that was new. It was a period of untiring experimentation in novel scenic forms. Anything was worth trying so long as it had not been done before and so long as it was in line with the theatre's principle of truth to life. The life-like sounds of crickets, frogs, birds, mosquitoes, filled the air, whole scenes were played by actors sitting with backs to audience, long and empty silences were the vogue; dozens of other tricks were tried.

Then came the Revolution of 1905. The Moscow Art Theatre went abroad for the first time and its beauty founded on simplicity and truth became appreciated by western Europe. When the theatre returned from its tour it entered upon the second period of its existence, a phase dominated by the tendencies then powerful in the art of western Europe—symbolism and mysticism. It was then that Dostoyevski, Hamsun, Andreyev, Maeterlinck, replaced in the repertoire the healthier and more social Ibsen, Chekhov, Gorki. The Art Theatre gave itself over to preoccupation with abstractions, negation of life, the meaning of death, and its stage was filled with strange music, darkness, and the "smoke of mysticism."

The progressive intellectuals found this theatre less to their taste, although its popularity with the great body of the bourgeoisie remained unchallenged, and when the Revolution broke, the Moscow Art Theatre had ceased to be revolutionary and was considered reactionary. Indeed, the Communists like to insist that the Art Theatre was in a state of irreparable decay and that these last preoccupations indicated a decadence which would have plunged the theatre to its destruction had not the cleansing and invigorating wind of the proletarian Revolution arrived to blow it back into sunny safety. It is true that the theatres of western Europe cannot be said to have recovered from the decadence of the early twentieth century. They remain today in a woefully pallid state, but it is doubtful whether the Moscow Art Theatre would have suffered their fate had it been allowed to pursue its artistic way untouched by the Revolution. Its art was too right and its leaders too wise for that.

The Moscow Art Theatre stood comparatively still creatively during the first period of the Revolution. Unable to apply the Marxian interpretation of art in the creation of new drama, it preferred to serve the Revolution by conserving its past for the service of the future. Of course, after the Revolution the Art Theatre might have changed its style. It could have much more quickly expressed the things which were wanted of it in the new society if it had been content to deal only with the externals—to perform as onlookers. But it refused to abandon its belief in a theatre of inner feeling. It preferred to wait until its actors could understand the psychological basis of these new feelings, for the Art Theatre remained an actors' theatre.

During this time, therefore, it occupied itself chiefly in pedagogical pursuits. Then the Theatre made its second trip abroad—to Europe and to America. When it returned it entered upon the final stage of its development. The Revolution had by this time been understood and accepted, at least by the younger generation which had grown up in the Theatre, and it was able to grasp the inner feeling of the new man with the same understanding with which it had penetrated into the heart of the life of Chekhov's landed gentry of thirty years before.

2

I have made several references to the Stanislavski system of acting, but I have not yet given more than generalized definitions of it. I cannot pretend to be able to offer a thorough analysis of the system, nor is it my desire to do so, for Stanislavski has himself been in the process of writing a book about it for the past five years, and it is that book alone which will be able to open it up properly to the understanding of the outsider. But it seems to me as important for a person watching the Art Theatre at work to know what the theatre expects of its actors as for him to understand the language it is speaking. The reader need not go through the ordeal of learning Russian, for I have, in a sense, done that for him; but he should know something about the system. Let me therefore make a very brief effort at exposition.

The Stanislavski system is really only a conscious codification of ideas about acting which have always been the property of most good actors of all countries whether they knew it or not. Its basis is the work of the actor *with himself* in order to master "technical means for the creation of the creative mood, so that inspiration may appear oftener than is its wont." That is what Stanislavski was seeking when he began to formulate his thoughts into a system. "This does not mean," he wrote in his *Life in Art*, "that I was going to create inspiration by artificial means. That would be impossible. What I wanted to learn was how to create a favorable condition for the appearance of inspiration by means of the will, that condition in the presence of which inspiration was most likely to descend into the actor's soul." Before proceeding further in an examination of the methods of production of the Art Theatre, I think it would be worth while to set down a few notes on the subject.

1. This work of the actor with himself is first expressed in physical development. Stanislavski is fond of saying to his pupils, "As a painter has his canvas and his paints, so an actor has his body and his voice." The actor must be master of all movement and all the senses. It is this dictum which is largely responsible for the attention paid in the curricula of all the theatre schools and technicums in Moscow to physical and voice culture, those courses in gymnastics, rhythmics, dancing, voice production, singing. One of the régisseurs of the *MXAT* told me that Stanislavski even now, in his seventy-fifth year, exercises his body and voice daily. How many actors in New York one-third his age and of one-tenth his experience consider such exercise necessary for themselves?

2. Work with the actor's personal psychology. This involves self-control of the nervous system. The first requirement of acting is muscular freedom. Nervousness must be overcome; there must be relaxation. The actor must be able to control his attention. For this the *MXAT* has a favorite expression: "the circle." In order that the actor may never be distracted from his playing he must put himself within an imaginary circle from which he cannot step as long as he is acting. This is a most important and difficult thing. Nemirovich-Danchenko, I am told, accomplishes this by looking at his cuff links; one actress closes her eyes for a minute, after that she is "within the circle" and nothing exists but the world of the stage. This is more than the erection of a "fourth wall" to shut out the audience from the actor's consciousness, for it is designed to protect him as well from distractions within that fourth wall, that is, on the stage itself.

3. Development of imagination and fantasy. These are the actor's most important weapons. The two words mean almost the same thing but not quite. Let me illustrate the difference. Suppose an actor must pretend that he is stand-

ing at a street corner watching a funeral procession pass by. He can, no doubt, recall a time in the past when he has done this. So now he recalls his impressions, re-creates the situation in his imagination and reënacts it. But suppose that he must pretend to be climbing a palm tree in northern Africa in chase of a monkey. If he has never climbed a palm tree, never been in Africa and never chased a monkey, he will be unable to use his memory to reconstruct the situation. Instead he must try to imagine what it would be like to do this. That would be called employing "fantasy." For the development of these two there are exercises which the actors and apprentices of the MXAT do. There is one, for instance, in which three words are chosen at random, "mountain," "shoe," "snow," let us say. The actor then creates a story around these words which he acts out. This develops his imagination and at the same time strengthens his powers of concentration.

4. "Offered circumstances." By this phrase is meant the situation presented by the author. The actor must learn how to master these circumstances, and this takes the most time. Let me illustrate with the "business" of writing a letter. The actor must know how to convince the audience that he is actually writing a letter, but he must be able to do more than that. The act of writing a love letter differs from that of writing a business letter. They are the performance of the same physical action: the body seated, pen and paper employed, the hand moving, the mind concentrated on the writing; yet there must be a different expression. Then if, in the offered circumstances of the playwright, the actor is required to write a love letter, he must not convey to the audience that he is writing a business letter, or that he is writing just any kind of letter. He must know how to fulfill only the required demand—he must write the love letter so that there can be no mistaking what it is.

5. Naïveté. The actor must be naïve—he must believe in what he does and says. Children believe in what they create in play. Actors should watch children and do likewise. There are exercises also for the strengthening of this naïveté and, in the production of "The Blue Bird" in particular, much attention had to be given to its development. This is almost the root of the whole system. Stanislavski has written:

I came to understand that creativeness begins from that moment when in the soul and imagination of the actor there appears the magical, creative if. While only actual reality exists, only practical truth which a man naturally cannot but believe, creativeness has not yet begun. Then the creative if appears, that is, the imagined truth which the actor can believe as sincerely and with greater enthusiasm than he believes practical truth, just as the child believes in the existence of its doll and of all life in it and around it. From the moment of the appearance of if the actor passes from the plane of actual reality into the plane of another life, created and imagined by himself. Believing in this life, the actor can begin to create.

6. Contact. In life, contacts between people are always dictated by a logical purpose. The actors must discover this purpose on the stage and bear it in mind. There the contact is necessarily repetitious, but this fact must be forgotten. Talk to your partner-actor's eyes, not to his ears, says Stanislavski. The person who talks produces a kind of rays; the person addressed absorbs these rays.

7. Memorizing of emotions. This is closely connected with the third point. A conscious effort to memorize certain emotions, both in large and small details, gives great strength to the imagination when the actor is called upon at some future time to re-create the emotion. The more the

actor can depend on the recollection of previously experienced and memorized emotions, the less he will have to resort to the uncertainties of "fantasy," and the more accurate will be his performance.

8. Rhythm. This must be developed in rehearsal and not by the actor independently, for rhythms must be based on the various "offered circumstances." Stanislavski used to use ten rhythms in a fractional arrangement. In rehearsing every movement was marked. The normal rhythm was 5. Rhythm 1 was that of a man almost dead, 2 that of a man weak with illness, and so on progressively to rhythm 9 which might be that of a person seeing a burning house, and to 10 when he is on the point of jumping out of the window. Tempo and rhythm must not be confused, for tempo comes from outside whereas rhythm comes from within. There may be one general rhythm of the whole stage while individual rhythms differ. The fractional system is no longer in use at the MXAT, but the principles of rhythm and the actor's understanding of their use are still a fundamental part of the system.

9. This is the final stage in the preparatory phase of the system and the word in Russian which is used to signify it is translated in our word "grain," the grain of the rôle. It means the collection of all the individual characteristics which make up the person. We might do better to call it the "kernel." It includes the internal qualities of the character as well as its external form. When this kernel is grasped by the actor, the character becomes real and there only remains to add to it

10. The aim. The aim gives motivation to the characterization. If one is conscious of the aim, all else is forgotten; there is no more consciousness of self, for the actor as the character can answer the question, "What do I want and why?"

There are half a dozen more notes on the Stanislavski system, but they are concerned with problems which arise during the period of the play's preparation—points such as "mastery of the rôle," "selection of the aim," "super-problem of the rôle," "perspective of the rôle," etc., and we would do better to talk about them when we are actually in rehearsal and can watch the master actors of the Art Theatre working them out. Then they will mean much more to us. A final admonition to the Stanislavski actor, not a part of the system but significant of its attitude toward the art of acting: never imitate your own good performance. The actor is not a machine and standardization is bad.

Many of these points seem exceedingly simple and obvious, almost childish. So, I might say, are scales in music; yet all musicians must know them and great artists practice them for years. Apropos of that, I should like to emphasize that this system of Stanislavski's is not something which beginners in Moscow learn and then forget. The exercises based on it are practiced constantly by even the great artists of the *MXAT*. Every week there is a class held at the Art Theatre to strengthen imagination, naïveté, contact, concentration and all the other things. The class is attended by Honored and People's Artists of the Republic; some of them have been acting for thirty years. Scales and études are as important as concertos.

3

The only way to understand the system and this Russian terminology is to go to some rehearsals, in fact, to many of them, watch a production evolve from beginning to end, and see whether and how these things actually work out. In watching this evolution at the *MXAT* we are at a disadvantage because of the time element. Many productions

there are in rehearsal anywhere from eight months to a
year and a half, and unless one can give that much time to
it one cannot be said to have observed properly.

This time element was something I was particularly
anxious to understand. In New York a play is rehearsed
for four weeks—perhaps six, if it is taken for a short trial
run out of town before opening. In Moscow I was told
they rehearse from three months to eighteen. What happens in all that time? The discouraged tourist who has experienced Russian ways, will nod a wise head and reply,
"Nothing," putting it down as just another example of
the Russian's famous procrastination, to his inability to put
anything through on time. If it takes the telephone opera-
tor in your hotel half an hour to get you a number, no
wonder it takes a stage director half a year to give you
a play. The Russians postpone all their openings—the
"Metro" was two or three years overdue.

If that were the whole answer we could dismiss the time
element forthwith, but I have concluded that it is not.
The Russian temperament does have something to do with
it; procrastination and the Russian's love of talk do enter
in, but rather more important is another facet of his temperament: his attitude toward workmanship. The Russian
artist says, "Nothing short of perfection is satisfactory. I
shall not, of course, attain it, but I shall work until I am
as close to it as possible." The end is everything and time
loses its meaning in the attainment of it. In many ways
the Russian seems closer to the East than to the West, and
his point of view is essentially Eastern. An Indian, I am
told, may carve away at a small piece of ivory for a year
or years until its form and pattern seem to be in every
way just what he wants. The aesthetic pleasure he derives
from perfect completion he shares with the Russian. It is
shocking to the Russian director to hear that a New York
producer will allow a play to open before he is completely

satisfied that there is nothing more that could be done with it. But how often does that happen? Simonov once said to me, in answer to the question, "When" (the interrogative most frequently on the lips of foreigners visiting the U.S.S.R.), "when will your play open?"—"My play will open when it is ready, when it is ripe, so to speak, not before."

There is a story told at the Art Theatre which illustrates this nicely. Stanislavski's illness in recent years has prevented him from doing much actual direction, and plays are prepared by the under-régisseurs under the supervision of either Stanislavski or Nemirovich-Danchenko, who come in at the last rehearsals to polish them off. Two or three years ago a new production of "Talents and Admirers" by Ostrovski was in preparation. Stanislavski had been ill and saw no rehearsals until the régisseur of the production felt that after three or four months of work he had done all he could with it and that it was ready, at least for the master's final touch. A run-through in costume and sets was arranged for the tenth of December and Stanislavski was brought to the theatre to see it. He was delighted; he saw very little that needed to be done. They could schedule full dress rehearsals for the fourteenth and fifteenth, an invitation performance for the eighteenth and open on the twentieth. Everyone went home much relieved —Constantin Sergevich, as he is known to his colleagues, was pleased. At the dress rehearsal on the fourteenth he returned. This time it was a different story. Quite a good deal seemed to him worse than before. Parts of the set were not perfect and needed correction. But they need not worry. While they worked on the set, he, Constantin Sergevich, would rehearse with the cast in his home—for ten days perhaps. They would postpone the opening only until the thirty-first of December. Stanislavski started his work with the actors at home. For the ten days they rehearsed. He thought of other things with the set which were not right. He found other things wrong with the cast. "We must postpone it a little longer," he said. "Talents and Admirers" opened the following September!

They tell another story of doubtful authenticity in Moscow about an Art Theatre production of several years ago in which the play opens with the hero's servant entering to shave his master's beard. For six months they rehearsed the opening line, "Shall I shave you now, sir?" and got no farther. Finally the play was abandoned because the actor could not learn to say the line correctly!

This is doubtless not true, but it very well might have been. I remember an afternoon in Stanislavski's study where I watched a rehearsal of "Carmen." It was the last act and the words Carmen utters when she comes in to find herself alone and face to face with Escamillo are, "*Ty zdyes?*" (You here?) For fifteen minutes Stanislavski and the Carmen discussed and repeated these two words, trying all the possible inflections and accents to discover the perfect one. The conclusion I want to draw from these instances is that time means nothing. No Moscow director ever said in my hearing, "We haven't time to do or to try that." Instead the two words one hears most in Moscow rehearsals are, "*yeshcho raz*"—once more.

The working of the repertory system also has an effect upon this time element in rehearsal. In New York the company is usually devoting its energies exclusively to rehearsal of the play in preparation. Rehearsals are often carried on for eight hours a day—sometimes all day and then far into the night. The schedule becomes stiffer as the dress rehearsal period arrives. In Moscow this is impossible, for many of the actors are performing every night and at matinées and in a different rôle at each performance. The demands of this system upon an actor are great. Therefore, even up through the final dress rehearsal he can only spend a certain part of his day in rehearsal on the new production; there must be time to prepare for his current evening performances.

My first-hand experience began in the rehearsals of Gorki's "Enemies." From most standpoints this production is a good example. It is an old play, almost a semi-classic, so that it is like much else that the Art Theatre has in its repertoire from point of view of text; that is to say, it is not a new Soviet manuscript. At the same time the Art Theatre has never tackled a production of it before. It is a deeply psychological play—there is little action. Therefore it is a good play for this actors' theatre. The actors who are cast are among the greatest in the company: Knipper-Chekhova, Kachalov, Tarkhanov, Tarasova, a dozen others. The director is Kedrov, perhaps Stanislavski's most able pupil. They should be a perfect group to interpret the theatre's principles of work.

We arrive for our first rehearsal at eleven o'clock in the morning. At the administrative entrance is a typed list of the rehearsals for the day. There may be as many as six or eight different plays being rehearsed at different hours in different parts of the theatre, for there are two other new plays besides "Enemies" to be done this season, rehearsals are already under way for a couple of next season's productions, and parts of the plays currently in the repertoire are constantly being rehearsed, either to familiarize an understudy or to keep the play fresh when it seems to be drying up. To guard against this latter, some member of the theatre's staff sits out front at every performance, whether the play has been in the repertoire for a week or for twenty years, to note any slips or any let-down which may be apparent.

We have arrived a few minutes ahead of schedule, so we must wait in the vestibule until the director comes, for no one not a member of the theatre is allowed to enter beyond without special permission. I have spent a good many hours sitting in that vestibule waiting for various officials and I have never failed to enjoy what I saw. It matters not what hour of day or night one is there; there is a constant procession of actors, régisseurs, young apprentices, business administrators, technicians, assistants, charwomen, and people who come to confer with them all (except with the charwomen). But we must remember that this theatre has almost one thousand people working in it. It is, I believe, from point of numbers, the largest dramatic organization in the world, excluding operas. There are three or four door-men always on duty at this entrance, and they seem to know everything that is going on in the complicated organization. Almost every artist that enters shakes hands with these door-men who address them all by their two first names. Then the actors pass within. The entrance does not lead directly to the stage, but through a *garde-robe* into the foyers of the theatre.

Now the director has come and we go in with him, leave our coats with an attendant and pass on to the first floor foyer where behind closed doors the rehearsal will take place this morning. As each member of the cast arrives he shakes hands carefully and formally with every other person in the room; the men kiss the hands of the women. We are in a theatre of actors, every one of whom carries himself with dignity and respects everyone else. There is an air of refinement and cultivation about the quietly and tastefully dressed company. No "Broadway stuff" here and none of the superficial earmarks of the proletariat either. This is a gathering of aristocrats of the Soviet Union!

Rehearsals of "Enemies" have already been in progress for about two months, but they are still in the first act and today they are just beginning to "walk" a section of it. Even in this early rehearsal all the props are at hand.

The tea table is completely set, including a cloth and all silver; there is even some real food. The actor is placed in as real or natural an environment as possible from the beginning. But there is a further value: the presence of the props at all rehearsals gives him a chance to make mechanical those little things which should properly be so.

The rehearsal is carried on very quietly. A low conversational tone is used, sometimes dropping almost to a whisper, as though the actors were but thinking aloud with each other. The director does not remain long in his seat by the green felt-covered table, but, leaving the script with the assistant stage manager who sits there too, and who prompts fairly constantly at this stage in the same pitch of voice as the cast, he stands in the group of actors. He talks with them quietly as they rehearse; he walks at their sides as they move tentatively about the extempore stage. We have difficulty in discovering when they are reading lines of the play and when discussing some mooted point with each other, for it is all done equally naturally and with equal quiet, and our Russian is too sketchy to understand remarks made *sotto voce*. We have to watch carefully. They are rehearsing only a small scene, perhaps six pages long, and they go over it again and again. There is a good deal of discussion, then the rehearsal is finished; it is only two o'clock, we discover. Setting six pages of script has been this one day's work, and we feel when it is over that those pages are only tentatively set, at that!

The rehearsal concluded, we come out into the rest of the theatre. Here the quiet of the rehearsal room is intensified. The Art Theatre is probably the quietest spot in Moscow. All speech in the heavily carpeted halls of the theatre is in whispers, for on the stage and in other foyers and rehearsal rooms other rehearsals are in progress. In the buffet some actors enjoying an interval in rehearsal are drinking tea and conversing quietly. Others, finished for the day, go downstairs to the dining room for dinner. The heavy meal for actors and for most Russians, for that matter, is served in the middle of the afternoon. We leave to ponder over the meaning of what we have just seen, and to consider how the morning's work fits into the plan of production which Kedrov, the director, has explained. Before attending another rehearsal perhaps it would be wise for me to discuss this plan and explain what has gone before in these two months of rehearsals.

4

What I have just given you has been an impression of the outward appearance of a Moscow Art rehearsal—a journalist's view; but it is the whys and wherefores, particularly in this theatre, which count. The play was begun two months ago with two or three readings. These readings differed from the usual New York first reading in that the play was read to the actors and they did not participate in the reading themselves. The Art Theatre considers these first readings very important. It feels that the moment when the actor is introduced to the person whom he is about to become is a most solemn one. The impression which he first receives is apt to influence his attitude very strongly toward the play and the rôle. Therefore these readings are taken slowly and are designed to arouse the interest of the actor.

After a while the actor is given his script, but the MXAT believes there should be no hurry about this. Then follows a period in which the régisseur stimulates enthusiasm for the play. The actor must fall in love with it; otherwise he has no faith and his work will not carry conviction. Stanislavski, they say, sometimes used to fall back on the trick of unreasonably criticizing the author's work as a result of which the cast would run to the playwright's defense, discussion would ensue, the actors in supporting the author would discover for themselves good things in the play to assist their arguments, and the interest which the régisseur wished the actors to take was aroused. This introduction over, they were ready to proceed to the next step.

The analytic period which follows is the first main division in the evolution of the production and it may take a month's work or, in the case of a great classic, much more. First there is an examination of the "sub-text." This simply means study of the lines taken up one by one and discussion of the meaning beneath each. The stage directions of the author are disregarded, for they sometimes lead one away from the true meaning of his words. But if the play is a new Soviet one, the author may be present at these round-table discussions to reveal his meanings.

From the interpretation of individual lines, the analysis passes to a consideration of the "superproblem": what the theatre wants to tell the world in this play. Then there is study of the "grain" of the play as a whole: examination of the period, its conditions, environment, tastes. Historical and scientific research and biographical study are part of this work. After that the cast returns to the text of the play. The régisseur has divided the act into a number of small pieces, or rather, he has taken up a short sequence of lines and grouped them together to create a small scene. Each fragment, *kusok*, has its place in the building of the act. It may be composed of four or five lines or it may be two or three pages long. The length is dictated solely by the unity of thought expressed therein. These *kuski* are definitely marked and numbered in the script and, during this analytic period and even into the period of rehearsal which follows, it is the rehearsal unit.

One might liken this dissection of the act to an analysis of a musical composition. Each speech is a measure which has its individual notes, here words; measures grouped to-

gether in sequence form phrases. Each phrase has perhaps its own tempo, its own little melody, its own meaning. It must be practiced separately over and over again to
be mastered. But it is only a phrase and in the composer's
mind has no meaning if cut off from the phrases which
precede and follow it. The long chain of phrases becomes
a movement to which we may liken the act of a play.
When all the movements are played, the sonata is completed, our play is finished. The right division of an act
into small pieces is very important, for, like improper
phrasing, if incorrectly done it may destroy the melody
and balance of the act.

This division of an act into minor scenes is not unknown in American production and I do not wish to hail
it in the Russian theatre as an innovation. But there is a
difference in its application. Usually the American director makes the divisions on the basis of action: a scene may
run from entrance to exit; often he picks up a new one
at the entrance of a character, using the physical act of
entrance as a motivation for the announcement of a new
scene. When repetition in rehearsal is necessary, the customary direction is, "Go back to your entrance." The Art
Theatre's divisions are much smaller and more frequent
because they are based not so much on movement as on
unity of thought and emotion. Each new facet of thought
or feeling requires separate treatment; often an entrance
of a character has nothing to do with his train of thought
or that of others upon the stage. A scene played across a
table between two characters who sit there quite still for
ten minutes would in all likelihood be rehearsed with us as
a single scene just because there is no break in action. In
the Art Theatre these ten actionless minutes might contain six scenes, divisions being made every time a new
chain of thought or a new emotional reaction is established between the two characters. It is very rare that two

people will converse for ten minutes without passing through many changing attitudes toward each other. Each of these with the Art Theatre becomes a separate entity requiring separate rehearsal and adjustment. This explains to us the meaning of that first rehearsal which we attended when only six pages of script were covered. Those six pages perhaps contained ten scenes, and looked at in this way one can see that really a good deal was accomplished.

In the period which follows this analysis, the actors work to master their rôles and then to "incarnate" them. Now comes practice of the final parts of the Stanislavski system. In mastering his rôle, the actor must first say, "All this has happened to me and therefore it is inevitable." This, of course, cannot be accomplished at once but bit by bit. Stanislavski himself likens the process to the passing of a day. As morning follows dawn, is succeeded by noon and it by afternoon and on to evening and night in inevitable progression, so the actor must feel that the life and action he creates on the stage has the same inevitability of sequence. "Remember the line of the day," says Stanislavski in rehearsal.

Next comes the "selection of the aim"—what I do and why. It is at this point that we come to realize that the Art Theatre and opprobrious "naturalism" are not exactly one, although in the mind of the casual student of the theatre they are linked. Naturalism is photographic reproduction. Pure naturalism and the camera both show you things as they are, but make no effort to show you why—you are left to draw your own conclusions. The camera does not reflect upon the meaning of the scene it reproduces and the naturalistic actor and régisseur when they become absorbed in that style are also apt to forget the "why." Naturalism tends to destroy inner profound emotions in its effort to mirror the outer manifestations of them. The selection and retention of an aim helps to define the action as well as the emotions and that is why it is considered of such importance at the Art Theatre.

Again sequence of action comes up, this time to help unfold the aim. "Let us suppose," says the régisseur to me, "that you want to go to Leningrad to see a play which they are performing there. You will pack your suitcase, you will board a tram to take you to the station, you will buy your ticket there, you will go out onto the station platform, when the train arrives you will board it, you will seek a vacant place and having found it you will seat yourself. When you reach Leningrad you will disembark, you will seek a hotel in which you may be comfortable, you will go to the theatre to make arrangements to see the play, when the time comes you will go to the theatre, enter, take your seat and proceed to watch the play, which has been the aim you had from the moment you started to pack your suitcase and which has continued to be your aim through the chain of actions that followed.

"If I am a naturalistic actor I shall be content to imitate these isolated movements of yours one after another and let it go at that. If I am an actor in the Art Theatre, I must know your aim, I must bear it in mind as I follow your movements. I must remember as I pack the suitcase, as I go through the action of buying the ticket, as I get off the train, that every act is part of my final purpose, which is to get me to see the new play in Leningrad. There is a reason for each thing I do and that reason is part of my final aim. For the purely naturalistic actor, it would be quite as possible to reproduce the action of buying the railroad ticket and then follow it with an imitation of you boarding the tram that would take you to the station. The Stanislavski actor could not do this because he would thus be destroying the logical sequence of events which lead to the accomplishment of the ultimate aim, and this he must know and remember at every step."

This simple little theory (but really quite fundamental and not always so simple as in this ABC illustration) has its name too. It is called the *krug,* which means circle, and Stanislavski suggests that it is like a necklace of pearls. No pearl is by itself a necklace, only when placed in a strand with others does it make one, and the necklace is only complete when all the pearls are there. It reveals that the physical and psychological problems of acting are one and must be solved at the same time, not divided as they were before the system.

In the production of "Enemies" which I studied, an experiment in this relation between the physical and psychological elements of acting was being made. They called it simply the "theory of physical action"—*physicheskoe deistviye*—and for the Art Theatre it represents a definite change of methods. Instead of coming to the incarnation of a rôle by thinking about it and arousing emotions about it, it is suggested to the actor that he try certain actions and then, from the doing of them, he discovers their meaning, their cause, and the truth therein. This is not really a departure from the beliefs of the Art Theatre, for the purpose remains the same—to arrive at an understanding of the psychology of movement.

Stanislavski is also making this experiment in the opera rehearsals he conducts. Before the first rehearsal of "Carmen" which I saw at his home, he explained to me what I was about to see. He now believes, he said, that the actor cannot get at the true psychology by thinking in terms of psychology. A hunter who is after a bird must try to decoy it out into the open, he must whistle gently and persuasively, coax it forth, then bag it. If he jumps at it rudely he has little chance of catching it. So the actor must be gently drawn out, whistled at, as it were, for the capturing of emotional truth is a subtle and difficult thing. Suggest to the actor what to do, then when he has done it, ask him why he did it. Make sure, of course, that he understands why, else the point is lost. If you say to him, "Your psychological state at this moment should be fear. Make movements to express it," you will doubtless be given action which is artificial or exaggerated, even though the actor may be approximating within himself the proper feeling. But if you suggest that he make certain movements and then ask him to feel as those movements dictate, you will perhaps arrive at a truer combination of psychology and action.

After the psychology of movement is grasped, the actor passes to the "superproblem of the rôle," to the dominant purpose in the life of the person he represents. To this he must carry a "perspective of the rôle." He must know how to apply his forces. The jealousy of Othello, the expression of which is perhaps the "superproblem" of that rôle, must not be spent in the early scenes but must be saved and built up for the climax.

Then comes the "incarnation of the rôle" which is the peculiar study of the Art Theatre. All the rest of the system ascends to this point. When the actor has found the nature and origin of his emotions, then he must say, "I am this person." There can be no separation between the actor and his part. It is in this final step in the system that the Art Theatre passes beyond other theatres. Upon arrival at this stage one comes to grips with the spiritual values of the play. Stanislavski says that we cannot relate things which we cannot see. We must, therefore, have our own spiritual vision. And if the actor sees into the spirit, then the audience will. Finally, when he has grasped the image in its physical, mental or psychological, and spiritual aspects, there remains only to work with his own will power, to will himself to act as the image would. Then is his character complete.

The effort to achieve the incarnation of the rôle occupies all the second period of rehearsals and it is here that the most time is required, perhaps two or three months, before the actor can lose his own personality in the personality of the character he is creating. We have seen that the expression of psychology in movement is an important part of this development. Therefore, when the actor begins to feel the need to move about in adding to his part, the round-table is dropped and the rehearsal moves to the stage. But it is the cast and not the director who will decide when the time has come.

It was at this point that we arrived in rehearsal. The period of analysis is over, the actors understand the meaning of what is being said; it is now their task to express these meanings. In doing this the rehearsal by small pieces, *kuski*, continues. All the pieces of one act are mastered separately and then put together before rehearsals begin on the next one. For five weeks I attended rehearsals of only the first act of "Enemies" before a full run-through of it took place and they passed on to the second. During the first part of these five weeks, rehearsals took place in a foyer or a rehearsal room and some were with action, some without; then the rehearsals were moved to the big stage where an approximation of the form of the set was provided.

At the Moscow Art Theatre there is more work done with individuals, the director and a single artist rehearsing alone together, discussing lines and trying movements, than at other Moscow theatres or than most New York directors do. Where the production is based on the principle of a collection of harmonized individual creations, with every part considered as important as the whole (the perfection of the whole being attainable only when every part makes its own perfect contribution), as opposed to the principle of the solo creation of the master régisseur who regards the perfect creation of the whole as attainable only through his own ability, such practice is quite inevitably necessary.

When rehearsals are held on the stage the director is constantly there with the actors; he does not sit out front. Throughout this period he seems only to be trying to help the actors. He walks about with them on the stage, whispers suggestions to stir their imaginations. If the actor wishes to make movements of which the director does not approve, he is allowed to try his way; perhaps he will eventually be led back to the director's way if it is best; but he is never forced at this point to do anything which is not comfortable for him.

Movement is now very slow in becoming set. At every rehearsal I used to see a slight variation of action tried by the actor as he felt his way toward what was "right." The director continues to watch the individual actor. A *kusok* may be repeated as many times as there are performers in it, the director concentrating on each actor in turn. Then on to the next *kusok* when every actor and the director feel that the "incarnations" of the rôles have been accomplished in that bit. So far there is no effort to bring all these individual performances together in outward form beyond the physical contacts provided in the action.

This process includes every actor on the stage, even to the supernumeraries who may have no lines. Every actor in a mob scene has his individual contribution, his own "incarnation," and the director helps them all. Each super must *be* a part of the crowd, understand its mob psychology and also reason out his own individual reactions which have made him part of it. All this takes time (another reason why plays are in rehearsal so long) but the end, convincing mob action, seems to justify it.

The middle stage in the production of the play the Art Theatre likens to the preparation of a bouquet of flowers. One can make a bouquet of artificial flowers very quickly —wire, paper, scissors, glue, and the thing is done. But if one is to have real flowers, then one must wait while they are planted, watered, sunned and tended before they will bloom. Only real flowers are acceptable to the *MXAT*, and the régisseur there becomes a sort of super-gardener-florist who must attend to all this. When the flowers are blooming he will pick them and arrange the bouquet.

It is the arrangement of the bouquet which becomes the third and final part of the rehearsal period. Stanislavski used to work out a very careful régisseur's plan which contained all the *mise-en-scène* [1] arranged in advance. Some directors continue to use this plan, but Stanislavski discarded the method some time ago and the director of "Enemies," Kedrov, uses none. This does not mean, however, that the production is allowed to take its own course. All during the preceding period he has had in mind the pattern of his play; he must have thought out all problems of movement and emotion in advance if he is to be of any help to his actors at all. All this he carries in his mind, however. There is nothing on paper. Incidentally, the prompt book of "Enemies" contains no stage directions or notes written in during rehearsal period. In other words, the mechanics of play production are cut to a minimum. During rehearsals no actor writes any business or directions in his "sides." Business is carried out and crosses are made, not because the actor has memorized them as he has his lines, but because they become necessary and unavoidable adjuncts to his processes of thought and feeling. For that matter, even in learning lines the actor is not rushed as ours must be. He has time to assimilate the lines as he examines their meaning over such a long period, and he scarcely has to make a business of conscious memorizing at all. Again the effort is to keep his work away from everything that is mechanical.

---

[1] *Mise-en-scène* in the Russian theatre means the pattern of action and "business" and does not refer to the *décor*.

During the analytic period and the rehearsals devoted to the incarnation of the rôles which followed, the director has worked from the rear of the line, he has not led the attack. He has been making constant suggestions, throwing out stimulating questions, indulging in discussions about meanings, and the actors have been free to speak their minds. But he has given few orders, it has been the actors' show. Now with the final stage in the rehearsal period, the director leaves the stage, drops his whisper, goes out into the house and becomes at the same time audience and full-voiced master. He must now give the performance unity and form. The danger which the "group of actors" theatre runs is that it may not recognize that eventually it will reach a point where it must yield its democracy to autocracy. Collective creation in art without a finally dominating hand is impossible and the Art Theatre knows it. When I have suggested that the *MXAT* is a theatre of actors, I have not intended to convey the idea that it is a theatre of actors alone and unled. What is significant about it is that the leadership serves the actors instead of the actors serving the leadership.

In this final period of rehearsal much will be changed in the appearance of the performance. There will be changes of tempo and rearrangements of movement and business. There will be a little cutting of the script perhaps. The director's word is now law and the actor's comfort is little thought of. But the point is that these rehearsals are begun only after the actor has become so completely established in his rôle that changes in the outward form of the play make no essential difference to him. There is, in this last series of rehearsals, very little tampering with characterization. If you, as an actor, have a complete understanding of the person whom you represent, if you are able to go so far as actually to think that he and you are the same, then externals can make little difference to you. That is why the actor's assumption of the character is the long and important process and why, once it is achieved, the director can in a fairly short time add shape to the performance and not disturb the actor in so doing.

When the director is satisfied with the pace of the performance, with its visual composition and its aural rhythm, when he feels that he has arranged the bouquet as adequately as the flowers he works with will allow, he is ready to turn it over to one of the two master directors of the Art Theatre. Stanislavski and Nemirovich-Danchenko are both elderly men, but they remain the final authority on all matters within their organization. It is true that much of the detail work is shouldered by a small committee, composed, in 1934-35, of the régisseurs Sudakov and Kedrov and the actor Podgorny—Sudakov concerned most with administration, Kedrov with production, while Podgorny represents the company. No production is presented at the Art Theatre, however, without being looked over by either Stanislavski or Nemirovich-Danchenko. There is no definite way of determining which will supervise which production; they decide informally between themselves and once the decision is made the other has nothing to do with the play. Usually comedy or fantasy will be under Stanislavski's eye, for his comedy sense is one of the finest in the world; Nemirovich is more apt to supervise drama or tragedy.

It is impossible to state definitely how much this supervising director will do in the production. During the season I was in Moscow, Stanislavski and Nemirovich took only a perfunctory part in the plays. They attended not more than half a dozen rehearsals of "Pickwick Club" and "The Storm," for which each was respectively responsible. Unfortunately I was unable to stay through the production of "Enemies" to see how much revision Nemirovich would do. Had I been there I should have seen an old and very distinguished-looking gentleman with the appearance of a Western ambassador wearing a very distinguished white beard, sitting quite quietly in the house. At the end of an act I should have heard some quiet remarks, perhaps suggestions about more effective staging, questions designed to make the actor consider a forgotten quirk of his character's nature. If there were many suggestions or many questions the director might go on rehearsing along these new lines for another month or so; if not, dress rehearsals would begin.

The dress rehearsal in Moscow is a much less feverish ordeal than in New York. This is chiefly because everyone is ready for it. It usually begins at the genteel hour of ten or eleven o'clock in the morning and is over by four or five in the afternoon, perhaps earlier. None of the all-day, all-night, intensive and frantic push to get a show on. In fact, the cast has probably been rehearsing for some time in various parts of the set as they were completed. There are six or eight dress rehearsals over which the work of our two or three can be spread. These are usually followed by three private performances, invitation dress rehearsals. The first is attended by the *Repertcom* which is the name of what amounts to the Board of Censorship of the government; the second is called "The Papa-and-Mamma," and the guests are the families and friends of the cast; the third is for various distinguished guests of the theatre. They are all held at twelve o'clock noon (the usual matinée hour in Moscow). At these rehearsals the director and his assistants, the designer and technical director of the theatre and usually one or two members of the *Repertcom* sit at a long table covered with a green felt cloth, which is set halfway back in the house. In all other respects they are like the regular performances to follow.

5

Before concluding this chapter, I wish to give you a short account of my first visit with Stanislavski. Space does not permit me to describe other visits, but because the first one left perhaps the most vivid impressions, and because few of my generation in the American theatre have had this privilege, and few others will doubtless be allowed it in the years that remain to this great man, I should like to make some record of it.

Stanislavski is no longer well and is compelled to remain at home most of the time, with a nurse in constant attendance. He is by no means easy of access and it took the combined direct and indirect influence of Mrs. Norman Hapgood, Mr. Philip Moeller, Mr. Lee Simonson, the Guggenheim Foundation, the American Ambassador to the U.S.S.R., the Ogpu (Gay-pay-oo), and my own untiring blandishments to secure from the charming but redoubtable secretary who protects him an invitation to a rehearsal at Stanislavski's house.

He lives on a quiet side street not far from the Art Theatre which he so rarely visits in person any more, in one of those large Russian Empire calsomine-tinted houses with which old Moscow is filled. One enters on the first floor the lobby from which opens the studio where the Stanislavski Opera Theatre presented performances in its early days. At the end of the cloakroom, across the lobby from the studio, is a tiny locked door. Miss Tamantseva, his secretary, had come over from the theatre to introduce me and my interpreter-secretary whom I had brought along, for Stanislavski speaks no English. She led me through this little door into a hall which led on down to further rooms, but we stopped before a late nineteenth century Gothic doorway and were ushered through it into Stanislavski's study, a huge high-ceilinged room with four long windows looking out onto the street. The room seemed filled with bookshelves and books and with small stage models, but there was room for a concert grand piano, half a dozen tables and chairs and a large divan besides. On the walls were a few pictures, an original drawing of Gordon Craig for "Hamlet," produced for the Art Theatre almost twenty-five years ago.

The room and its furnishings fade into insignificance beside the man who stands at the far end and comes forward to greet us. He is the most leonine figure I have ever seen, well over six feet tall, perfectly erect, with snow-white hair and heavy white bushy eyebrows, large strong-featured face which seems to have incorporated into its permanent composition the characteristics of all the rôles which its owner has ever played, with hands like those with which one imagines Michelangelo to have chiseled his Moses.

There are a few people whom one meets in the course of a lifetime, if one is lucky, whose greatness one feels directly one is brought face to face with them. I knew that Stanislavski was such a man. His regal bearing is combined with an ineffably gentle smile and completely understanding eyes. You instinctively wish to bow before him, and yet at the same moment to stand erect and smile back into those eyes. He was most gracious, put himself and his entire theatre at my disposal while I was in Moscow. I had come into the room emptied of my usual verbosity. For me to ask this man questions about his "work" would have been impertinent. I could only say, "I have come six thousand miles to see you and now that I am here, I have nothing to say." He understood, patted me like a little dog, and started to talk. Much of what he said I have paraphrased in earlier parts of this chapter.

After half an hour, a stage manager came to say that

the opera rehearsal was waiting. We crossed out of his study through the lobby into the large brightly lighted studio room. It was crowded with all the principals and chorus of "Carmen" assembled there. When Stanislavski entered, all stopped talking and rose to their feet. He shook hands with the principals with that same *ancien régime* formality I had observed at the Art Theatre, presented me to the company, then seated himself in a large armchair with the régisseur on one side of him and the conductor beyond; a stenographer sat ready to record everything that he said, and the rehearsal began. For two and a half hours it lasted, the maestro completely lost in the work. As the action progressed his whole body was thrown into the action—he leaned forward in his chair, his hands alternately clutching its arms and relaxing, his face working with excitement. When the scene had been sung through, he talked with the cast, asked questions, showed them bits of movement, then abruptly rose and left the room. I followed and we returned to his study for tea and biscuits and jam and more conversation. Then after a little respite the rehearsal began again. This time the principals came into the study, sat about in a semi-circle before him, and work on another scene without its action began.

It was six o'clock and the Russian night had fallen when the score was closed and the singers bowed themselves out of the room. My first afternoon with Stanislavski was over. One often wonders whether the things whose grandeur one has always heard about will be as grand as he has imagined when he finally comes face to face with them. One approaches the Parthenon for the first time with a little trepidation lest one may be disappointed. The Parthenon is no disappointment. Neither is Constantin Sergevich Stanislavski. Neither, I may add, is the Moscow Art Theatre.

CHAPTER FOUR

Régisseurs at Work

GENIUS is a word to be used carefully. Enthusiasts are in danger of over-populating their world with geniuses and of confusing Allah with Mohammed. Other reluctant souls, their opposites, would deny the appellation to any living man. I shall not have occasion to employ the term often in this study, but when introducing a personality so monumental in Soviet art as Meierhold, I think it best to say at the start that here, I believe, is a man of genius. Like most of them, he has aroused a storm of criticism and misunderstanding. He has had his share of debunkers who view him only as an artistic charlatan, he has had blind worshipers who foresee a future theatre which will contain nothing that is not "pure Meierhold," and he has confounded critics and disciples alike by the intricacy of his movement. His development is not easy to follow.

The name of Vsevolod Meierhold appears on the program of the Moscow Art Theatre's original production of "The Sea-Gull" opposite the rôle of Treplev. Considered in retrospect, no other Russian artist could have more appropriately delivered that fine rebellious speech which was Chekhov's own battle cry:

To my mind the modern theatre is nothing but tradition and conventionality. When the curtain goes up, and by artificial light, in a room with three walls, these great geniuses, the devotees of holy art, represent how people eat,

*drink, love, move about, and wear their jackets; when from
these commonplace sentences and pictures they try to draw
a moral—a petty moral, easy of comprehension and convenient for domestic use; when in a thousand variations I
am offered the same thing over and over again—I run
away as Maupassant ran away from the Eiffel Tower which
weighed upon his brain with its vulgarity. . . . We need
new forms of expression. We need new forms, and if we
can't have them we had better have nothing.*

The Art Theatre itself was running away from the old
forms, but young Meierhold ran farther and faster. Very
quickly he found himself passing beyond the Moscow Art
Theatre and as his demands for more freedom were greater
than the Art Theatre's ensemble could grant, he fared
forth alone.

For a time thereafter we find him directing and acting
in the south of Russia; thence he went to St. Petersburg
where he managed the theatre of Kommissarzhevskaya.
Here he worked on Maeterlinck's "Sister Beatrice," Alexander Blok's "Gypsy," Andreyev's "Life of Man," in an
effort to translate the new literary tendencies of the day
into some sort of parallel scenic form. Then he was appointed stage director of the Imperial Opera, the Marin-
ski Theatre, and the Imperial Dramatic, the Alexandrinski
Theatre. In opera he produced "Tristan and Isolde," the
"Electra" of Strauss, creating plasticity of movement in a
composition which became part of the music. At the Alexandrinski he produced his famous "Don Juan," and on the
night of the February Revolution in 1917, the last and
magnificent art expression of the old régime, his equally
famous "Masquerade."

Probably the most profound influence on Meierhold
during these years was that of the French symbolists who
led him to his belief that the actor should become on the

stage a sort of visible symbol of poetic thought. This is far removed from Stanislavski's belief that the actor should portray actual human experience: symbol versus representation, poetic thought versus human experience. To find the appropriate medium of expression for this symbol of poetic ideas was Meierhold's task. He turned for inspiration to the conventionalization of the Commedia dell' Arte, of the Oriental and Medieval theatres, of the marionette, of the Greek theatre. Some kind of stylization was necessary. His whole career seems to have been a search for a style which would completely satisfy him. He has never found the perfect form.

Throughout his life, Meierhold has been powerfully influenced by painters and by *décor*. Just as in the post-war years he was the first and the most strongly to be influenced by the constructivists, so in the early twentieth century he was affected by the mystic and symbolist painters among whom were Soudeikin, Anisfeld, Bakst, Korovin and Golovin. From them probably as much as from elsewhere he took on a mystic coloring. Komisarjevsky, who was also working in St. Petersburg at that time, believes this and further writes, "Whether he was dealing with 'Tristan and Isolde' or with a play by Pinero, or Lermontov's 'Masquerade,' or with a Harlequinade, a somber mysticism pervaded all his productions and the symbolic artificiality of the acting and *mises-en-scène* was their important feature." [1]

Meierhold's second preoccupation brought him into still closer contact with designers: the solution of the problem of space on the stage. Dissatisfied, like many other artists at about the same time, with the picture-frame, box stage, he sought ways of bringing action out of it and of fusing it more with the auditorium and the spectators. His work with the spatial stage has continued through the period of

[1] *The Theatre*, p. 147.

constructivism which was in one way an attempt to solve this, and is finally embodied in his plans for the Meierhold Theatre which is about to be built according to his specifications. Here there will be no architectural barriers between spectators and actors. There will be no proscenium arch and no wing space. The stage will be set in the middle of the space and the audience banked around it. The actors will emerge from their dressing rooms directly into the view of the spectators where they will remain until the time for their performance arrives.

In every conventional theatre, when the spectator accepts the spirit of the conventions he is automatically received into a sort of conscious alliance with the artist. The artist plays directly to the spectator, bearing in mind always that he *is* a spectator. The spectator watches, always bearing that in his mind too. It is rather like a circus. The clown talks to the audience. His white face and red circles for cheeks are not supposed to be his natural complexion. The audience is not asked to imagine that it is. So, likewise, the conventional theatre asks you to remember that that is what it is and all it is.

All theatres up until the late Romantic period—practically up to the time of Antoine, to be precise—have been of this kind. Meierhold, in seeking for conventionalization on the stage, has therefore really been looking for a way back to the theatre of the ancients, of the East, of the Middle Ages and of the Renaissance. He has been seeking a way to create a form of new theatre from the forms of the old.

Meierhold wished to invent conventions which would go beyond making the spectator simply a conscious witness to the self-conscious creation of the artist, to a point where he would be drawn into closer emotional contact. Stanislavski said that this could be done only by destroying both conventions and self-consciousness, by making both spectator and artist forget that their emotional experiences were being created artificially in a theatre. Meierhold disagreed with this and was seeking another way when the Revolution came. At once he plunged eagerly into its eddying stream. The rebel was awakened in him to its full strength. Early he became a Communist. He seemed to understand the demands of the Revolution as no other artist in the theatre did at that time. He was placed in charge of the Theatre Section of the newly created Commissariat of Education.

In the first five years or so of the Revolution Meierhold held full, although not always undisputed, sway in the Soviet theatre. The academic theatres were neglected and the populace thronged to his playhouse. It was a marvelous opportunity for Meierhold to experiment with his artistically revolutionary theories. It gave him a theatre where he could hurl artist and spectator together under the most emotionally stressing circumstances. It gave him a public unacquainted with all formal theatre expressions and therefore untouched by the previously prevailing naturalistic style of the theatre. He used the opportunity to deal a strenuous blow from the left at the Moscow Art Theatre.

It is doubtful whether his audiences in those early proletarian days had the slightest conception of the aesthetic revolution which they were witnessing, but in these same performances Meierhold was laying the foundations of a theatre revolutionary in form as well as in content. The Revolution had destroyed, as far as he was concerned, not only tsarism but every vestige of theatrical realism—a destruction he had long been trying to accomplish singlehanded. His appeal to the audience was at once direct and indirect. He addressed it frankly as spectators, as really more than spectators—as a living force in the drama which it took the whole of his playhouse, stage and auditorium, to create. But at the same time he appealed to his audience

not by the direct words of literal translation of life, but
through the indirect medium of suggestion, of emotion
conjured up through symbol, of intelligence provoked by
abstractions.

With actors in blue denim, as I saw in "The Magnificent
Cuckold," without benefit of footlights or curtain, he
talked straight to his hungry but excited audience in the
words which were on its own lips. In those days there were
propaganda posters and slogans on his walls, the action of
the play was interrupted from time to time by announce-
ments of news from the civil war front. Certainly at that
time life needed no heightening. But Meierhold took the
drama of the hour men were living in and, heated through
by the fire of his genius, turned back to the people their
own experiences etched in sharper and more vivid strokes.
At such moments life and the theatre were one; the spectator was the actor—it was his own drama.

In this new theatre for the new masses, let us turn away
from all that the theatre of the old régime offered us, said
Meierhold. The *MXAT* asked its bourgeois audiences to
forget that they were in a theatre and to imagine that
they were living through the experiences with the artists.
We ask you to remember always that you are in a theatre.
Since we don't for a moment imagine that we are living
through these experiences which we depict on the stage,
there's no reason for you to imagine it either. See: this is
the back brick wall of the stage; this is the way we change
our scenery—for this is only scenery, don't think for a
moment it's real. We have thrown away our curtain especially so that you may see that, and so that we may feel
that you are close to us—no barriers here. We actors are
not extraordinary beings apart, we are people like yourselves. We dress as you are dressed. We are just as concerned as you are in what is going on outside this building.
When we hear any fresh news from Samara or Odessa,

we'll let you know. Now let us get on with the play, for we have some exciting things to tell you. We exist, you know, only to talk to you and to help you face this new life we share together. And by the way, that is not sunlight that floods our stage; you know as well as we do that it is night outside and that the light is only electric. Therefore you see? This is where it comes from. There's no point in hiding it and pretending, is there?

At one blow Meierhold had destroyed the naturalism of the Art Theatre, had brought in a stylization, had created what seemed to be a proletarian theatre, and had bridged the gulf between actor and spectator as he had so long wanted to do.

It has been said that every production of Meierhold creates a new theatre and this is true, so that it is hard to trace his path without stopping to consider his accomplishment with each play which he undertook. But time forbidding that, I may say in a word that Meierhold's rôle since the Revolution has been that of arch-destroyer of all that is old in Russia. Not only old theatrical conventions have been laid low under his scythe, but the old society has had in him its most brilliant critic and its most vitriolic condemner. The later 1920's saw him advancing from the early agitational plays, through a phase of poetic Revolutionary tragedy, to a genre of production which made him the scenic Voltaire of the Soviet Union. With marvelous comic genius he lifted the old Russia to heights of ridicule and absurdity and hurled it with cruel and bitter force upon the rocks of his poetic and social disillusionment. His power was devastating, and into his famous productions of "Woe from Wisdom" and "The Inspector-General," he threw all the weight of his satire and the beauty of his artistic formalism.

It is difficult to divide Meierhold's work into periods, but if it were possible, then we might say that the first period after the Revolution, which began with a production of Verhaeren's "Dawn" in 1921, is marked by the development of constructivism, dynamic action, and a movement toward simplification. The very use of these three terms suggests that Meierhold continued to work in abstractions and this was true. Constructivism, the scenic essence of abstraction, had been tried in the theatre, as a matter of fact, before the Revolution. In 1914 Meierhold produced Alexander Blok's "The Unknown" with a setting that held the seeds of it. But it was the Revolution that gave it its significance. Meierhold is sometimes thought of as its creator but this is not true, for constructivism existed in art before it was adapted to the theatre. It was he, however, who introduced it to the stage, for he appreciated that there was a style which would make a complete break with all previously existing scenery.

This scenery, with its ladders and scaffolds, its ramps and steps and slides, its colorless backgrounds, based on abstract form which would provide it own meaning (abstract in the sense that it was non-representational), paralleled his attempts to create the same kind of art with actors and their movements. It was apparent to him that it would be this sort of scenery only which could complement his actors. However, constructivism did not accept pure form empty of function; it must be part of the action. A slide, if it was to be used, must be on the stage in order to help the actor express a special meaning, like the slide in "The Magnificent Cuckold." Since Meierhold had long sought unity between actor and setting, he was further delighted with the dynamic constructions of this new art which were in closest harmony with his theories of bio-mechanical movement, for bio-mechanics bears the closest possible relationship to functional movement.

Constructivism has been considered by some writers to be an attempt to depict a mechanical era in scenic form.

This is perhaps true in part—particularly true in the German theatre—but I do not believe that it was in Meierhold's mind at the beginning. His use of it in plays like Ostrovski's "The Forest," which have nothing to do with the machine age, indicates to me that he used constructivism first because of its non-representational functions and only later did he come to use it to suggest the mechanization of society or as a symbol of the modern Soviet materialistic mind.

As constructivism developed it became more and more absorbed in the function of materials. This was an obvious preoccupation for art in a country which was passing through such a materialistic phase. The constructivists sought new uses for various metals, wood, glass, in forms which expressed their use. These elements had never been so employed before in the Russian theatre. Meierhold became interested in the emotional effect which certain raw materials might produce, and we may trace the movement away from the first bare scaffoldings and uncovered runways through the *décor* for plays using these various raw materials, which were created almost entirely of corrugated metal, for instance, or of wood, or bamboo, until we reach "The Inspector-General," wherein Meierhold, as Komisarjevsky puts it, "almost gave up constructive ideas and followed, partly the methods of the German expressionists, partly the old picturesque and naturalistic methods of other pre-war and modern producers." In this play jumpers were banished and his people wore period costumes; a few tables and chairs appeared, but on a stage still without curtain or proscenium, in a sort of permanent setting composed mainly of a semi-circle of a dozen doors. In this production he used also a smaller moveable stage which advanced toward the audience in the full light and with the actors and props in place upon it.

The use of dynamic movement in abstract rhythms to

arouse emotions and convey ideas is as old as art. The primitive origins of the theatre in aboriginal dances and ceremonies, where movements are symbolic and yet direct in their appeal to the spectator, are based on it. Bio-mechanics is a partial return to that kind of art, but with modern interpretations derived from Taylorism and from the reflex action theories of Pavlov which alter it. In so far as it attempts to substitute mental or nervous motiva-tion of action for emotional it is something new in the theatre. The Art Theatre actor had said, "I make these movements because my feelings force me to." The bio-mechanical actor says, "I make these movements because I know that, by making them, what I want to do can be most easily and directly done."

The practice of such a theory of movement leads quite obviously to the simplification which was Meierhold's third early revolutionary characteristic. By removing what he considered to be all the mumbo-jumbo of emotionally dic-tated movement, he got down at last to bare action which had no relation to the traditional, emotionally explicable action. It was entirely rational and physiological. When a person pricks his finger or sits on a tack, he jumps. He does not do this dictated by his emotions. It is a nervous reaction and that only. A tiger springs not in answer to its emotions but because it instinctively knows that its spring will bring it at once to its prey. Observation of these facts, of behaviorism, led Meierhold to his new system.

By the adoption of such a theory Meierhold came to what were abstract Marxian principles in art—the substi-tution of rational, functional, utilitarian creation for emo-tional, intuitive processes, and it was at this point that Meierhold came closest to being a revolutionary leader in both senses of the word. The reason I do not think that he was—a point which I shall develop later—is that he arrived at this as a *result* of his purely aesthetic experiments and was not using it as a motivation for the development of them. If in the process of applying Marxian principles to art, he had found his bio-mechanical theory, then I might be mistaken, but the knowledge which we have of his previous searches for abstractions leads me to believe that his aim was to discover an aesthetic convention, and that he came first to his bio-mechanics and then discovered that it coincided with a Marxian attitude.

In contrast to this first period when his devotion was to movement, Meierhold's second period is static. Now he works for conventionalization of pose to replace conventionalization of action. His great production of "The Inspector-General," which may be taken as the high-point of this period, was designed as a series of poses, one blending into another, but the whole composition essentially static. When movement is used the principles of bio-mechanics direct it, but the greater influence is now the Commedia dell' Arte again. With it Meierhold returns to a kind of symbolism. There is reintroduction of real details in setting to replace the constructive, and great attention is paid to the sensuous effect of various materials and objects, but they are used with an intellectual purpose. *Things* are used to arouse emotional reactions by their associative power, and, by their effect on the senses, to stimulate rational reflection. A cigar or a fan in the hand of an actor is no longer simply a cigar or a fan, but a symbol for all the qualities which the observer can associate with those objects and their users. The Moscow Art Theatre, with all its attention to the subconscious in its acting, yet makes its appeal solely to the consciousness of the spectator. Meierhold, with all his emphasis on the rational, appeals directly to the subconscious.

Meierhold's characters also are symbols. Although dressed now in realistic costumes of period, but with some exaggeration of detail and a definite exaggeration of make-up, they continue to be as they have been since the Revolution, completely depersonalized representatives of type. He wipes all expression from their faces, except the permanent stamp which their make-up gives to them. They are empty masked automatons. Here the Sovietized Commedia dell' Arte is most apparent.

When the earlier period of destruction was over, and the old régime had been "liquidated," there remained no need to worry the dead rat. But the line of march of the Revolution Meierhold has seemed unable to follow. The new socialistic realism has no expression in his repertoire. In 1934 and 1935 he still looked backward—to Dumas, Chekhov, Pushkin. Good Communist critics say Meierhold's day is past. So long as the Revolution needed a winnowing sword, Meierhold wielded it, but now the call is for plowshares and pruning hooks, and they mournfully predict the spear he continues to carry will eventually be thrust into himself.

2

This champion of proletarian art is for me, paradoxically enough, a complete aristocrat. Although Meierhold may never have borne a title—I neither know nor care about his birth—he has the tastes, inclinations and temperament which, for want of better definition, we call aristocratic. Soviet critics are, I suspect, just beginning to realize this as they become aware that a theatre *for* the proletariat, which is what Meierhold's is, is not at all the same thing as a theatre *of* the proletariat. Now that real proletarian art, by which I mean art created by proletarian artists, is just beginning to appear, it is plain to see how far from being proletarian Meierhold's art is and always has been.

By retracing the career which I have just outlined I can show what I mean. First there was Meierhold's break with the Art Theatre which was always essentially bourgeois. The latter's preoccupation with commonplace domestic life—portrayed in a realism that closely approached naturalism—its lesser success when it essayed symbolism, expressionism, and other sophisticated intellectualities, its great popularity with the intelligent theatre-going public which was essentially middle class in the days before the war, all this points to that bourgeois tendency in the Art Theatre.

When Meierhold left the Art Theatre he cast off his tie to bourgeois art and its literalness. But where did he turn? He forsook Moscow, the merchant city, for St. Petersburg, the imperial city. There he found himself more in sympathy with and better understood by the artists of the *Mir Iskusstva* ("World of Art") school and their sophisticated and aristocratic following. He became devoted to the theatrical forms of those remote times and places when the theatre was either clerical or aristocratic. His best work before 1917 was done at the imperial theatres. He has never been particularly popular with the bourgeoisie, nor with the proletariat either, after the first hysterical days of the Revolution. Nowadays he is adored by certain sophisticated and acutely sensitive artistic spirits, of whom there are a few among the Russians and a few more among foreigners in Russia.

The middle class in Russia was never strong, perhaps partly because it appeared so late. By the middle of the nineteenth century it was just beginning to rise and with it the realism of Ostrovski appeared. By the first years of the twentieth century it was in its short-lived ascendancy and the Art Theatre created in those days an art which was its true expression. In doing this it did more than Meierhold has ever done; he has never created an art which was the expression of his society or age: in the pre-war days, as in the post-revolutionary ones, his constant desire has been to escape from the theatre of a material and utilitarian present. The Art Theatre is like bread: simple, fundamental, not too imaginative, necessary. Meierhold is like olives: piquant, a little bitter, unnourishing, appetizing and stimulating to the palate, unnecessary. The enjoyment of his work is definitely an acquired taste.

Meierhold is not the artist of the masses because he is a complete individualist. That he greeted the Revolutionary hour with enthusiasm seems to me more an act of opportunism than of welcoming a long-awaited Messiah. It gave him the chance to legitimatize and give tremendous impetus to the revolution in the theatre which he wanted, and because of his dynamic personality and through liberal use of Communist terminology, he could make the two seem one. He played with the idea of a Mass Theatre because, like Max Reinhardt (who uses the term in a different sense), through the use of the Mass Theatre his own egoism could be exalted. But he is no charlatan; if in his theatre he expresses Meierhold and not a proletariat, he does what any strong artist or poet has to do. I consider it no slander to suggest that he is more aristocratic than bourgeois or proletarian. A man must be as his temperament dictates. Furthermore, I do not deny that it is possible for an aristocrat to be a Communist. His personal political views I do not question; I do not say that he is a bad Communist. All I contend is that, given sympathy, his kind of art could have developed wherever and in whatever society Meierhold had found himself.

The Moscow Art Theatre is essentially a prose theatre. When it has essayed poetry it has given empty vestment to the poetic scheme and decorations of Gordon Craig for "Hamlet," or of Alexander Benois for "Boris Godunov." It has rhythm certainly, but it is the rhythm that is found deep within great prose. Meierhold lacks a conception of what we might pompously call the "rhythm of life," and that the Art Theatre has. But for sheer expression of poetry in all its other implications, Meierhold has a sensitivity that the Moscow Art has always lacked.

When we study the development of the Meierhold Theatre we study only one person, Meierhold himself. He *is* his theatre, and this cannot be otherwise considering his attitude toward the stage. Previously I stated that his earliest influence, that of the French symbolists, required that he consider actors as symbols. Only the individual creator of the whole scheme of expression can invent the symbols —the symbols cannot invent themselves. A theatre of conventions and stylization—unless the conventions are traditional—can scarcely conceivably be a collective theatre. Even if it is so, when it comes to practice its conventions, it is the régisseur who, putting himself in the position of the observer, must give form to the production. The individual actor may understand his own emotions and in a theatre like the *MXAT* where he is called upon to act in accordance with them, he may need only guidance from the director. But in a theatre where outward form is the important factor, the actor by his very physical position on the stage is unable to see the form of the whole and must depend upon the man who sits in the auditorium to tell him how and when to fit into the picture.

It seems to me therefore quite natural that the Meierhold Theatre and likewise the Kamerny Theatre, which is also a theatre of outward form, should be dominated by a master who creates with actors who serve only as animate clay for his modeling.

3

The production of Meierhold's which I studied in Moscow was hardly typical, but then no production of his ever is. This one was called a Chekhov Vaudeville, and it consisted of three one-act plays of Chekhov, "The Proposal," "The Bear," and "The Jubilee," which Meierhold was putting together in a triple bill and presenting in the manner of the French eighteenth century vaudeville.

The first rehearsal of the plays took place on the stage of the Meierhold Theatre, for, as I have said, there is little space in this makeshift playhouse and no rehearsal room is available. The stage was crowded, for almost all of the members of the company were present and all the apprentices. Meierhold sat in the center at a large table. His stooped shoulders give his head a slightly forward thrust which adds prominence to his prominent nose. His thinning gray hair stands on end, apparently held in that position by the electric current generated within him. His movements are rapid, his speech is voluble. In rehearsals he appears to be almost in a state of spontaneous combustion! This first rehearsal simply consists of a talk by him on his ideas for the production.

"Two things are essential for a play's production, as I have often told you," Meierhold begins. "First, we must find the thought of the author; then we must reveal that thought in a theatrical form. This form I call a *jeu de théâtre* and around it I shall build the performance. Molière was a master of *jeux de théâtre*: a central idea and the use of incidents, comments, mockery, jokes—anything to put it over. In this production I am going to use the technique of the traditional vaudeville as the *jeu*. Let me explain what it is to be. In these three plays of Chekhov I have found that there are thirty-eight times when characters either faint, say they are going to faint, turn pale, clutch their hearts, or call for a glass of water; so I am going to take this idea of fainting and use it as a sort of leit-motif for the performance. Everything will contribute to this *jeu*."

Meierhold reads the script to the company, pointing out his thirty-eight illustrations. The designer, Victor Shestakov, is called in and he draws on the blackboard

his tentative idea for the set which in plan looks like a
biologist's enlarged drawing of an eye with just a suggestion of a tear dropping from either end of it. Meierhold
suggests that the music must be reminiscent of Chopin.
"In fact, we shall use Chopin in rehearsals," he declares.
Now that he has stated this basic idea about the production
he adjourns the rehearsal.

As a prelude to our study of the methods of production
at the Art Theatre, it seemed wise to consider the system
of Stanislavski, which was the preparation of the actor for
his work. In the Meierhold Theatre we do not study a
system of acting, for all that he asks of his actors we have
already discovered in the statement of his under-régisseur.
Instead, we must study Meierhold's personal preparation
for his work, for here it is the director's work which is
important.

Meierhold has a little notebook which he has had for a
good many years. Throughout that time he has noted
down in it various plays which he would one day like to
do. Whenever he has seen a performance of one of them,
he has made further notes about that production which he
did not like, changes he would make. He was spurred to his
recent production of Chaikovski's "Queen of Spades"
through his indignation at the way it used to be produced.

Meierhold prefers to read a play only once at first, for
thus he feels that his interpretation is clearer and his judgment surer. He believes firmly in the correctness of his
first impressions. Then he allows these first impressions to
ferment in his mind. He takes no notes. He ponders long
over the thought of the author. He tries to penetrate the
playwright's meaning, he tries to decide what he himself
would have meant if he'd written such a play. In the end,
he may give to the writer by such a practice a false meaning, but it is a meaning never inconsistent with Meierhold.
In his production of, let us say, "The Inspector-General,"

he has tried to express the thought of Gogol. He has tried
to show what he believes to be Gogol's disgust at the
hypocrisy of the time, Gogol's ridicule of the provincial
government of early nineteenth century Russia, Gogol's
condemnation of the middle class's watery morality.
Whether he has succeeded, or whether Gogol even intended
these things, no one but Gogol, dead these hundred years,
could say; but that Meierhold has definitely succeeded in
expressing his own thought through "The Inspector-
General" there can be no doubt. This effort to get at the
meaning behind the word of the dramatist is one cause of
his drastic rearrangement of texts. If only half the lines
of "The Inspector-General" express what he considers to
be the author's purpose, then the other half he cuts or else
revises so that they may become part of that same purpose.

Once he decides actually to produce the play and has determined the motivating idea, he starts to plan the *mise-
en-scène*, again in his head. He does not write out his *mise-
en-scène* at any time, or any of his definite ideas of a production, because he seems to feel that in the writing they
lose their purity. "A thought once uttered becomes a lie,"
he remarks. At any rate, an idea written out loses its charm
for him. Meierhold puts the play into rehearsal still without any notes in writing. He declares that as he works he
must take the physical qualities and abilities of his actors
into consideration, and if a set plan were created before he
started, it would only have to be changed when he faced
the material at his hand. For he uses actors, as he himself
says, as a sculptor models his clay, working with them to
get various textures which will create various effects, as
does the sculptor. Therefore the actor who is most mal-
leable becomes his best actor. Ilinski, for instance, is considered by most people to be Meierhold's best actor today.
Ilinski is to my mind not a great actor at all; he simply
has a remarkably pliable face and body with which Meier-

hold may do what he pleases, a perfect "dead pan" which the director may fill with meaning or empty at will. Of course, he must have some more subtle sympathy for Meierhold's style than the other actors there, since he can grasp more quickly and fully what the director wishes him to express, but without Meierhold's direction, he would be only a very mediocre actor.

Meierhold's company of actors is rather like a collection of rubber balls. He throws them and they must be able to bounce; if they cannot, he has no use for them. But that a ball should bounce itself is impossible. An intelligent rubber ball is unheard-of nonsense; so is individual intelligence in the Meierhold Theatre. The maestro supplies all the intelligence just as he supplies all the artistry. But there are many actors—all the good ones—who do not want to be rubber balls, to be thrown about by no matter how good a player, so naturally Meierhold has difficulty in keeping a good company.

Meierhold is a profoundly well-informed, intelligent, and sensitive musician and he not only sees his production but hears it. The laws of musical construction and of musical contrast, the effects of sound and tempo, are all applied by him in working out a play. "The Inspector-General" was built as a sonata. "La Dame aux Camélias" was composed as follows:

ACT I

1. After the Grand Opera and strolling at the Fête	1. Andante Allegro Grazioso Grave
2. One of the Nights	2. Capriccioso Lento (trio) Scherzando Largo e mesto
3. The Meeting	3. Adagio Coda. Strepitoso

ACT II

1. Dreams of a Rural Idyll

    1. Allegretto
    Tenerezza
    Intermedietto

2. The Money of the Count de Girey

    2. Moderato. Secco
    Agitato

3. Confession of a Courtesan

    3. Lamentoso
    Molto Appassionato

ACT III

1. Bougival

    1. Giocoso

2. Bourgeois Morals

    2. Freddo
    Dolce
    Impetuoso
    Lacrimoso

3. Shattered Dreams

    3. Lento con dolore
    Inquieto

ACT IV

1. Olympe's feast

    1. Tempo vivo
    Tempo di ballo

2. Again in the rôle of a Courtesan

    2. Tempo di valse
    Allegro agitato

3. Parole d'honneur

    3. Espressivo
    Piu mosso
    Lugubre

ACT V

1. Abandoned

    1. Tempo commodo
    Largo e mesto

2. A late returning

    2. Amoroso

3. "And life goes on"

    3. Coda. Spianato

The right-hand column was not taken from a musical score played behind the scenes or in an orchestra pit as an accompaniment to the action. Indeed, there is little music played in the whole production. It is rather a key to the movement, to the timbre and pitch of voices, to the tempo of action, and, of course, when there is music, to its quality. In fact, a sensitive impressionist artist could light the production from study of this column, and as Meierhold is such an artist he uses this column as a key to lighting and to color in sets and costumes as well.

The left-hand column illustrates another characteristic of Meierhold's method: his division of a play into many short episodes. In "La Dame aux Camélias" there were but fifteen; in "The Inspector-General" there were many more internal episodes, although the program announced but eleven. These scenes are not like those into which the Art Theatre divides its acts, either in purpose or in effect. At the MXAT these *kuski* are segments of text which are rehearsed separately but when performed flow without a break, so that one is aware only of the continuity of the act. Meierhold divides the act into small episodes so that each idea of the dramatist (or each Meierholdian interpretation of an idea of the dramatist), or else each example of the *jeu de théâtre,* may have individual expression. Each *kusok,* as we see, has its own title; sometimes it will be played as a separate scene in performance with a pause before and after it, sometimes with music to introduce it, sometimes even with its own setting (none of this specified by the author, be it understood). Sometimes, on the other hand, the scenes will blend one into another so that the audience, as at the MXAT, does not realize that a new scene has begun. Thus the whole production becomes like an "improvisation" or "variations on a theme." Meierhold, taking a few lines of text, sometimes only a stage direction, will build up a whole pattern of action, usually pantomime, which develops the idea therein. One line may become the motivation for five minutes of cadenzas which the virtuosity of Meierhold will have invented, before the theme—that is, the text of the play—is continued. In "The Proposal," for instance, the simple direction, "He drinks a glass of water," becomes a small scene. Ilinski breaks off his speech, clutches his heart with one hand, his coat lapel with the other. The father rises, steps back a pace and holds out both his arms, as though Ilinski were about to swim to him. The maid in the background raises her broom and holds it poised in mid-air over her head. There is a pause. The Chopin music begins to play. Ilinski, still holding his lapel, reaches out with the other hand for the glass on the table. He holds it at arm's length from his mouth; his eyes grow bigger; the music plays louder. The father and the maid stand motionless. With a quick jerk Ilinski draws the glass to him and downs the water. The music stops, the maid returns to her sweeping. Ilinski carefully smooths his lapel and returns the glass to the table. The father continues with the next line.

Since I have made such a point of the fact that Meierhold works without pencil and paper, the reader may wonder whence that double column of notes on the "Dame aux Camélias" production. The answer will draw forth another contrast with the Art Theatre and further point to this being a theatre of the régisseur. To assist Meierhold in rehearsals and in the routine of the production generally, is what is known as a "Régisseur Brigade" which consists of from eight to fifteen under-régisseurs. These are what we should call in America stage managers, for their work is only to a very slight degree creative. Their chief concern is the preparation of a sort of super-prompt book which shall be a record of Meierhold's work on the production. The brigade divides itself into three groups: one which works on lines, records line changes, inflections, tempo of speeches, all the vocal side of the production; one which records business; one which handles all other notes on production which Meierhold makes in the course of rehearsal. At the end of each rehearsal the brigade meets and its work is compiled into what is practically a stenographic record of all the creation of the director. The result is probably the most elaborate and detailed prompt book which is made anywhere in the world today.

When Meierhold is absent from rehearsal the régisseurs, one of whom always acts as a sort of assistant director, can carry on his work with perfect exactitude by reference to this book. But no effort is made to create anything new which Meierhold has not done. As we study the work in rehearsals further we shall see how necessary such a record is, whereas at the Art Theatre a prompt book was only of use if the actor had an unfortunate lapse of memory.

In composing a play Meierhold builds not only a musical but a pictorial structure. He applies the laws of space in his theatre. I have talked about his preoccupation with space before but it has been in a general sort of way. Now I mean the actual spatial composition within a particular play. This is one of the chief problems of painting, and Meierhold makes a careful study of it as well as of music. He is particularly fond of the Italian primitives, a predilection which is quite understandable, since we know his love of conventionalization of emotion, of a sort of combination of mysticism and symbolism, all of which he can find in the early Italians. Giotto is his favorite because, as Meierhold says, "He knows the art of not filling in the empty spaces."

In producing "La Dame aux Camélias" he tried to infuse the quality of Manet and of Renoir into his stage pictures. This pictorial influence has appeared only in his later revolutionary period; it helps to explain the recent static quality and the constant use of posing. It shows how far he has moved from the early dynamic and constructivist days and it suggests that he is closer to his still earlier period of intimacy with the painters of the *Mir Iskusstva* when together with Golovin he created almost entirely through the medium of sensuous stage pictures. When he moves into his new theatre, however, he will doubtless be influenced less by painting than by sculpture. He has always accepted his actors three-dimensionally, but at times he has tried to make them two-dimensional and fit into two-dimensional scenery; at other times he has tried, like the painters, to make a two-dimensional medium appear three-dimensional; again, he has looked for the day when he could create with actors who would appear only three-dimensionally in empty space.

Even his pictorial compositions have been geometric. This is the hold-over of the constructivist influence which was of course entirely geometric. In "La Dame aux Camélias" he used diagonal lines almost entirely. I have described the stage as being divided into two principal parts by the use of a curtain which worked diagonally from lower right to upper left hand corner instead of parallel to the front edge of the stage. His pieces of scenery were arranged along diagonal lines either running parallel to this central line or intersecting it. This forced the furniture into diagonal positions and all this finally brought the actors into diagonal compositions, which was the end he had in mind. This geometric use of space was only apparent on analysis, like the geometry in a Leonardo painting, and it was, in this period of his development, so subordinated to the pictorial effect that one is scarcely conscious of it.

The next rehearsal of Chekhov's "Proposal" which I attended was a reading of the play by the cast. I sat in a front row of the auditorium with the rest of the company who were not performing and with the apprentices. On the stage sat Meierhold facing the actors. "Let us begin!" he ordered. The opening line was read by Chubukov, or rather only the first four words.

"Wait!" said Meierhold. "You must read the line this way," and he illustrated. Chubukov read the line again.

"Stop," said Meierhold. "You are not giving it quite the same reading as I did. I wonder if you know why you are saying those words? To read it the way I just did, you must understand what sort of a character I want Chubukov to appear."

Then Meierhold started in on a brilliant dissection of the line, of the juxtaposition of words and sounds that made up the line, of the meaning of it, of the characterization, of the style of the play as it would be set by that opening speech. "The sort of character *I* want Chubukov to appear." Not the sort of character which the actor visualized, nor his interpretation of his part at all. Instead, "Watch me! This is the expression Chubukov must wear to point his absurdity. My expression now. . . . Do you see? Now you try it."

Again and again the actor repeated the line. Each time Meierhold's keen ear detected some slight variation from his preconceived idea of the way the line should sound. Finally he was satisfied. "Proceed," he directed. And the next speech was read. Again came the same explanations and the same repetitions. Stanislavski, in the "Carmen" rehearsal, had worked for fifteen minutes with the actress to find the correct reading of a single line. But he had been simply trying to help her find the reading which came most easily and truly from her. He did not know himself what was needed until she gave what sounded true to him. Meierhold is not searching for a reading that will satisfy the actor, as was Stanislavski, but for one that is as close as possible to the way *he* would read the line. He knows in advance the exact speed and intonation of each word; it simply takes time for the actor to catch it exactly.

For three hours this continued and not more than a dozen pages of one of the one-act plays were finished. But when finally the play had been read through, it seemed to me that it was already set. All this was so different from the Art Theatre. Here there was no seeking the underlying meaning, no discussion of the real thought or emotions which some speech conveyed, no feeling the way. Meierhold had analyzed it all out in advance.[1] He was leading his actors along a brilliantly lighted path, pointing out all the curves and pitfalls and bringing the cast swiftly around them all. They had only to follow. Once they reached the end, they were through; they must memorize the route they had taken and then they could present the performance. Of course, there must be a few more line rehearsals to help this memorizing process and to give polish to the flow of dialogue. But in almost no time at all—at least compared to the *MXAT*—we are at what is the final stage of the Art Theatre's production plan, at the point where the director begins to give the play its outward form.

The next rehearsal I attended was devoted to setting "business." The stage was crowded. The center part of it was set for the action. Meierhold sat at one table at the edge of it; his assistants sat at two other tables; the usual crowd of onlookers filled the wings and footlights. The actors took their places for the opening scene. "Let us begin!" said Meierhold. The first two speeches were read. Meierhold was at once on his feet.

"As you say 'Ivan Vassilyevich!' the second time, clap

---

[1] A verbatim stenographic report of Meierhold's directions in a rehearsal of "The Inspector-General" appears in the appendix to this volume. It might interest the reader to turn to this for comparison at this point.

your hands—so," he directed. "And you, Ivan, turn your
head slightly to the left . . . just a little further. The audience must see only the tip of your ear coming out from
under your hat. A little further. . . . There! And at the
same time, distend your neck. Watch me do it. . . .
That's it! Now let us try it again. . . . That was better.
Only your handclap, Stepan Stepanovich, must be more
affectionate. Place your wrists directly opposite each other
as you clap, instead of side by side. That will make a
smoother, more sliding clap. . . . That's the way. And
you, Ivan Vassilyevich, will be having a hat that is slightly
too large, although it will not appear so at first to the
audience. You are a country bumpkin and you have borrowed your father's best hat to pay this call in; his head
is a bit bigger than yours. Then when Chubukov claps,
you will allow the hat to slip down and cover your ear
as though it were involuntarily coming to the assistance
of your weak heart. That is why the audience must see a
little more of your ear under the hat than it did the first
time just now. And let your eyes—just your eyes, for your
head must not move again now—let your eyes rove the
room hunting for the glass of water, and when they find
it, rest upon it. That is the first suggestion of fainting
which will accompany the clapping at once here in the
first speech. There will be a pause when your eyes find it,
so that the audience observing the direction in which your
eyes are turned, will follow and see the glass and decanter
of water. After a count of two, so: one—two—there will
be a gentle minor chord played on the piano, no more, as
though sight of the water brought that music with it.
That will be the first musical sound. Then when two
speeches later you reach for the glass the first time, the
music will begin to play again, picking up the same
chord as before. But we shall work that out when we
come to it. Now let us try that sequence once again. But

before we start, will the pianist give me a chord. . . . No, that is too low. Its top note should be E flat, I think. . . . There, that's it. Now while we repeat this business, see if you can be finding a Chopin prelude that has a theme beginning with that chord, or at least in that key. Now repeat the action once again, please."

All this direction is on but the first two lines of the play, you must remember. The work proceeds in this fashion for an afternoon. At the end of it, three pages have been finished. But they have been completely set, every movement, every flicker of an eyelash, every chord of music, every prop or article of costume that will be part of those three pages has been indicated. The play could be presented tomorrow in finished form up to the top of page four! That is all for today. Tomorrow another three pages and the next day three more. Finally the entire play will have been gone through once.

In integrating music with his production, Meierhold is guided by his episodic divisions of the play of which I have spoken, and seeks to find a musical expression for each. In the Chekhov, as we see, every reference to fainting becomes a music cue, and because each reference is a variant of the same theme, the music is in the same key. The pianist brings to rehearsal a great pile of music. Meierhold hums the sort of thing he wants, the pianist leafs through his sheets and tries to find it; in this play it is either Chopin or Chaikovski. When all the music is collected, it is turned over to the composer of the production who has been carefully listening at rehearsals, and he works out a score from the assembled material and according to the musical pattern which Meierhold has indicated by his choice.

These rehearsals at which business is created are perhaps the most interesting in the whole evolution of a production at the Meierhold Theatre. Meierhold seems to know what every position and every movement is to be. He knows the inner reason for it, the outward effect of it, the audience's reaction to it. All these he explains to the actor and then proceeds to show him how to do it. Step by step, gesture by gesture, he builds up the action. The actor remains standing perfectly still until Meierhold gives him a movement; then, as in the reading of lines, he makes his approximation of Meierhold's example.

From the first rehearsal Meierhold has had a vision in his mind of the completed production, the vision of what the audience will see, and this he holds always before him. As Huntly Carter puts it, "Stanislavski told the actor he must forget that he is on the stage. Tairov told him he must remember nothing else. Meierhold told him he must remember that he is one of the audience."

Since Meierhold is constantly looking at the stage picture as a whole, he creates all the characters in rehearsal simultaneously and does not work with each actor individually for more than a speech or two. The speed with which ideas pour out is such that one understands how a dozen stage managers can be kept busy making notes of them. For in the creation of business Meierhold is a master. He must be, in a theatre based on externals. His business seems to be invented entirely on the spur of the moment. In fact, all of Meierhold's work seems to be inspirational, although we know that he works out a great deal in his own mind in advance. I am told that during the production of "La Dame aux Camélias" rehearsals would advance for two or three weeks without a word from Meierhold, and then suddenly just when the cast was getting most discouraged, a long and complicated idea would come out in full form.

It is this inspirational work of his that makes Meierhold's rehearsals so engrossing and so valuable to his students. He could never give them formal lectures about his methods, he could never set down a system like Stanislavski (although he once did attempt to formulate some of his theories in a book called *The Journal of Dapertutto*). All that is done for him, and sometimes incorrectly, by his commentators. But by watching him work his students can learn about acting and directing and pantomime—a very great deal about pantomime—and something about painting and music and mathematics too. In the course of every rehearsal, often perhaps in his final bit of directing, he will compose some piece of business so remarkable that it brings a round of applause from the apprentices and the attendant company. I shall never forget one of the later rehearsals of "The Proposal." Meierhold had been inventing a dozen pieces of business to point his *jeu*, the fainting-water-drinking motif. Ivan Vassilyevich had done as much with the glass and carafe of water as seemed possible. Finally, as the rehearsal drew near its close, Meierhold rose suddenly. "Watch me and do likewise," he ordered. Then he read the line: "If it were not for these terrible agonizing palpitations, Madam, if it were not for the throbbing in my temples—" He paused, looked about him wild-eyed, seized the carafe, held it in his outstretched hand a moment, then lifted it and emptied its entire contents over his head! With his hair and nose streaming water, he finished the line: "I should speak to you very differently!" The apprentices and cast cried, "Bravo!" Meierhold bowed, wiped his face and head and adjourned the rehearsal.

It is a pity that Meierhold never appears in any of his performances any more, for he is, in my opinion, the greatest actor in Russia today. He is great because he gives to his outward forms, which are superb, the inner spiritual meaning which his actors many times cannot give but which must be there if his theatre is to be of any dramatic force at all. The emptiness which so many of his performances have is because the soul of Meierhold is missing and only the body has been reproduced. Whenever his performances are moving it is because somehow his actors have caught up the whole of their master-creator and have arrived at his spiritual subtlety; but this rarely happens. His rehearsals are such exciting experiences not only because Meierhold is ever the showman but because in them he himself acts every character, combining the virtuosity of Heifetz with the soul of Kreisler.

When the Chekhov play had been in rehearsal six weeks or two months, Meierhold had not yet chosen his final cast of three characters. Every week or so he tried a new actor as the father or the daughter. (Ilinski seemed set as Ivan Vassilyevich.) Such a procedure would be possible in no other theatre, but here, so long as he has an actor to work with, Meierhold can go on with creation unimpeded. The régisseurs have made a detailed record of the progress so that if one actor finally dissatisfies him and he changes to another, the new one may learn what has already been done from the prompt book and go on from there.

Although I have said that Meierhold has the finished production in his mind at the first rehearsal and always thereafter, I do not mean that the play takes its final form at once and is never changed. After the long period during which all the details of action and movement are created, there follows another when Meierhold leaves the stage and goes to the auditorium to begin his revisions and additions from there. For a time he makes constant interruptions and is continually dashing up the runway to the stage from his seat by a little table in the center of the house. All this time he is building, adding new movements, new pieces of business. Then he begins to run an entire act, in this case the whole short play, without interruption. He is working now for the tempo of the whole and its form. There are many more run-throughs here than we saw at the MXAT, two or three times through the one-act play at one rehearsal. Between run-throughs Meierhold talks with the actors and his corps of régisseurs about business and tempo, drinks tea and eats a sandwich—then back to it again.

At this point the lighting begins. American theatre workers light a play only after the setting is on the stage. To Meierhold, however, light has its own part in the production aside from illuminating scenery and actors, and it must be orchestrated into the performance just as is the music. Consequently it can be begun whenever he is ready to turn his attention to it. A month before its opening I attended one of his rehearsals of "Queen of Spades" at the Maly Opera in Leningrad. None of the scenery that would be used in the production was on the stage, the actors were without costume or make-up, but while the rehearsal with full orchestra went on, Meierhold devoted his entire attention to lighting. He went from spotlight to spotlight adjusting and focusing each one himself, returned to his center aisle seat to relay cues from there to the operators, and to observe the effects of his experiments with colors and intensities of beam. Meierhold does not look upon light naturalistically. He considers that in the theatre it has only aesthetic value; that there is an emotional power from light whose extent if explored is far greater than that to be derived from the use of amber gelatine for sunset effects or steel-blue in night scenes. Sources of light need not be natural either and the pattern of light beams against darkness is often part of his visual composition. For these reasons he need not wait until the set is in place before creating and rehearsing his light plot. It can quite as well be done in a bare theatre with only his actors and music to guide him.

As Meierhold is sometimes practically the author of the piece, as he is to a great extent the composer of its score, as he enacts all the rôles by creating everything for his actors, as he invents the lighting, it is only natural to suppose that so also he has a hand in the designing of the scenery. This is quite true. In the constructivist days it was more or less necessary, for the setting and action had to be one. In his later productions he has continued to have a hand in devising the *décors*, for he believes that he himself must still correlate them with the action. As his complete domination of his theatre has prevented the best actors from joining him, so the most original designers are not eager to work in the Meierhold Theatre where they would be little more than master-draughtsmen.

Thus it is that Meierhold reigns supreme in his domain. Just as he is responsible for its weaknesses, so its greatness springs from him alone. Meierhold is as completely bound to the past as is the Art Theatre—the latter to the bourgeois conceptions of a literal art of the days of its foundation, Meierhold to the past in art which stretches from the beginnings of the theatre up to the Russian Revolution, but no further. But the Art Theatre has this advantage: it may carry its past into the future because it is a collective adventure in art and the descendants of Stanislavski and Nemirovich-Danchenko are as much a part of the collective as are the generation that dies with them. They may change it eventually from bourgeois forms to proletarian ones. They are already on that way. Meierhold's adventure into art has been solitary; when he is gone there will be no one to succeed him. His contribution was that of providing the impetus to theatrical revolution, and it is a contribution which has been completed. The influence of his style will certainly continue and perhaps in expressions more adequate to the needs of a proletariat whom he may have represented but one of whom he never was. At any rate, the American theatre has had no Meierhold and that, I think, is a pity.

4

The Kamerny Theatre is another autocratic theatre in which Tairov and his consort and leading actress, Alice Koonen, hold undisputed dominion. It is as impossible to imagine the Kamerny without Tairov as to imagine the Meierhold Theatre without Meierhold. If my belief that a theatre built on external form must always be a one-man theatre is correct, then that explains this second theatre of the régisseur in Moscow. For Tairov has constructed a formalism of his own creation and the practice of it requires his personal direction and interpretation.

The Kamerny Theatre was founded by Alexander Tairov in 1914. Economically speaking, Tairov chose a difficult time to found a theatre. Just on the eve of the Great War money for new artistic ventures was scarce; aesthetically, however, Tairov felt that the time was ripe. The Art Theatre was becoming constantly more petit-bourgeois and its naturalism and its symbolism alike revolted him. Stanislavski had said that it was his aim "to chase the theatre from the theatre." Tairov wanted to bring the theatre back into the theatre: a theatre theatrical. *Kamerny* means "chamber." The new group was to be a *théâtre intime*. It did not expect to be a theatre with a wide public appeal; it demanded a sophisticated audience. A certain small group of intellectuals and students, of the type which usually supports new ventures in aestheticism, acclaimed Tairov's excursion.

With what was Tairov to replace naturalism? The young director knew more definitely what he did not want than what he did. It seemed to him, however, that instead of a theatre of everyday life, his should be a theatre of heroics. His aim would be the exaltation of the hero. This hero was to lift the audience above the realms of life into a region of pure aesthetic harmony. His plays would be heroic plays; hence in the center of his performance would be the actor, but now a "new actor equivalent to the full meaning of the word." By that he meant that his actor was always to remain an actor; he was not to fuse his personality with that of the character he was portraying—a fundamental conception of the Stanislavski method. Stanislavski had told his actor to forget that he was on the stage; Tairov told his actor always to remember that he was on the stage.

Tairov then began to create new keys for this new kind of actor to play upon. The aesthetic harmony he sought could be found only through the development of new rhythms. Movement became formalized by him into aesthetic abstractions which were to strengthen the rhythms and lend them that unreal color which he sought. He developed a system of intoned speech which heightened what he felt to be the abstract definition of heroics. He created gestures which by their formal and unreal rhythms would further heighten the theatricality. It is probable that Tairov had in mind the Greek theatre, where the outward paraphernalia of heroism were the mask, the high-heeled buskin, the formalized gesture and intonation. He wished to re-create its theatrical monumentality. This technique of the new actor began to minimize the importance of the rôle as attention was diverted from the play to the actor. In this Tairov made his greatest departure from Stanislavski.

In its search for a pure formalistic style, the Kamerny necessarily discarded naturalistic decorations, and innovations in lighting and scenery were made. Futurism and cubism entered the theatre and constructivism as well, but a constructivism based on form and not on function. Herein it differed from that which Meierhold made use of.

"Salomé," by Oscar Wilde, has been considered to be the masterpiece of the early days of the Kamerny Theatre. I was privileged to see a performance of it on the occasion of the twentieth anniversary celebration of the Theatre in January, 1935; it is no longer in the regularly performed repertoire of the Theatre. Its artistic composition is exquisite and it rightly takes its place among the chief museum pieces of the Russian theatre—but that is all it is today. With its original performance the Theatre received the recognition of the Soviet government, now come into power, and it became a state theatre. At the same time it became influenced by the aestheticism of Wilde which caught the artistic imagination of the Theatre and probably did as much as anything else to retard its progress along the line of the Revolution.

The Kamerny, like the other theatres founded before 1917, found difficulty in accepting the implications of the proletarian Revolution. In fact, it was particularly hard for Tairov because his art was by its very nature devoted to the cultivated taste of a small group of people. To comply with the demands of the new audience he would have to concern himself with the Revolutionary message and content of plays, and to do that he would have to change his belief that the play is only a pretext for the art of the actor. Such a profound change was very difficult for this theatre. A couple of the new Soviet dramas were tried but both were failures. The playwrights were too naturalistic to suit the style of Tairov, and to accept naturalism and abnegate his artistic principles was unthinkable to him.

It was necessary, however, that he produce some contemporary drama, so Tairov turned to foreign authors. He tried Shaw, G. K. Chesterton, then Eugene O'Neill. In O'Neill he found what he needed. O'Neill was not a revolutionary, it is true, but certain of his plays brought out labor problems and race problems which, although not solved from an orthodox Marxian point of view, were yet near enough to the required social approach. To these plays

Tairov did not need to apply the principles of pure naturalism. Encouraged by his success with O'Neill, particularly when he went on tour abroad ("The Hairy Ape," "All God's Chillun Got Wings," "Desire Under the Elms" were the plays he chose), Tairov went further in the field of American drama and produced Sophie Treadwell's "Machinal" and Dos Passos' new "Fortune Heights."

In the production of these plays Tairov gradually discarded certain elements of his previous formalism and approached a neo-realism which, while far from naturalism, yet made it possible for him to produce Vishnevski's "Optimistic Tragedy," the first Soviet play with which he has had any eminent success. With its performance the Kamerny claims to have arrived at the line of the Revolution. Tairov says, "Our theatre is still the theatre of heroics, but the conception of a hero differs. Now he is the natural son of his environment." His present purpose is to "take the heroic elements of this new hero and create a great scenic whole," a something which, with the Russian love for high-sounding titles, he will call "synthetic realism."

How far the Kamerny Theatre has succeeded in understanding the Revolution is uncertain, for in spite of its recent declarations, this theatre seems to stand outside the main stream. Its earlier years of Wildean aestheticism, its later excursions into foreign material, have given it a stamp which is not purely Russian. It is quite the most cosmopolitan theatre in Moscow, which perhaps is one reason why most foreigners are attracted to it, and also perhaps why many Muscovites distrust it artistically. Excellent in its own field—and its field is a broad one, for in building what he calls a synthetic theatre, Tairov has created a company which can present equally well, within its own style, comedy, tragedy, pantomime, light opera, and a curious kind of musical revue—and led by a master of unquestionably great artistic feeling, it is, I feel, essentially sterile. Is it a coincidence that no theatre in Moscow claims the Kamerny as its direct progenitor?

My study of Tairov's methods was limited because of this conviction of mine that his work lay outside the typical line of the Moscow theatres, and because the particular production in which he was then engaged, "Egyptian Nights," was, because of its magnitude, so atypical even of him that observation would be of little value in discovering his normal practices. "Egyptian Nights," which was a production based on a combination of Shaw's "Caesar and Cleopatra," Pushkin's poem, "Egyptian Nights," and Shakespeare's "Antony and Cleopatra," was in rehearsal off and on for three years and I arrived in Moscow for only the final three months of preparation. Therefore I could get little idea of Tairov's methods except second-hand. Here I shall record only my few firsthand impressions.

The rehearsals of "Egyptian Nights" which I did see were exceedingly interesting. About six weeks before the scheduled opening—the actual opening took place a month late—I went to my first rehearsal there. The production was beginning to be assembled on the stage after months and months of work on small scenes with small groups of actors. There must have been one hundred in the cast, and Tairov, working personally on the stage, was correlating the movements of the crowds with the individuals. This is the part of production at which he excels. In any Tairov performance the mass movement is superb. Where Meierhold takes a single character and puts into his features and his movement generalizations which make him the symbol of a mass, Tairov takes a group and, galvanizing it into unity, makes it move and seem as one.

Although Tairov tells us that his theatre centers about the hero, when it comes to actual performances, I find his supers more effective than his heroes. The great scenes of "Optimistic Tragedy" and of "Egyptian Nights" are scenes of mass movement or when the mass and an individual are set in juxtaposition. The memorable moments are ones like that in which Cleopatra sits at the apex of a pyramid of steps; below her stand or recline her court and attendants, first distinguishable on a dark stage by the points of light which are their glowing torches; like the fleeting scene when two ships are joined in the battle of Actium and the fighting legions overrun the stage—the finest staging of Shakespearean "alarums and excursions" I have ever seen; or like the moment when Cleopatra's terrified attendants fleeing from her presence, scurry down long narrow flights of steps in seemingly endless number, and make of the whole stage an agitated anthill of movement.

In comparison with these mass effects, scenes of dialogue between two or three characters become weak and watery. Tairov seems to have become bored. This contrast to Meierhold may be explained, I think, by the fact that Meierhold brings the actor's eye to the theatre and Tairov does not. Meierhold lavishes creative inventiveness on individual performances because he thinks in terms of the actor's technique. He must project himself into the performance and this he has to do through the medium of each actor. Tairov, not feeling this urge, considers the scenic whole more objectively and so creates more telling ensemble stage pictures.

I was particularly pleased, therefore, to see this rehearsal where, on a stage set with the skeleton of the scenery and with all the steps and levels in place, Tairov worked with his mob. Coming from the Meierhold rehearsals where the régisseur is constantly acting himself, Tairov seems passive. He does little acting, only once in a while shows an actor a move. Instead he walks about, talking his directions, beckoning or pulling his crowds into position. Although

standing within a few feet of a battalion of Roman legion-
aries, he seems able to visualize the effect they will produce from a distance as well as though he were sitting
beside me two-thirds of the way back in the house. He
treats the mob as one person, regulates its movement and
tempo as though it were but one, and it reacts to his directions like one man.

Tairov was already synchronizing the Prokofiev music
with the mass movement and was watching that the time
which the crowd took to perform certain action did not
drag beyond a definite cue in the score. This time there
was only a piano accompaniment but by the next rehearsal which I attended five days later, there was a full
orchestra in the pit. There was also the beginning of lighting, for the dress rehearsals were soon to be upon them.
At them Tairov sits at a little table set in the first row of
the orchestra with his staff of assistant régisseurs beside
him. There are numerous interruptions and the dress rehearsals are far from being smooth run-throughs yet.
Later Tairov will move his table back to the center of the
house, run the acts without pause, taking notes during the
action and criticizing and changing at the end. The mul-
tiple changes of scenery which must be accomplished during a certain number of bars of music and on a darkened
stage with the curtain raised, are rehearsed for about a
month so that when the first night comes the shifts may be
as smooth as the performance.

If rehearsals like Meierhold's have never been seen on
Broadway, the Kamerny dress rehearsals, at least in Tairov's
present mood, are technically carried on very much like
our own, and if the Russian language only sounded a little
more like English one could easily imagine himself in a
theatre on Times Square!

CHAPTER FIVE

Actors and Régisseurs Meet

THE FUSION of the principles of Stanislavski and of
Meierhold may be considered as the creation of a
Center median theatre which will be a combination of the
Left revolutionary with the Right reactionary theatres.
Or it may be thought of as the combination of outward
form with inner meaning and feeling. Or, as a development from that, it may be considered the creation of a
theatre in which the actor and the régisseur will work side
by side with a balanced share in creation.

Those who wish to behold in the theatre only a reflection of political evolution will see in such a development
the arrival of a compromise which carries the Soviet Union
away from the original radical program of the Communist
Party. They can support their theory by citing retrench-
ments and modifications of the Party in other fields and
point to the day when in the theatre as elsewhere the influence of bourgeois conceptions will return.

While it is possible to look upon this very apparent
movement in the theatre as an indication of externally
moderating tendencies, I prefer to consider it solely from
within the theatre, and to explain it as an effort to take
what is good from Meierhold and what is good from Stanislavski and weld them into a new form that will contain
elements of stylization with elements of psychological
realism. I further see in the compromise an effort to weigh
the importance of the régisseur against the value of the

actor's personal contribution and to make use of them both in such a way that the production will get full value from the contributions of each. I believe that the apparent way to the future Soviet theatre lies along such a path. If Vakhtangov had been able to lead the theatre down this path of compromise, he might have brought about the creation of something new that would no longer be in itself a compromise. Perhaps it will be accomplished anyway.

In the theories of Vakhtangov are the seeds of this compromise, the effort to reconcile Stanislavski and Meierhold, contained in a criticism of them both, and a prophecy of the form which a living Russian theatre must take. We have, however, far more than that, something which the politically minded brethren may chew on. I propose to discuss Vakhtangov first as a sort of symbol of the artist of the theatre in his relation to the past and the future in Russia.

Eugene Vakhtangov came to his artistic maturity at almost the exact moment when the Revolution broke. Behind him he had the training of the system of Stanislavski whose most brilliant pupil he was. He had beside him the full development of Meierhold's art which was at that moment in its most advanced revolutionary expression. He had all around him the opening vistas of the proletarian Revolution and before him a new society creating a new civilization. He had the advantage over both Stanislavski and Meierhold, for the roots of each of them were in other soil. Vakhtangov's creative influence derived from all these sources, but the influence of the Revolution was the strongest. He had, however, strong ties to the past. Let us consider them first.

Vakhtangov had learned from Stanislavski that the preparatory stages of creation in acting were conscious—the collection of material, the study of life, the other things which form the first part of the system. Then, on top of this and really more essential, came intuitive creation. When the Marxists arrived, they opposed this, calling it "subjective idealism." The Marxian theatre said that intuition could not work independently; all creative processes must be conscious and rational. At first Vakhtangov could not agree with this Marxian approach. He held a Tolstoyan belief that every play should serve the good; this was combined with a certain mystical attitude toward art. He believed that the theatre was like a monastery isolated from the human world. This isolation existed in order that the actor might be cleansed through his separation from the "world of sinners." He would be as a priest in that "Temple of Art" which Stanislavski called the theatre. Oblivious of the world and its problems, he could devote himself to the perfection of the art in himself.

It was with this attitude that he undertook the direction of the Habima Theatre, that Jewish company which New York saw many years ago in its production of "The Dybbuk," produced by Vakhtangov. Huntly Carter suggests that in his direction of the Habima he was influenced by the Tibetan mysteries. This may be, and if it is so, we see what a long way Vakhtangov had to go to become a Marxist.

To rid himself of these mystical tendencies, and undertake the new conception of art and the theatre, was a struggle for Vakhtangov, as it was for all others brought up in the artistic beliefs of the early twentieth century. But during the months when he lay dying in a hospital (he died in 1922, still a young man) criticism of the existing systems in the theatre occupied all his thoughts and finally the change in him was effected.

Vakhtangov did not want small things in the theatre; he demanded grandiose, revolutionary, philosophical themes. The theatre must tackle the deepest things in the life of the time. For it seemed to him that the whole fate of the human race was then at stake. One could not stand by like the reactionaries and miss the opportunity to participate. But participation through the production of melodramas such as were being put out by the early Revolutionary writers was entirely inadequate. There was not enough criticism and too much naturalism. He wanted something to contrast with these unimportant plays, and if big plays were not being written, one must turn to the classics. In this he was following the conclusions of all other intelligent workers in the Soviet theatre. But he demanded not the contained romantic classicism of, say, Schiller, but rather the rebel attitude of Byron.

His chief trouble earlier had come in trying to understand how it was possible to present one's personal attitude in and toward an *obraz* (the image of the character an actor creates) without its limiting one's art. Vakhtangov now said that the actor must have a critical attitude toward the part he enacts. He must be able to present both the action and his ideological attitude toward the action. In other words, he must both give the image of the character and then make his own comment upon it. In order to do this he and his *obraz* can no longer be one. This method requires subjectivity plus objectivity. Without doing this a classic remains only a study in literary archeology. By adding one's own criticism (which may be in agreement or disagreement with the author's point of view), one makes the play live in the spirit of the present.

From this Vakhtangov passed to his conception of the form of the performance as a whole. First comes the idea of the play; then the artistic characteristics of the company, which are the vehicle for the conveyance of the idea; then the contemporary ideological problems of the period. Every play must have its own method of expression, its own style, but never, whatever the play and whatever the style, must the theatre be forgotten. There was to be no fourth wall in his stage; one actor talks to another, but only in order consciously to tell the audience something. In all this he followed, as you see, close to Meierhold's theories.

The theatre must find the truest form for the performance, Vakhtangov believed, and that form must come from the content of the play. But the content must be reinterpreted through the eyes of the collective to accord with the difference in time. Given a production of "Julius Caesar," by way of illustration, the collective should not attempt a reconstruction of Roman civilization and Roman thought as the Art Theatre had done; neither should it attempt a reconstruction of Elizabethan civilization and an approximation of Shakespeare's contemporary thought. Rather it should pay the classic the great compliment of acknowledging its universality in time and try to make "Julius Caesar" an expression of the collective's own civilization and its own thought. Only thus can it live in today.

The conclusion which Vakhtangov draws from this is that revolutionary method therefore harmonizes with revolutionary content. After ten years you could not do the same play with the emphasis in the same places. Performances must grow and change. A decade hence "Julius Caesar" will have a still different meaning from what it has today. The form of the performance must also correspond to the creativeness of the collective and its contemporaneous ideas. "The Life of Man" could not be produced today as it was twenty-five years ago at the Art Theatre, he said, because it is decadent from the standpoint of our life now. But this attitude does not involve the same criticism of the Art Theatre as Meierhold leveled against it, for it is not essentially aesthetic criticism. Meierhold would have criticized its production as much at that time as after the Revolution. Vakhtangov, however, would have had to say that actualism, the realism of the Art Theatre, on the one hand and the mystic and pessimistic "Life of Man" on the other, were expressions of the artistic characteristics of the *MXAT* and of contemporary thought at the time that it was produced, and that therefore it was correct.

Consequently, Vakhtangov broke with the Art Theatre not because he was opposed to its artistic principles as such, as was Meierhold, but because he believed that naturalism and the style of the *MXAT* had limitations in the new régime and were not the correct expression of it. For some time Vakhtangov had felt that from a technical point of view, the Art Theatre's concentration on the inner meaning of a rôle and the "sub-text" of a play, which was perfect for Chekhov, was not always successful when applied to authors who did not write like Chekhov. The theatre, furthermore, now played to the people and not to a small group of bourgeois intellectuals. Vakhtangov wrote in his diary, "The red line of Revolution has divided the world into old and new. If an artist wants to create after the Revolution, he must create together with the people— not for their sake, not out of them, but together with them. People are creating new forms of life. They are creating through the Revolution because they have no other means to shout into the world about injustice. About which people are we talking? About the people who are creating the Revolution!" With the assumption of this attitude, Vakhtangov had completed his break not only with the Moscow Art Theatre but with Meierhold as well. Let me explain.

Vakhtangov demanded maximum sharpness and definite form to bring out the substance of a play. The productions which were his personal creation, "The Miracle of St. Anthony" and "Princess Turandot," bear the stamp of that sharpness. This style called forth a special form of thought in art—active thinking closely connected with actual life. Class and Party characteristics must be combined with psychological depth. It was at this time that Meierhold was developing his constructivist methods. Vakhtangov did not entirely understand them, but he sounded out certain weaknesses in them. He objected to such complete technical formalism as Meierhold sought. He objected to Meierhold's seeking a form for the new theatre that would be taken from old theatres. He felt that Meierhold's art was all externals and no substance. He objected to what he considered was his mechanistic materialism. Meierhold was making a distinction between the truth of emotions and theatrical truth and denying the former; this Vakhtangov could not accept. In his theatre Meierhold worked, as part of his mechanistic conventionalization, for complete depersonalization; on his stage every soldier looked and acted like every other soldier—one soldier or ten were alike the symbol of all soldiery; every aristocrat and every "comsomol" were like every other on his stage, for they were but stylized symbols for aristocracy or the Young Communist Party. This Vakhtangov objected to, feeling that Meierhold was wasting valuable material when he threw away individuality from characterization.

Vakhtangov felt (and I agree with him, as I have said) that Meierhold did not understand those times. Perhaps, he had already jumped to the future (there I do not agree), but that was very nearly as bad as hanging on in the past, for the theatre above all must feel the moment of the present; and the *obrazy* of the future, said Vakhtangov, must be built on concrete elements from the present day. And when Vakhtangov leveled this criticism against Meierhold, we must remember that he was criticizing the work of the whole Revolutionary theatre of that day, for Meierhold was its dictator, and beside his there was no proletarian theatre of any consequence; the rest were academic. Thus Vakhtangov was, in a sense, the creator of a new kind of Revolutionary theatre, made in protest against the first (Meierholdian) one; a theatre which was, as I believe, much more actually proletarian and much more in the spirit of Marxian art.

Vakhtangov also made certain pronouncements on method in the theatre. The whole collective of the theatre must participate in the plot of the régisseur and of the dramatist. If the actors do not accept the régisseur's plan, then it is inadequate, for the actor is the one who must realize the plan. The régisseur, however, must give unification and line to the play. That "maximum sharpness and definite form" which Vakhtangov underlined are necessarily the responsibility of the régisseur. He must, nevertheless, develop the creative initiative of the actors. This theory is not far removed from Stanislavski's attitude toward rehearsal, but there are some differences in its practice as we shall soon see. Vakhtangov did not accept a passive attitude on the part of an actor. The spirit of the new Russia must have its expression in the theatre collective where all are to share in a common creative experience. In the theatre of Meierhold, leader of the Revolutionary theatre, this was denied the artist.

This analysis of the evolution in the thinking processes of a leading artist in the theatre of the early days of the Revolution, when as yet it knew not what course to pursue and when not all men could follow the erratic genius of Meierhold, reveals, I hope, the profound change which came over the art of the Russian theatre both in ideology and in practice, and the change which was effected in the attitude of the individual artist. I hope, too, that it makes clearer the reason why the younger theatres, while learning their lessons from the Stanislavski system and Meierhold's ideas, have looked back at Vakhtangov as their real progenitor. In him we have, it seems to me, the translator of the great theatrical heritage of Russia into the terms of the modern Soviet stage.

Although Vakhtangov never entirely severed his connections with the Moscow Art Theatre, he became active in the work of its First Studio and was one of its guiding intelligences for several years. Then he himself organized another studio group which became the Third Studio of the Moscow Art Theatre. This he directed until his death. Afterwards, this Studio, like the First, severed its association with the MXAT and became a theatre in its own right, calling itself after its founder.

2

When Vakhtangov died, his disciples set to work to carry on his principles. They have not been entirely successful: too often there have been small and mediocre plays, and to cover up the shallowness they have had recourse to rather empty decorative forms. Occasionally they have done the sort of thing which Vakhtangov would have done: Moscow critics cite "Débâcle" and "Egor Bulichev" as two.

The ten disciples who remain in the Vakhtangov Theatre have kept one fundamental demand of their master close to their hearts. "Look at life," said Vakhtangov, "and make that your guide in creation." When he said that, he was not advocating naturalism. He meant, "Let the theatre never consider itself an end in itself. Let it always go hand in hand with the current of life and be a contribution to it, as it receives its color from it." Neither Stanislavski nor Meierhold have been able to do this consistently throughout their careers. The Vakhtangov Theatre has tried hard to keep this commandment. As life has changed in Russia during the years since his death, so necessarily their theatre has changed, and those critics who say that Vakhtangov's theatre today is not doing what he would do, do not realize that they don't know what he would be doing today, for it certainly would not be what he was doing fifteen years ago.

The ten followers of Vakhtangov have remembered another admonition of their leader: "Each play should have its own style." Through these years they have tried to approach each production with a fresh attitude, ready to work out new forms and ever fearful of getting fixed in one style. They have felt the weakness of the Art Theatre to be its insistence on weighing down every play with its psychological feelings and inner meanings; the definite form and the maximum sharpness they value so much have sometimes disappeared in that way. They have felt the weakness of Meierhold on the other hand to be his continued refusal to use any psychology at all.

Within their own theatre they have established two trends. One is chiefly psychological and the other decorative. They have tried to give to plays which needed sound character analysis the kind of treatment which would emphasize these inner qualities. They have tried to invest plays chiefly theatrical with a vivid colorful spectacular form. "Egor Bulichev" and their late 1935 production of "Aristocrats" were planned as psychological studies. "Intervention" and "Love and Intrigue," equally effective pieces of theatre, were approached from the opposite angle.

The result of this effort to give each play its own style has resulted in making the Vakhtangov Theatre exceedingly flexible, in making it almost "all things to all men." This has been possible chiefly because individual régisseurs within the organization have been allowed to develop each according to his own inclinations. Zakhava has become the leading régisseur for plays which require psychological handling, and Simonov and Akimov (the latter not a regular member of the theatre but a frequent guest-director) have shown the greatest talent for devising productions of

outward theatrical effectiveness. When a play calling for
one kind of treatment is decided upon, it is turned over
to that director who can realize it in the most telling way.
The decision as to what the treatment will be is a collective
one, for the Theatre remembers that it was another of
Vakhtangov's beliefs that the whole collective must participate in the creation. Let us see how this works out.

I have chosen the Vakhtangov Theatre to be the first
representative of the theatre of the future because it is a
theatre where régisseurs and actors meet and share in the
creation of a production. This meeting suggests that the
style will be one in which the actor will contribute psychological portrayal of character (inheritance from the
Art Theatre) to which the régisseur will add a more definite outer theatrical form than do the Art Theatre régisseurs (influence of Meierhold). I have already pointed out
that Vakhtangov wished this to be so. Thus there will be
collective plus individual creation in the process of production. In that the Vakhtangov is like the majority of
Moscow theatres today, although certain parts of its collective functioning are unique.

First, of course, comes the choice of a play; this is the
collective's responsibility. The Artistic Director of the
Theatre, together with the Literary Adviser (every good
Soviet theatre has its literary adviser who is really the play-
reader and also in charge of the repertoire) having found
what he considers to be a likely script, invites the author
to read it to the Theatre. The entire company assembles
to hear this reading and afterwards votes. If many of the
actors dislike the play, it is abandoned forthwith and the
search for another play is begun. If the play is acceptable
to the company, the Artistic Director chooses a régisseur
for the play. His choice must be confirmed by the Artistic
Council of the Theatre which consists of thirteen other
members beside himself. Ten of these are part of the original group personally associated with Vakhtangov. The

others are elected by the collective. They form a representative body of the "actors' shop," as the acting company is called.

The régisseur's first work is the preparation of a report based on a formal questionnaire which all régisseurs are supposed to fill out. This *enquète*, as it is called, has the following form:

1. Theme of the play
2. Chief ideas in the subject
3. Social meaning
4. Chief points showing this social meaning
5. Chief points of form:
    a. Principles
    b. Methods of work with actor
    c. Relation between actor and character
    d. Principles of acting, speech and movement
    e. Mass scenes
    f. Creation of *mise-en-scène*
6. Setting
    a. Construction
    b. Architecture
    c. Painting
7. Visual impressions to be received which unite the performance
8. Rôle and meaning of the properties
9. Costume and make-up
10. Musical setting
11. Faults of previous productions to be rectified in this one
12. Whither in this production?
13. An analysis of the contents of each scene and its meaning

When this report is prepared,[1] the entire actors' shop meets to consider it. The author is also present and if he dis-

[1] I have included as an appendix to this volume the régisseur's report of Zakhava for Pogodin's "Aristocrats," based on the points of the *enquète*, to which I wish to call attention at this point, and I recommend that the reader

agrees with the régisseur's interpretation or proposed method of handling any point, this is his opportunity to express his opinion in the presence of the entire theatre. After the collective has discussed the report and has accepted it—and only then—work on the play begins.

Once his plan of production is agreed upon by the collective, the director is in full charge. There will be, however, frequent meetings of the Artistic Council during this period of rehearsing, usually following the run-through of an act in its presence. At these meetings it will discuss with the director the progress which is being made and make suggestions which he is, however, at liberty to disregard if he sees fit. This periodic overseeing by the Artistic Council would remind a member of the New York Theatre Guild staff of the "death watches" of Guild productions, those run-throughs attended by the Board of Managers of that organization which are held for the same purpose as these at the Vakhtangov. The Council continues to advise with the director about the sets, music, and all the details of production as they are worked out, and since its membership is large, they can bring a good deal of pressure to bear upon the director if they agree among themselves, and when they do not, he has at least a variety of ideas to assist him.

With this organization and plan of production in mind, let us go to rehearsals at this theatre as we have gone at the other theatres, in order to see the plans work out.

3

The play which I watched is a new Soviet one, "Shlyapa," which has a colloquial meaning rather like our word "booby." It is one of those modern Russian comedies of factory manners with which the Moscow stages abound. It

skip to it before continuing with this chapter, for from it he can discover all the elements that go into the creation of a Vakhtangov production.

is a long, complicated and, for the most part, dull opus
with innumerable characters and scenes which tell us about
the problems of factory management. Because the newly
appointed factory director seems to devote his entire attention to planting flower beds in the courtyard, to re-
painting the workshops, and to carrying on a campaign
against dirt, his fellow workers think he is a fool. When
he fires an old laborer—thirty-five years in the factory—
for chronic drunkenness, their dissatisfaction reaches its
peak. But the manager sticks by his decision with sudden
unexpected firmness. They soon discover that their "gar-
dener" knows more about industrial problems than they
thought, and the factory is not only cleaned up and beau-
tified, but it raises its standard of production and its output. The "booby's" chief accomplishment, however, seems
to be the change of heart which he effects in the workers.
From a surly, lazy, bibulous crew they become conscien-
tious, enthusiastic laborers. The old drunk is the major
object lesson. Under the application of the manager's per-
suasive methods of applied psychology, his habits of a lifetime are transformed, he is accepted back into the laboring fold, a sober man, and the iniquitous bottle is replaced
by a healthful glass of tea which he waves aloft in triumph
during the joyful finale that celebrates his return to grace.

    With such bromidic ideas and with characters who de-
velop as obviously as the ideas, there was really little that
could be done with the play but make it as bright as possible. There was no deep psychological study necessary.
Reuben Simonov was the logical director. If we watch it
from first rehearsal to last it will occupy us four months,
which is about the average length of time for preparation
of a play. Rehearsals are prompt in this theatre and run
from eleven to twelve-thirty and from one to two-thirty
daily except "free-days," which are the Soviet counterpart
of Sundays.

When the parts are distributed at the Vakhtangov, the actor is not told what type he is to impersonate or anything about the rôle. Instead, he goes home and after examination of it, comes back and in a round-table discussion outlines his idea of the character. He has probably chosen some type which he has observed; his descriptive analysis, at any rate, will be of external qualities. The director may disagree or have further suggestions; perhaps the fellow actors will have an idea for their partner's impersonation. Together they will talk about the quality of voice he shall use, his gait, idiosyncrasies of manner, facial expressions, even the clothes he shall wear. Shall he wear a beard, does he carry a cane, does his suit fit, does he speak loudly or softly, does he walk on the heel or the ball of the foot? They paint a vivid and minute verbal portrait of every finished character. It is quite objective, to be sure, but Vakhtangov's demand for sharpness can best be fulfilled by looking at the outside of the man. If you try to get within him too soon, you lose perspective and get muddled up in the inner complexities of his soul and your portrait is apt to lose its contours. Approach the inner man through his external form. This is more or less along the line of that recent experiment which we saw the *MXAT* making in their theory of physical action, except that here they say, approach, but never become, the inner man.

When this preliminary work with the *obraz* has been done, the reading rehearsals begin, a scene at a time. It was at one of these that I made my entrance. A dozen or fifteen artists were seated about a long table in the white Empire foyer of the theatre. The first thing that astonished me was their youth. Hardly any actor seemed to be beyond thirty, some looked as though they were still in their teens. But youth in the U.S.S.R. holds much more responsible positions in every field than it does in America and this is true in the theatre too. Outside of the Maly and the Art Theatre, I dare say that no theatre in Moscow has more than half a dozen members who are over forty. In this rehearsal all were modestly, even drably dressed. All were very quiet and very serious. There was nothing glamorous there. No one would imagine that these poor, unassuming boys and girls were the same swashbuckling romantic dandies and sophisticated ladies in satins and velvets whom I had seen the night before re-creating the lush Paris of Balzac in "The Human Comedy." They must have added a cubit to their stature, ten years to their age, and an unbelievable amount of *savoir faire* to their manner!

The acts of the play were divided into a number of scenes and these were again subdivided so that the work was taken up in small sections as at the *MXAT* and Meierhold's, except that the *kuski* here were on the whole a little longer and were more often divided on a basis of form and action than of thought, emotion, or idea. As at the *MXAT*, one act is completed before work is begun on the next. That day's rehearsal covered only two pages, but from them was drawn everything that the director wished the cast to get. The passage was read through once without stopping. It was the beginning of a scene in which the workers return to their old shop to find that the manager has replaced their old lathes and machines with new ones, has cleaned up an old smoking corner which was their favorite, has lightened and freshened the shop. The director took it up line by line, discussing the effect to be produced—their surprise, their pleasure mixed with apprehension, their discomfort. He outlined the business which he had planned for it—the way the crowd would enter, which men would form little groups together, which would be solitary figures. Already he began to work on tempo in the delivery of the lines. He wanted to have many lines delivered simultaneously, and this he worked out forth-

Illustrations

INTERVENTION. Designed by Rabinovich for the Vakhtangov Theatre

PICKWICK CLUB. Two scenes designed by Williams for the Moscow Ar Theatre

THE IRON FLOOD. Staged by Okhlopkov at the Realistic Theatre

Socialistic realism at the Realistic Theatre! ARISTOCRATS staged b‑
Okhlopkov

Banquet scenes as Stanislavski and Meierhold stage them. DEAD SOULS at
the Moscow Art Theatre; WOE FROM WISDOM at the Meierhold Theatre

Meierhold today: LA DAME AUX CAMELIAS at the Meierhold Theatre

Meierhold in 1922: MASSE-MENSCH

THE OPTIMISTIC TRAGEDY. Designed by Ryndin for the Kamerny Theatre

EGYPTIAN NIGHTS. Model of setting designed by Ryndin for the Kamerny
Theatre

EUGENE ONEGIN. Duel scene designed by Rabinovich for the Bolshoi Opera

PRINCE IGOR designed by Fedorovski for the Bolshoi Opera

THE STORM as produced at the Moscow Art Theatre by Rabinovich in 1934
and at the Kamerny Theatre by Stenberg in 1924

INTERVENTION. Final scene designed by Rabinovich for the Vakhtangov Theatre

THE HUMAN COMEDY designed by Rabinovich for the Vakhtangov Theatre

LOVE AND INTRIGUE designed by Akimov for the Vakhtangov Theatre

Stage Model: EUGENE ONEGIN at the Bolshoi Opera

Stage Model: THE SPANISH CURATE at the Second Moscow Art Theatre

TWELFTH NIGHT. Designed by Favorski for the Second Moscow Art Theatre

with. He seemed to be setting the aural effects of his performance from the beginning.

"I want to work in this production for the psychological motivation for mass movement rather than for abstract groupings," Simonov tells his cast. "The problem will be to fix the concentration of the audience on one man in a crowd of which all the members are in movement. This we tried to do in the café scene in 'Intervention' and we succeeded, but we had an unusually tense situation to assist us. Here the audience will be colder. In this scene with the lathes when the workers return to find their shop remodeled, there will be much movement, but we must concentrate the audience's attention only on the effect it produces in a few of the men, on Bubinsov, the drunkard, in particular. There are other scenes like this one throughout the play. I remember once watching a street fight from the opposite sidewalk. Naturally a crowd gathered. People would stop as they walked by; little boys would run out from near-by doors. But throughout all this complicated pattern of moving forms, coming and going, stopping and moving on, my attention, like everyone else's, was concentrated on the two struggling figures. When I suddenly realized this, I began to consider the whole picture and to unravel the movement of the onlookers. We must build up a comparable situation on our stage if we wish to focus the audience's attention where we will it to be."

With this problem before them, which they will jointly seek to solve, the director and his cast proceed with rehearsals. After the whole scene had been rehearsed in sections in this way, the actors began to "walk" the scene and the work on action and business began. This takes the most time here as at the Meierhold Theatre. The director orders the arrangement of furniture and props at the first rehearsal, for as in all theatres, props are at hand from the beginning. The actors then proceed to run through the scene without direction from the régisseur, working out their own business and "crosses" based on his remarks during the readings. After rehearsing through once, they start again and this time the director begins to make alterations in what they have extemporized and in what he originally planned. He introduces more business.

These rehearsals continue until the entire act is covered. All this time the actors are expanding their own characterizations, they are introducing bits of business and spinning out action which will define them, they suggest certain props which would be useful to them. The actress playing the scrub-woman in the factory's offices rehearses with something in her mouth to suggest the absence of teeth. The old clerk works out, on a suggestion from the director that he might be tubercular, an elaborate system of coughs and business with an overcoat draped about his shoulders as he walks through the factory's corridors. They are making what I call a collective creation. Together with the director they build up the act with everything that both he and they can contribute. After some five weeks of work on this one act, they are ready for a run-through before the Artistic Council. It is apparent at this run-through, which takes place in the large foyer, that the act has been built up too much; they have overloaded it with their inventions. This was consciously done, however, and now must come a cutting and simplifying process. Simonov believes, like many good playwrights, in putting forth all his ideas on a subject to start with, then paring away what is least important and effective.

The designer has arranged for his first showing to follow this first run-through, so the entire company adjourns to the Scenic Department offices where they are shown the *maquette,* or stage model, with every scene depicted and some approximation of the lighting. The designer explains his ideas and the technical mounting which he plans. The exterior of a lighted factory at night, with its large, dirty, small-paned windows, will form a background for the prologue. In the foreground a single tree in a field of refuse suggests the conditions there before the arrival of the new manager. Later scenes, most of them played against a black cyclorama without ceiling or side maskings, show various parts of the factory—the manager's office, workshops, other offices. There are smaller scenes showing two workers' families' quarters. The final scenes show the improved factory, modern workers' apartment houses, blue sky and bright green grass. The many scene shifts will be handled by two or three wagon stages, for the Vakhtangov does not use a revolving stage. All these plans as well as the run-through are discussed by the Artistic Council assembled in conclave afterwards. To its meeting in the high-ceilinged Conference Room with charmingly painted French rococo wall panels the designer is invited, and their criticisms, which are many and which go down into the smallest details, show that the Council, although almost entirely composed of actors, has more than a superficial knowledge of all aspects of the production. Few groups of a dozen actors assembled in an American theatre could discuss as intelligently the problems of scene design as can these artists of the Vakhtangov—but then there is no need, for there are still fewer groups of a dozen actors who are running theatres in the United States.

The second act is now taken up in the same way as the first. While Simonov is rehearsing it, his two assistant régisseurs hold rehearsals of the first act in another part of the theatre. These assistants are very different from Meierhold's, for they make their own contribution to the creation of the production, and have been allowed from the first rehearsal to offer suggestions and help in planning the action. Now they tackle the problem of cutting, and every few days Simonov reviews scenes from the first act and considers their proposed revisions. What cuts he does not approve of he restores and then makes other changes himself. The actors have by now ceased their improvisations in the first act and allow the director to mold them as he wishes. With the second act completed there is a run-through of it, and again the pruning shears are applied as the work on the next act goes forward.

Now the production meets with delay from a cause which I am prompted to mention because of the frequency with which one experiences it in Moscow. One of the principals is ill. The Russian artists are always getting sick! Yet with the rehearsal period extending over such a long time it is understandable how the health of a whole company might not remain unbroken throughout it. The artists lead very rushed and hectic lives, their energy is demanded sixteen or more hours a day, the climate is rigorous; no wonder illness overtakes them. When it does and an important actor or a number of the lesser ones are sick, rehearsals are simply called off for the time being. This is difficult in New York where time means money. But the possibility of postponing rehearsals pending the recovery of various actors is one of the contributing reasons, though a homely one, why the Russian theatre takes from four to five times as long as the American to produce a play.

You may have wondered, as I did, when I first heard of their development of the play act by act, whether the first act might not be apt to get a great deal more attention than the last. Directors in New York fear such a system, feeling that if they take up their play and perfect one act before proceeding to the next, they will spend more time than they should on the beginning and leave too little time for the end. I have to report that this occurs to a degree in Moscow, but less so than it might in America. For again, you see, the New York director works against a time limit which his Moscow colleague does not know. There he can postpone his opening until the last act has been rehearsed as long as the first if he feels it needs it. In point of fact, if one works as carefully on the psychological motivation of action as do the *MXAT* and all theatres which practice in some form or some part of its system (and the Vakhtangov is one), during the time spent on the first act certain problems are solved for the whole play and need no further consideration when they appear thereafter. The subsequent acts are much more easily rehearsed. If the actor follows the "line of the day" theory of Stanislavski, his emotions and his mental processes develop logically and easily. He reaches his climax only when he has passed through all the steps which lead to it.

Often American actors have to struggle with a climactic scene which should be as easy as any other scene for them, simply because they come upon it almost "cold." The director is trying to work on the whole play at once, and after a week of rehearsal he has to begin on his most dramatically emotional scenes. Since these are customarily in the latter half of the play, the Soviet actor doesn't come to them until he has lived with his part for at least a couple of months; by then he is ready to meet and conquer them.

Now that the whole play has been rehearsed act by act with periodic reviews by the Artistic Council, the assembling process begins. This lasts about a month and in the course of it much that has been created is revised, in outward effect at least. This last stand at the Vakhtangov is very like the last few days of a New York production.

For some time, as various skeletal parts of the set have been completed, rehearsals have been taking place on the stage. Because the sets are being built in the theatre, a cast has the same opportunity to familiarize itself with the form of the stage as it has to grow accustomed to the props. By the last two weeks it is able to work in the completed set—completed, that is, in accordance with the designer's original plans. After the set is finished, it will undergo the same amount of change as the action.

Almost every day from eleven to four the company works in the settings. After the regular evening performances there are scene and light rehearsals. At these the designer and technical director preside and then show their work next morning to the director who approves or changes various details himself. One of these days is devoted to an inspection of costume and make-up. A parade takes place and every actor's appearance is criticized as he passes before the director and his assistants. There is nothing very unique about this procedure save that it takes place a month before the opening night and thereafter the cast rehearses off and on in make-up and regularly in costume, so that these become as familiar to them as have the setting and props. Here, it seems to me, is another important reason for the excellence of the Moscow theatres; by the time the first night arrives, the actors are completely at home with their performance, physically as well as spiritually. There is no fumbling, only complete confidence and assurance. At the same time, they have not gone stale, for there has been constant progress up to the opening, not mere empty repetition in which things become mechanical —the obvious danger.

The orchestral accompaniment is now being added and with the introduction of music (which comes here much later than at Meierhold's theatre) many rearrangements in action must take place, for the two must blend. The music in this particular play consists chiefly in variations on a street song to which some of the factory workers compose a simple doggerel about Bubinsov. The tune, with its peculiarly Russian minor cadence, is sung, is played on an accordion, is built up by the orchestra in the hidden pit, is repeated by one or another of these time and again throughout the play, now sadly, now gayly, as the mood changes. The fact that music is not part of the production from the beginning is illustrative of the fact that the first concern of the Vakhtangov is for the element of psychological characterization—the actor's contribution. When it has been set, then the form and punctuation of the performance, in which music is of great importance, are added on top of it by the régisseur.

The last minute drive—here a last week drive—will be to speed up and tighten the production. Even up to this point the performance has been allowed to run much too long. Now the prologue with its stark tree will be eliminated, one or two short scenes will be cut out entirely. Simonov, in the last three or four days, puts in a dozen final touches which give the play his signature: he is distributing the action over more area—sending actors up to the stage boxes for sharp surprise effects, a young trio of workers with guitar and accordion to sing the Bubinsov song again from there, bringing actors in from doors in front of the proscenium, pulling scenes down onto the Vakhtangov's sloping apron while scene shifts go on behind the drawn house curtain as I saw in "Intervention" (incidentally, Simonov also directed this latter play); he is emphasizing a bar of music here, picking up a bit of business with a sharper spotlight there. One whole inset is repainted, a door is rebuilt, one shift done with moving platforms in view of the audience, is entirely rearranged to make for more smoothness and speed.

Most of the rehearsals now are run-throughs, one each day, without interruption and with the directors taking notes. The Artistic Council is in regular attendance at the last three or four rehearsals and the play takes its final form at its collective consultations. As in the beginning stages, so at the end, the play is a collective creation executed through a single intelligence. Finally the *Repertcom* is invited, then follow the invitation dress rehearsals and at last, four months after its first reading, "Shlyapa" is shown to the Moscow public.

4

"For a long time I sought the kind of theatre which I wanted my own to be," Nikolai Okhlopkov, director of the Moscow Realistic Theatre, told me, "but nowhere was it to be found. The theatre of Stanislavski was not it, for there the audience was forgotten behind the fourth wall which its artists threw up to separate themselves from it, and that I did not want. The theatre of Meierhold was not it, for there the actor vulgarized himself, he played directly to the audience as a clown does, and that I did not want.

"One day during the Civil War I stood on a railway station platform. From one direction a troop train drew in and stopped. In a moment another troop train arrived from the opposite direction and halted across the platform. Soldiers poured out to refill their tea-kettles, buy a bun, or stretch their legs. Near me one man alighted. From the other train came another soldier. They saw each other, ran forward and embraced, unable to speak for emotion. They were old comrades, dearest friends, whom the war had separated. There on a station platform, as one went one way and the other another, they met for a moment, clasped hands, and parted. In that instant I knew that that was what I wanted my theatre to be—a meeting where two dear friends experience an emotional union, in which for that moment all the rest of the world may be forgotten. Ever since I have worked for that. In my theatre, actor and spectator must clasp hands in fraternity. On my stage, when the mother cries, a dozen in the audience must be ready to spring forward to dry her tears."

Okhlopkov has created such a theatre. He has succeeded in effecting the meeting which he wanted between artist and spectator, or between playwright and spectator, and he causes it to be intensely emotional. There is no fourth wall here—no wall at all, save the ones which enclose actors and spectators alike. The spectator is always swept into the stream of action, just as I was at "The Iron Flood," but at the same time the actor seems not to be acting to the audience; he seems somehow to take it for granted that the spectator is a fellow actor and performs with him and not for him.

Okhlopkov's method of accomplishing this is a direct one, but it is by no means original. In theory he has borrowed a great deal from Meierhold, and the form of his theatre is just that set down by Adolphe Appia in his last books, *L'Œuvre d'Art* and *Art Vivant ou Nature Morte,* where he said that "the new theatre should be a large bare empty room without stage or auditorium. A platform with steps leading up to it, of the size and shape required by the action of the play, should be placed therein where necessary, and the spectators should be seated according to the position of the stage."

Okhlopkov has not followed Appia further, but so far his theatre literally fulfills Appia's description. It is a small one with a balcony across one end. The rest of the hall is completely empty and there is no proscenium arch. The stage is composed of moveable "parallel" platforms which may be set up in any arrangement in any part of the hall. The seats are also in moveable sections which may be set up around the stage according to its position. In "The Iron Flood" they were grouped along one side and end of the hillside which was the stage. Sometimes the form may be circus-like, with the audience sitting in a circle around the stage; sometimes the stage may be at one end of the room like a dais in front of which the spectators sit facing it as in a lecture hall; at other times, the stage may be lozenge-shaped, the audience sitting in the four empty corners of the room; again, they may sit on three sides of the stage as it extends out from the fourth wall. In one production Okhlopkov placed much of the action on bridges set up over the heads of the audience. In "Mother" by Gorki the stage was a circular one set in the center of the house; then from this center there were four runways extending out at right angles to one another, like spokes from a hub. The runways connected with other runways that ran along the four walls of the auditorium. Actors made all their entrances and exits to the center stage along these runways.

All these devices are designed to bring about the meeting of actor and audience so that it will be impossible to separate the two—to surround the audience with actors just as the actors are surrounded by audience. In "Mother" Okhlopkov carries this so far as to have one actor hand to any spectator sitting beside the stage a loaf and a knife for him to hold. This fusion of the two he makes much more natural than has any other director whom I have ever seen attempt the same thing. Whereas Max Reinhardt, Meierhold, and all other régisseurs have simply made the spectators more self-conscious by mingling audience and actors in ways which have seemed to me to destroy much illusion and theatrical unity, Okhlopkov makes the unity and the illusion stronger.

The reasons for this are, I think, to be found less in the method than in surrounding circumstances. In the first place, there is a much stronger bond between actor and spectator. Okhlopkov chooses only the most fiery revolutionary themes—plays wherein the playwright talks of things which the theatre's working class audience has itself experienced. The bond is also material. Whereas the movement of actors in medieval robes up and down the aisles in Reinhardt's "The Miracle" only accentuated the fashionable but anachronistic evening dress of the audience seated in Geddes' reconstruction of a cathedral, in the Realistic Theatre spectators and actors look much the same and as one faces across the stage another part of the audience, it seems as though it might be another group of participants: there will be Red Army uniforms on the stage and in the house; there will be shawl-shrouded women and rough-bloused men in both places.

Meierhold was seeking much that same end in his early Revolutionary theatre, we are told, but if it existed then he has lost it now through "aestheticizing" away the psychological union. Although he talked directly at his audience, he spoke with a subtlety of speech and a use of symbol which estranged them, perhaps ever so slightly and it may be subconsciously. Still he talked *at* them rather than *with* them, and in doing so he lost his chance to win them. Okhlopkov's actors seem to talk *with* their hearers.

Okhlopkov has felt that to make his meeting real he must keep his style realistic, almost, at times, to the point of naturalism. Abstractions, when such an end as his is in view, are dangerous, at least if the audience is a proletarian and not very sophisticated one. Therefore, although using great freedom in the architectural form of his theatre, he has continued to use real objects in their accustomed functions; he has suggested reality in the surroundings, just as in "The Iron Flood" the audience found itself in the midst of trees and bushes, tents and covered wagons, rocks and camp-fires.

Suddenly in his last production of the 1934-35 season, "Aristocrats," the play about the building of the White Sea Canal by Gay-Pay-Oo prisoners, which Zakhava also directed for the Vakhtangov, Okhlopkov set aside this realism for a stylization again reminiscent of a Meierhold experiment, for it largely derived from Commedia dell' Arte and from Japanese and Chinese sources. The action took place on two completely bare rectangular platforms set tangent to each other in the middle of the hall, with the upper left hand corner of one connecting with the lower right hand corner of the other. There was no scenery on these two stages. The only decorations were painted screens done in the Japanese manner which lined the walls of the house. These suggested the changing seasons with oriental sparsity of detail—an owl on a snowy pine bough against a gray blue sky indicated that it was winter; apple blossoms against a lemon yellow background suggested that spring had come. The actual props required in the business were brought on in the full light by blue-masked and dominoed attendants who in function suggested the Chinese property man. They would run on in full stage light carrying a telephone, for example, and would hold it while a character made his call; when the business was completed they would run off taking the phone with them. Or when a table was required two of these men would enter with a piece of green baize which, squatting on the floor, they would hold taut between them to suggest the table top. The rest of the play, the dialogue, the costumes, were realistic, and the combination of these conventions with the realism I found disturbing. However, this production was hailed by most Moscow critics and many foreign ones as the Realistic Theatre's finest performance.

Nikolai Okhlopkov is now only thirty-four. The American finds something familiar about him. Perhaps it is that his appearance slightly suggests that of Lindbergh. There is the same long, lanky body, the same mop of unkempt hair, the same firm chin and eyes which the American has seen so often pictured in his newspapers over Lindbergh's name. He has tremendous energy, is an indefatigable worker. His decisive manner of speaking, his rapid and emphatic gestures, as much as his ever-present gray suède zipper sweater and his gray flannel trousers, seem American.

When the Revolution came eighteen years ago, it found young Okhlopkov a sandwichman in a little Siberian town. After a short time he entered the theatre, first by working in a theatrical furnishing shop, later by doing a little acting. A mass spectacle there on May Day was his first production as a régisseur. Later he came to Moscow, worked with Meierhold as a pupil, and learned a great deal from his methods which he applies in his own rehearsals.

The Mass Theatre has always interested him. It may have influenced him in his decision to work out of a proscenium theatre into one which might be a small likeness of an arena theatre of the future. Tretyakov, prominent Soviet man of letters and of the theatre, says that he envisions a future Mass Theatre which Okhlopkov will create, where this energetic style of his, which now seems at times as though it would burst through the tiny theatre that houses him, will have room for proper expression before thousands of spectators. This, I think, is Okhlopkov's own vision too, as it was Meierhold's before him. Meierhold is the Moses who has led the theatre to the brink of this promised land, but it may be given to Okhlopkov to be the Joshua who will realize the true Mass Theatre.

Okhlopkov is an ardent Communist. He is one of the most striking examples of the new social artist in the Moscow theatre; he is certainly more completely the product of the Revolution and more completely under its influence than any artist we have studied. He would very much resent it, therefore, if I should suggest that his theatre be classed among the theatres created out of an artistic dictatorship rather than among those which are collective creations. But I must admit that, although his theatre, like all other Soviet ones, is collectivist in form, in fact it exists entirely through his own ability. If we study his theatre at work we shall see that this is so.

5

The Realistic Theatre has effected two meetings—not only one in which artist and spectator may join and share an emotional catharsis, but a technical one in which certain elements of the Stanislavski theatre and of the Meierhold theatre are joined again, but this time in different proportions.

I have explained how Okhlopkov is continually changing the form of his stage in every production. The architectural arrangement of his theatre space is one of this régisseur's first considerations in planning a production. This stage form becomes a sort of Meierholdian *jeu de théâtre,* and Okhlopkov works it out himself before any rehearsals are begun. He himself will decide whether the stage will be round, square or oval. Again, as in Meierhold's theatre, the designer's work is subordinated to the concept of the director and is chiefly one of executing details.

When the actual rehearsal period begins, there is no time spent working on the psychological image alone. Movement and the development of the *obraz* advance together. In fact, from my own observations, I should say that the movement is set down first and the psychological motivation is supplied afterwards. This is somewhat similar to methods now practiced at the Vakhtangov and to the new Art Theatre experiment, but it is still closer to Meierhold because often the psychological motivation is explained and supplied by the régisseur for the actor. In fact, at many rehearsals of Okhlopkov's one might imagine himself at the Meierhold Theatre. Every gesture, every move, is as carefully demonstrated to the actor by the régisseur, and the prompt-book plays almost the same important part. The principles of bio-mechanics are not unknown in this theatre, and Okhlopkov demands the same flexibility of body in his actors as does Meierhold.

Okhlopkov composes all the movements himself and these he teaches to his company with the precision of Meierhold. Since his actors are seen in the round—sculpturally, so to speak—because the audience views them from many sides, his problem is more complicated than the régisseur's in a picture-frame theatre. He must design his groupings and his movement so that they will be as effective from behind as from in front. It is obviously impossible under these circumstances for the actor to work inspirationally on his own. When movement is being considered, he must turn himself over completely to the régisseur who can see him from as many different angles as will the spectator.

Okhlopkov considers his stage pictures from one angle of view when setting action and business. Then when rehearsals have advanced a little, he walks about the room and when movement seems incoherent to him from another angle, he re-creates it. I was surprised to see how similar to that of others was Okhlopkov's direction. Composing for a space stage seems to make less difference in mounting a play than one would think—that is, if one does not compare it to the stereotyped staging of the early twentieth century box-set drama with a sofa left, a table and two chairs right, all facing the footlights. The chief thing to be kept in mind is that there must be almost constant movement. His performances are studies in *perpetuum mobile*.

From early in his rehearsals Okhlopkov works, like Meierhold, with music. His score, however, is written and is played in its final form from the start. Music is here, as in most of the non-naturalistic theatres of Moscow, an integral part of the production, and since it serves as an accompaniment to action, it must be carefully rehearsed with it. For regular rehearsals, the piano alone is used, but full orchestra is used at all run-throughs, even those of a single act which may take place a month or two before the opening.

After all the movements are worked out and business and action are set, one begins to hear Okhlopkov say, "Consider now why I have told you to do this; what do you feel at this point?" If the actors merely imitate his movements their performances will ring hollow, as Okhlopkov knows, so he tries to have the actor now make his own contribution from within himself. I am told that sometimes Okhlopkov has his cast prepare character sketches based on their rôles which they will work out and present to the company. It is, however, in this phase of creation that the Realistic Theatre is least successful. What the actor contributes in the way of psychological reality is too often inadequate, his performance too often does ring hollow; there is a tendency toward overacting and ranting. This would never be if the actors could couple their director's talented *régie* with a sound inner contribution of their own. But though they have remarkably well-trained bodies (I have watched strenuous acrobatic exercises which all the company practices in their foyer in the mornings before rehearsal starts, and it gives them superb body control), the Realistic Theatre unfortunately has few intelligent actors and Okhlopkov apparently cannot sharpen their minds and their emotional sensitivity.

I suspect that one reason the Realistic Theatre has so few capable actors (there are some, I do admit) is perhaps the reason that Meierhold has so few—Okhlopkov is a dictatorial régisseur. His demands must be executed to the letter and his temper is impatient. *Régie* first and acting afterwards. Many actors will not submit. In a theatre built along the lines of his, *régie* has to come first, but the director must give his actors a share in creation and perhaps a larger share than Okhlopkov is willing to allow. It is unquestionably the dynamic personality of Okhlopkov alone and his talent for the stage which has made his theatre so interesting, but might it not be still more interesting if other talent could be joined with his own? Let someone bring a little sense of humor, for instance, to lighten his ferocity.

You may wonder, after I have seemed to insist that the Realistic Theatre is a theatre of one régisseur, why I place it in this chapter called "Actors and Régisseurs Meet." I do so because I believe that Okhlopkov wishes that meeting and that perhaps it will soon be accomplished more completely than at present. His theatre is working to find a combination of Stanislavski's system of acting with Meierhold's system of directing, just as is Vakhtangov's. Okhlopkov does know what the Art Theatre teaches and he is trying to teach it to his company. In time when it is maturer (the theatre is only six years old and its actors are all quite young), the company will, I think, be able to make its contribution to the synthesis. After all, Stanislavski himself has been something of a dictator in his theatre and has yet built an ensemble of actors who are individually actively creative. So long as Okhlopkov earnestly desires that his actors share in his creation (and herein he differs from Meierhold and Tairov), one must await the day when they can and will, and the day when Okhlopkov will temper his own directing with a greater consideration for their contribution.

CHAPTER SIX

Designers at Work

IN JANUARY, 1934, an International Exhibition of Theatrical Art was opened at the Museum of Modern Art
in New York. There in a dozen rooms one might view the
assembled work of outstanding designers for the stage from
the seventeenth century to the present day. An exhibition
from the Soviet Union was—not very surprisingly—late
in arriving, so that for visitors at its opening, Russian stage
decoration was not represented. Those who returned later
saw a modest collection of stage models or *maquettes*
downstairs and a few sketches in an upper room. But one
wished to see more.

In January, 1935, an exhibition entitled "Seventeen
Years of Stage Design in U.S.S.R." was opened at the Historical Museum facing the Red Square in Moscow. There
one might view assembled in two dozen rooms the work
of outstanding designers of that one country during
the last two decades. If those whose appetites had been
whetted by the New York exhibition had journeyed to
Moscow they might have seen enough glory to last them
a lifetime. I was one of the few privileged to see both exhibitions. I listened at the opening ceremonies of the Moscow exhibition to People's Commissar of Education Bub-
nov repeat the government's pride in the Soviet theatre,
to Artists Fedorovski and Akimov and Director Tairov
reaffirm the theatre's pride in its own accomplishment.
Now one regularly hears in Russia expressions of pride in

accomplishment; they are repeated so often as to weary some foreign visitors whose broader bases for comparison make it difficult for them to share the Bolsheviks' satisfaction in all their handiwork. However, none of the dozen or so foreigners who were present in this large assembly of Moscow's intelligentsia would have denied the justification for the Russians' pride in this exhibition. They could defy any country to present such a quantity and variety of conceptions for *décor* in the theatre as Soviet artists had here presented.

What conclusions about Russian design could one draw after seeing the exhibition? First, that the excellence of the theatre in the Soviet Union is not entirely dependent upon its acting, as most of the world has been led to believe, but in some measure also upon its *décor*. Second, that there is as much variety of expression in design as we have seen that there is in styles of producing and acting. Third, that the Russian designer is primarily a painter and afterwards a man of the theatre. Fourth, that the designer's work is almost entirely done to fill a need, by which I mean that artists have either not the time or not the inclination to design "projects for the theatre"—there are no Gordon Craigs among them, nothing like Geddes' famous "Divine Comedy" project is represented in the exhibition—only settings for plays actually produced. Fifth, that the Russian designers show sometimes more courage than skill in seeking novelty of expression, but that that courage always reveals a fertile imagination at work to find some resource for the theatre which it has not possessed before. Good taste and a knowledge of interior decoration can equip a New York designer for setting the average show quite adequately there. Moscow requires more, for its designers do not follow patterns. If we study the history of the designer in the Russian and Soviet theatre, we can see that some of these conclusions may be explained in the light of that history.

Sergei Diaghilev, whose name one associates primarily with the ballet, was probably as great an influence in the development of the arts of the theatre in Russia in the early twentieth century as was Stanislavski. Particularly in the field of stage design was he influential. It was in 1898 when he founded the magazine *Mir Iskusstva* ("World of Art") that the Russian painters of the time first came into active collaboration with Diaghilev. He invited such painters as Roerich, Benois and Bakst to do the illustrations for it, and the "magazine became the semi-official organ which particularly defended and furthered the work of those artists who expressed fantasy or archaism."

Diaghilev had even earlier arranged the first exhibition in Russia of contemporary French impressionist and symbolist painters, and these Russian artists all came more or less under the influence of the French. They and also Golovin, Korovin, Anisfeld, Vrubel and Serov, with whom Diaghilev was from time to time associated, were one in their opposition to naturalism in painting. They were, however, less symbolists than they were colorists and anti-naturalists.

Diaghilev it was who also led them to the stage, for he brought them into collaboration with himself in the production of his ballets. In their work with him and in the work which some of them did for the private opera theatre of the Moscow millionaire, Mamontov, they avoided the current naturalistic trend and turned stage sets into great canvases on which they painted their broad, bold pictures with an unparalleled flow of color. In order that it might be a complete picture they all designed the costumes which were to fit into their scenes. They were all influenced by the exotic: Bakst by orientalism, Roerich by recent Scythian research, Benois by eighteenth century baroque.

The "legitimate" dramatic theatre of the early twentieth century was, as we have seen, absorbed in naturalism. Therefore, these great painter-artists had little to do with it and their work was mostly seen on the stages of ballet and opera. In the Moscow Art Theatre the chief painter was Simov and it was he who was the leader of the naturalist designers in the theatre. The two schools grew up side by side. It was not until Meierhold went to St. Petersburg that the colorist-impressionists began to work in drama to any extent, and at first it was chiefly in the music-drama productions of Meierhold that they collaborated. Then Meierhold formed a sort of artistic collaboration with Alexander Golovin, and with him produced "Don Juan," "Masquerade" and several other plays. After that the colorists were commissioned regularly to do sets for the Imperial theatres, though their work was seldom seen in Moscow.

The Revolution brought an end to the painter-artist influence in the theatre, at least for the time being. Meierhold, as we have seen, was practically the only man who created new productions in the early years of the Revolution and he turned abruptly from his collaborator, Golovin, and plunged into constructivism. Both the naturalists and the impressionist-colorists had kept in their settings a geographical actuality; this they had in common. Meierhold now wanted to abolish all suggestions of *place* and substitute scenery which would provide no representational connotations whatever but which would be as abstract as the theory of movement which he was creating. I have tried to show earlier how constructivism suited his purpose.

"The constructivists were concerned least of all with the stage picture and most of all with the dynamics of action," writes Margolin, the Soviet critic.[1] They did, however, have concern for the content of the play, for, as Margolin points out, "The constructivist artist being little concerned about the decoration of the stage or about the spots of color in the performance, endeavors to put the whole of his energy into disclosing the social aspects of the play."

Although constructivism was the chosen scenic art of the Revolutionary theatre in Russia during its early period, other styles continued simultaneously. The academic theatres—the Moscow Art and the Maly—never abolished representationalism, and the few new plays which they produced during these early years were as naturalistically set as ever. As the 1920's progressed and these theatres started to swing into the prescribed leftward line, they began to partake somewhat of the outward form of the more leftward theatre, and their scenic effects began to reflect the influence of greater stylization. Productions like "The Fruits of Enlightenment" and "Don Carlos" at the Maly showed a departure from naturalism as did Golovin's charming settings for "The Marriage of Figaro" at the *MXAT*, done in his best colorist style, and the production there of "Three Fat Men."

Beside constructivism and naturalism, a third school of design carried from the Russian into the Soviet theatre was the formalism of Tairov's decorations at the Kamerny Theatre. This was in the main derived from the futurist and cubist painters, and although certain developments of it resemble constructivism, there is this fundamental difference which is the characteristic of the futurists and the cubists: this formalism had no function "either representational, social, ethical, didactic, religious, sentimental, or even rationally logical." It was designed to evoke purely aesthetic reactions. It was the last stand of the preachers of "L'Art pour l'art" in Russia. Hence it was as welcome

---

[1] *The Theatre in the U.S.S.R.*, p. 44.

in the theatre which Tairov was creating as functional constructivism was to Meierhold. When constructivist elements were used at the Kamerny, as in the production of Ostrovski's "The Storm" or in parts of "Giroflé-Girofla," we must remember that they were not used functionally, but as pure form—they were static and not dynamic; so they differed from Meierhold's use.

Exter and Vesnin were the artists who gave the Kamerny its scenic stamp, and in the productions of "Phèdre," "Salomé," "Romeo and Juliet," and "The Man Who Was Thursday," the influence of futurism and of cubism in costume and scenery is at its height. As the Kamerny has moved away from its aestheticism into a more leftward position, so its scenery has lost the forms of its past and now, in the hands of Exter's successors, the Stenberg brothers and Ryndin, it becomes more symbolic and allegorical with at the same time many more realistic details. Ryndin's settings for "Machinal" are typical of this unexpected juxtaposition. Against a background of projected skyscrapers which mount in rigid corrugations of light into the sky, are set small scenes without ceilings or side maskings, realistic rooms with beds and lamps, desks and typewriters, sinks and dirty dishes, rooms which huddle symbolically beneath the towering monuments of capitalistic construction.

The latest reconstruction phase of the Revolution has called forth that new style of art given the name of "socialistic realism" which is talked of and is being created in all branches of the theatre: in staging plays, in writing them, in devising backgrounds for them. It is the artistic slogan of the hour, but it is hard to find a definition of it. Soviet artists seem only able to say that it is "the artistic expression of the new life and the building of the socialist state." Accept such a loose definition, and it seems easier to tell you what it is not than what it is. Meierhold's satire was not socialistic realism, for it was backward-looking and hence negatively rather than positively Revolutionary; likewise his style was not, for it was abstract. The new life and the building of socialism are concrete and call for concrete representations. The formalism of Tairov was therefore equally not it, for all theories of pure aesthetics were out of touch with the new or any other life. The naturalism of the Art Theatre, on the other hand, was just as far from being the expression of the new life and the building of socialism as abstractions, for it was essentially passive and non-committal. An active art form is required to express such an active idea as building, and photographic literalness is static. The new style therefore seems to require active, real representations of ideas that have bearing on the new life.

Socialistic realism which began as an attitude toward art thus ends up as a style of art. In the field of design its practice, as I have suggested, requires the abolition of all entirely non-representational art, including constructivism and cubism, the latter long condemned by the Marxian theatre as an essentially negative art. It means the abolition also of pure naturalism. The socialistic realism of the stage designer therefore seems to be a style which has elements borrowed from many sources. There will be some forms of a filled-out constructivism; there will be simplified naturalism; there will be occasional use of non-realistic color brought down from the *Mir Iskusstva;* there will be some of the formal arrangements borrowed from the space stage and from expressionism. It seems to be a highly eclectic style—anything may become socialistic realism so long as it is not too definitely and completely something else, and so long as it is used actively by the designer to express in some way "the new life and the building of the socialist state." On the whole it seems to an outsider to be merely leading to a simplified representationalism such as the best imaginative Western theatre has been creating for the last ten years or so.

2

The study of acting and *régie* in Moscow led us to particular theatres where actors and régisseurs are permanently associated in creation. The study of stage design leads us to individual artists who have no permanent tie with any specific theatre and each of whom is working out his own private salvation. Collective creation in the theatre which is so uniquely an achievement of the Russian stage breaks down when we come to the designer's place in it.

Several times I have asked Moscow authorities why theatres do not have designers regularly and permanently associated with their organizations, why the Central Theatre Technicum, when it trains a complete collective theatre of actors, régisseurs, managers, literary advisers, to send out to provincial centers, trains no designers to go with it. No one knew a satisfactory reason. There were in 1934 no schools of stage design in Russia and no art courses in which one could major in designing for the theatre. This would not seem so surprising were it not for the many courses, schools, institutes and technicums which exist in the U.S.S.R. for the preparation of actors and régisseurs.

The answer seems to be that the Soviet Union does not yet look upon stage designing as a profession in itself. The designer for the Soviet theatre is a painter. His training in art school is for painting and the stage becomes for most of them simply an enlarged *atelier*. I appreciated this when I visited that Exhibition of Theatre Art in January, 1935. One-third of the rooms were filled with what seemed to be illustrations of engineering projects set behind proscenia. The other two-thirds were hung with exquisite paintings which gave no suggestion that they were done for execution in the theatre. The painter had been interested in making a good easel picture; afterwards he thought of transposing it to the stage. He is first an illustrator. That is why so many of his *maquettes* and later his finished settings seem clumsy and awkward when they are realized. That is why many admirers of the decorations of Russian artists which they have known only from reproductions of the original sketches, are disappointed when they see the finished products on the Moscow stages.

I have said that we must go to individual artists and not to theatres if we are to study design, and that is what I propose to do now. There are no more than eight or ten outstandingly fine stage decorators in Moscow this year, if one excludes painters like Favorski who have done one or two isolated plays, beautifully mounted, as a sort of recreational sideline. It is possible to say of these eight or ten that they know the requirements of the theatre, and remember that they are creating for it when they make their sketches, so they should be excepted from the general criticism which I have just made of the Soviet stage picture-painters.

The "dean" of scene designers in Moscow is Fedorovski who is the chief colorist of them all. He learned many lessons from the lush Byzantinism of Bakst and the primitivism of Roerich. His brush is broad and his palette vivid. His style is heavy and monumental, what we should call operatic, and it is no wonder that his work is rarely seen except at the Bolshoi Theatre for which he has designed the gorgeous trappings of "Boris Godunov," "Prince Igor," "Carmen," "Lohengrin." He is the perpetuator of the tradition of the *Mir Iskusstva*.

Among the leaders of the constructivist movement in the Soviet theatre, Dmitriev, who designed Meierhold's first Revolutionary production, "Dawn," and Shestakov, who designed Meierhold's "Woe from Wisdom," are intelligent artists who comprehend the effect which the changing age has upon their art. They appreciate that constructivism is dead and that they must create a new and living style upon its structure. In his swing back, Dmitriev has gone to an extreme of naturalism, as one can see from his production of "Egor Bulichev" for the Vakhtangov Theatre, and in his *maquettes* for "Enemies" for the Art Theatre. Even so he is closer to the new approved socialistic realism than before. Shestakov in his 1934 production of "The Good Life" for the Second Art Theatre shows that he knows what is meant by the new style and gives a very satisfactory illustration of it. He uses modern furniture, flat bright color for interior walls, modern lamps and fixtures. He is attempting to show the kind of environment which the new Russian intelligentsia is on the point of creating for itself and for others.

Simov, the same Simov who designed the first productions of the Moscow Art Theatre almost forty years ago, continues to work and might, in fact, challenge Fedorovski for the title of "dean" of scenic artists. Simov's style has changed little in all these years and his new productions are chiefly those of the First Art Theatre.

Isaac Rabinovich is one of the finest designers modern Russia has produced. I spent an exciting two hours one afternoon over coffee in the attractive new and very bourgeois-looking café opposite the Art Theatre listening to him talk about his work and about some of the things that good Soviet design is attempting. Rabinovich considers himself a theatrical-architectural designer and so opposes the painter-artists to begin with. He has studied constructivism in the past and his settings for the Nemirovich-Danchenko "Lysistrata" were based on the principles of constructivism given architectural body. It was his arrangement of white, slender, Greek columns with only their entablature set in swaying curves against bright blue space that New Yorkers who saw this production there remember. He has continued to work three-dimensionally and architectonically, and his aim is to create "form in its expression of the meaning of the play," a doctrine close to that of the constructivists'. The difference lies in the kind of form he will use.

Rabinovich calls himself a régisseur-designer, for his sets are so created that to be complete, the actor must take his place in them in such positions as he, the designer, indicates. He sees the actors as sculpture set in his scene. The duel scene from "Eugene Onegin" illustrates how he designs for and with people. The curtain rises upon empty space, but an emptiness that is white, not black. On one side of the stage is gradually revealed through increasing light the dark outline of a deserted mill and a leafless tree. The rest is snow, snow that stretches out to the horizon, that blends itself with a white sky—all this visible as through the haze that precedes dawn. But this illimitable whiteness has no meaning and no depth until the black figures of the duelists and their seconds appear. Then his picture is complete only when they assume positions in the frame which fulfill his composition.

Rabinovich believes that a régisseur-designer may have other contributions to make to a play. He illustrates this by his work on the Vakhtangov Theatre's "Intervention." He had gone off to the country in the summer to prepare his *maquettes,* and there he read the play for the first time. When he laid down the script at the end, he felt that something more was needed. So when he returned to Moscow in the fall and exhibited his sets to the theatre, they found that he had created a set for a final scene which did not exist in the play.

They said, "What is this?"

"A representation of the great steps of Odessa," he answered.

"But there is no such scene called for in the play," they said.

"No, but there should be," he replied. "The play must not end with the three soldiers who have decided to forsake the Interventionists for the Reds, standing on the quai, but with their ascent of this great flight of steps of mine into a new future for them."

The theatre and the author agreed, perceiving that this gave the play stronger significance, so without the addition of a single line, just in a simply executed set and with one piece of business, the play was given by its designer a new punch and a climactic ending which has been hailed by Moscow playgoers as one of the most dramatic moments of the production.

Rabinovich composes with light also, for he believes, like Meierhold, that light has an aesthetic contribution to make to a performance if its use is carried beyond simple actualism. He says that scenery should be a kind of "visual music." One of the few effective lighting innovations in Moscow is his illumination from behind of a cyclorama of translucent glazed material, like tracing-linen. With the projection of soft, half-tone and quarter-tone silhouettes coming from other materials hanging between light sources and cyclorama, he builds up the misty quality necessary to many scenes, best illustrated, perhaps, in some of his sets for "The Human Comedy" and "The Storm" and (without the silhouettes) in some of the sets for "Eugene Onegin."

Our conversation brought out another point about designers' work in Moscow. While designers are free to do settings for any theatre they choose (Rabinovich has worked for the Vakhtangov, MXAT and Bolshoi all in one season), and although theatres employ as many different designers as they wish (the Art Theatre had Rabinovich, Dmitriev, Williams and Simov all working on settings for its different productions simultaneously this last season), the better designers do loosely associate themselves with some particular theatre whose artistic theories most closely coincide with their individual talents. Therefore, while the Vakhtangov does not have Rabinovich on its staff, it frequently calls him in to do a show, and he more readily agrees to collaborate with it than with other theatres because he recognizes that the Vakhtangov's sharp, vivid, witty and slightly stylized methods come closest to meeting his own. So it is with Akimov and the Vakhtangov, and so it is with other designers and other theatres: Simov and the Moscow Art Theatre, Fedorovski and the Bolshoi, Ryndin and the Kamerny, Tischler and the Jewish, Shlepyanov and the Theatre of the Revolution. The association is completely informal and reminds one of Robert Edmond Jones' past collaboration with Arthur Hopkins, Lee Simonson's work at the Theatre Guild, Jo Mielziner's association in so many of Guthrie McClintic's recent plays.

Nikolai Akimov is another artist who considers himself a régisseur-designer, but in a more actual sense than does Rabinovich. It would, in fact, be more accurate to call him a designer-régisseur. He wishes to create in the theatre an entire production, believing that one artist must be responsible for the synthesis of the visual with the intellectual elements of a play. Most of his work as artist-régisseur has been done in Leningrad, Moscow knowing it principally through his brilliant production of "Hamlet" for the Vakhtangov. When he works on the *décor* alone, as he has done for many other plays in Moscow, he shows his love for the theatre theatrical and for artificiality. He shows us, too, a keen intellectual understanding of the meaning which a particular production is to convey, a marked sense of irony and humor, and a desire to explore all the possible ways of mounting a play, achieving as a result remarkably fresh and novel effects. It was he who designed the Vakhtangov's production of "Love and Intrigue" in which the whole stage became a huge silver disc, tilted at a sharp angle up from the audience and surrounded by blackness. On this disc the action was played and what scenery was used—and there was little—was set. His also were the settings for "Débâcle" in which he made an inner proscenium in the shape of a cinema screen which, as in movie closeups, showed only the upper two-thirds of the actors' bodies.

Ryndin, whose work is most often seen at the Kamerny Theatre where his outstanding productions have been "Machinal," "The Optimistic Tragedy" and "Egyptian Nights," is an architect-artist who shows little interest in color and great interest in form. Working almost in monotone which he punctuates with color derived from light, he creates massive architectural effects which are always formal and sometimes tend toward abstract symbolism. This abstraction is strongest in "The Optimistic Tragedy"; in his last work, the settings for "Aristocrats" at the Vakhtangov Theatre, he shows a tendency to adopt a simplified realism which is at the same time powerfully impressionistic. He seems to have been influenced more by Appia than by anyone within Russia. He makes much use of light projection, sometimes for abstract emotional effect and sometimes for illustration of points in the text of a play, as I have described in "Machinal."

Space prevents discussion of the other good designers in Moscow—of the painter Favorski, who gave to the Second Art Theatre its charming decorations for "Twelfth Night"; of Shlepyanov, in whose work at the Theatre of the Revolution we can trace the emergence of good socialistic realism out of a good constructivism, of the brothers Stenberg who preceded Ryndin at the Kamerny; of Tischler whom someone has called a "revolutionary romanticist," whatever that means in the U.S.S.R.; of Williams, a recent arrival in the theatre but a man who shows himself an able graphic artist and a fine colorist in his sets for "Pickwick Club" and the forthcoming "Molière," both for the Moscow Art Theatre.

3

It is difficult to make generalizations about the technical processes of work of the Soviet designers, for it has never been systematized like the work of Russian actors and directors, and it is largely a matter of the individual's temperament. To study it properly, we really should go from studio to studio and report what we find in each. That being impossible, I shall have to attempt generalizations.

There seem to be two ways in which the designer tackles his problem. Either he will develop his ideas in the form of *esquisses*, beginning with rough thumb-nail sketches and carrying them through to highly detailed colored plates, or, after a rough sketch or two made only for his own eye, he will proceed at once to work on the *maquette*. Different designers use the different methods at various times. Certain ones prefer the former system, and in this they betray themselves as painter-artists. Many of those whose conceptions are essentially three-dimensional and architectonic or constructivist go at once to the stage model. A few versatile designers work in either medium, depending on the style they are adopting for the commission at hand.

It is possible to say, however, that the *maquette* is much more generally used in the Moscow studio than in New York. There are several reasons for this. The first is the ever-present one of time. The Moscow designer has usually anywhere from eight weeks to a year to prepare his production. The New York designer rarely has more than the same one month that the director and cast are allowed in which not only to design but to execute his plans. During this month he may even be working on one or two other plays. The *maquette*, if it is to be of any value, must be carefully and exactly made. It is long and tedious work. The American designer, while usually acknowledging the value of it, rarely feels that he has the time to complete one before its practical use will have passed.

Another reason for the use of the *maquette* in Moscow is that Soviet stage design is principally based either on some kind of definite architectural form or on some derivative of constructivism which, to be understood, must be seen in the round, in space. The possibilities of the spatial stage cannot be adequately explored by the régisseur or the designer from a two-dimensional rendering. The realistic convention of the New York theatre, because of the kind of plays which are being produced, requires that about seventy-five per cent of its plays shall be mounted in some adaptation of the box-set interior. There is little need for a *maquette* to illustrate such a staging. The box-set, however, makes rare appearances in Moscow.

Almost every theatre in Moscow has a revolving stage; even the smallest stages have their turntables. These are regularly used because so many Soviet productions are of many scenes. Therefore, the audience also will be called upon to see the scenery in the round, and the designer must ascertain what the effect will be. If revolving stages are not used, then some kind of moving wagon or platform stage must be devised, and here again the *maquette* is of use in working out the feasibility of the designer's scheme. New York has few revolving stages; the majority of its plays have had, until the last season or two, no more than three sets, and there is little need for rapid-shifting devices. When the American designer is called upon to mount a production of many scenes, he is apt, incidentally, to make use of a model, which proves that he appreciates its value under such conditions as he then must work—conditions which are the daily ones of the Soviet artist.

The *maquette* has come to be so depended upon in Moscow studios that if the designer has not seen fit to make one, then the working staff of the theatre for which he has prepared his *esquisses* may very probably make one-inch scale models for itself from his sketches. Some theatres even provide permanent models of their stages which the designer is expected to use in his work. All these *maquettes* are carefully and beautifully executed. Photographs of them might easily be confused with ones of the finished product. All furniture and the tiniest props are made to exact scale and there is usually an effort to work out the lighting as well, although the electrical equipment of the models is not usually very complete. I am sorry to say that often the *maquette* of a setting is more effective than the finished set.

His final drawings or his models having been completed and turned over to the working staff of the theatre, the designer's work is theoretically finished, for they are supposed to be so accurate in every way that their exact reproduction will give the designer what he wants without further bother on his part. Actually, however, the designer's duties continue, for he wishes to supervise the execution of the setting, props and costumes, and he will oversee the final arrangement on the stage. He will also supervise the execution of the actors' wigs and make-ups for which he will have made sketches.

Although the designer is not on the theatre's staff, the staff does include a permanent "artist," a technical director, an assistant technical director, and sometimes one or two art assistants. It is to them that the production now goes. They are directly responsible for executing the designer's plans, and it is with them that he works. The designer himself makes no architectural drawings, no working or mechanical drawings of any kind. He employs no assistant or draughtsman of his own to do this for him; his work is done alone, usually in his home, and it does not involve ground plans, elevations or detail sheets. If there are any, the technician or the artist of the theatre's staff will do them. But in most cases there are no formal working drawings made by anybody for a setting. The technician simply applies a scale rule to the designer's scaled model or the one which he has made himself from the designer's sketch, jots down the dimensions he finds there, makes, if need be, a few constructional notes or perspective sketches of details on a piece of scratch paper or the back of an envelope. These he then turns over to the carpenter or the property man. There are no blueprints to be shown to the inquiring visitor because no blueprints have ever been made.

In America dimensions must be down in black and white (or rather, in blue and white) so that scene shops may have them as a basis for estimates of cost to regulate their bidding for contracts. That is one reason why accurate blueprints are so important in New York's professional theatre. But since every theatre in Moscow has all its own shops where it does its own building and painting of scenery, manufactures all its furniture, props and effects, there is no advance estimating and bidding and no contracts let. These shops are all situated in the theatre's building and are manned by a permanent staff of workers who execute all that theatre's scenery only. This is another reason why working drawings are so little used in Moscow. The technician who is executing the settings may have his office just adjoining the shops, he can pay them twenty visits a day, he can if need be show the workers personally how every piece is to be made and finished, and the *maquette* or sketches are at hand for any workman to see at any time.

The technical department of the Moscow Art Theatre is the largest and most complete of any dramatic theatre in the city. There are 260 members on its staff and it occupies parts of four buildings. A five-story scene "factory" is being built which will have much better equipment than the present shops, and into it they will be transferred within a year or two. The technical director is today a little apologetic when he shows an American visitor the equipment, for much of it was purchased before the Revolution. But in extent there is nothing in America comparable to this department save perhaps the "warehouse" of the Shubert Corporation in New York.

We should start a tour of the technical department in the studio and offices of its director and his assistant, in which the staff artist lays out certain details, patterns for upholstery for instance, and where the models are made and exhibited. These rooms open off the foyer of the balcony and are far from the scene of execution which is half a block up the alley. We go first to a low building which contains the carpentry and iron-working shops. In the carpentry shop we see that much heavier lumber is being used for frames of "flats" than the American theatre uses, that there are a great many more solid units being built, that probably because cloth is expensive and scarce and wood is plentiful, canvas yields to plywood in covering many surfaces. In the iron shop we discover that the theatre makes its own lighting units—floodlights, stands, clamps, etc.—as well as its own rails and corner irons for building support. The department supplies any metal fittings that may be needed in a production: it will turn out a sixteeth-century hanging lantern, an eighteenth-century musket barrel, or a twentieth-century door latch or pair of handcuffs as the play requires.

From this building we go to the other buildings along the alley which house the other departments. The Art Theatre has its own paint shop, where we observe that the Soviet scene painter does all his painting with the material lying flat on the floor; no paint frames or vertical scaffolds are in evidence. In the prop shop we find complete wood-working equipment, a little antiquated but quite adequate, and we see a dozen Russian Empire chairs being made to match a single original, all of them to be used in the new sets of "The Cherry Orchard." All kinds of props are being manufactured there. Adjoining this is the upholstery shop where all upholstering is done. In the artificial flower department are artists of that craft who have been working there ever since they provided the first cherry blossoms for "The Cherry Orchard" thirty years ago. In another room many women (wives of the men who work elsewhere in the MXAT shops) are making artificial leaves for trees.

There is a dye shop where all kinds of materials are colored in quantity—goods for costumes, velvets for cycloramas, carpeting, drapery material, sky drops. Special dyes are mixed here to be sent to the paint or to the upholstery departments for use in particular painting-with-dye processes. In the same little house with the dye shop is the theatre's laundry which shares with the theatre's dry-cleaning shop, also installed there, the responsibility of keeping the costumes and draperies for all the plays in the repertoire fresh and clean. This is quite a task in a theatre which may continue to perform a play for ten or twenty years without changing its costumes.

The costume shops are situated in the theatre building itself, and here all costumes are made, both men's and women's, which are to be worn on the stage, including modern gowns and men's suits. Some of the period costumes are refashioned out of materials already at hand in the costumes of plays which have been withdrawn from the repertoire (Stanislavski has never allowed the robes of the original "Tsar Fyodor" production to be touched), some gorgeous materials are available from confiscated ecclesiastical and royal regalias, but most costumes are completely new creations. Adjoining the costume shops on one side is the hat shop where all kinds of hats and headgear are made, save metal helmets which come from the metal-working shop; on the other side is the bootery where shoes and boots of every style and period are manufactured. The wig department has a dressing room situated near the stage door, for the wigmaker creates his wigs and beards at home and uses this room only for dressing and caring for those wigs which the actors bring to him at the theatre before or after performances. As part of the equipment and staff of the technical department must be included two scenery trucks and the truckmen who haul sets back and forth from the shops and from the large *MXAT* to its small affiliated stage six blocks away.

This part of the technical department is concerned only with the preparation of a production, with the execution of the artist's designs in their dozen different aspects. It is possible for these shops to be preparing three productions simultaneously—"Enemies," "Molière," and the new mounting of "The Cherry Orchard" were all in work there in January, 1935. The shops may require from four weeks to four months to do a complete show, depending on the complication of its designs. We have now to consider the assembling of the production on the stage and the organization of the technical crew which runs it. I should like first, however, to describe the stage of the Moscow Art Theatre on which they have to work. It is not very new or unique, but it is, I believe, the largest and one of the best equipped dramatic stages in Moscow.

(The Kamerny's stage is the largest of the newer ones and it has much better lighting equipment than the *MXAT*, the best in Moscow, in my opinion.)

The most spectacular feature of the Art Theatre's equipment is the huge turntable, fifty-five feet in diameter. To encompass so large a revolving section, the stage is sixty-three feet deep, which makes the space of the stage floor very nearly a square. (The average depth of a stage in New York is about half that.) This characteristic the Art Theatre shares with almost all Moscow theatres, for they have uniformly deep stages. Within this revolving space are two rectangular sections which are capable of rising six feet above the floor level and of sinking six feet beneath it. The turntable may revolve in either direction and at various rates of speed. The rising and falling sections may be in movement while the turntable is revolving.

There are sixty-six sets of lines on the gridiron, sixty-eight feet above the stage floor. There are two basements, the revolving stage being controlled electrically from the first. Here also is the furniture storage, with an elevator which brings props up from there to the stage level during a scene shift, thus allowing the stage floor to be free of unused furniture and props. Here also are some of the sound effects; others are elsewhere. There is a pipe organ in the back wall of the stage itself and a set of full-sized church bells hangs from a gallery. From the first basement one enters the booth which contains the switchboard, situated next to the prompter's box beside the footlights. From here the electrician may see the entire stage and control his lights accordingly. He is in telephonic communication with the stage floor. In this the *MXAT* has served as a model to most other Moscow theatres, for almost everywhere the switchboard is in a box under the stage with an opening which commands a view of it. Rarely is it found in the wings. The Art Theatre has also set an example to

the other Moscow theatres in the matter of the house curtain. The Maly is the only theatre I have seen in the city
which has a drop curtain; in all the others, like the *MXAT*,
the curtains part.

Of the 260 members of the technical department of the
Art Theatre, considerably less than half form the stage
crews in its two theatres. These crews are divided into
two sections; one which is on duty on the stage by day,
arranging sets for rehearsals, preparing for the evening
performance, and one which runs the show at night. It is
obviously much more difficult from a technical point of
view to present a different play every night, as the repertory system requires, than to keep the sets of only one
play indefinitely on one's stage. That is why two crews are
required—many "lines" must be cleared each day, new sets
hung, lamps rearranged, flats restacked, old props cleared
and new ones stacked—enough work for one whole crew,
considering that this must be done before eleven or after
four in the afternoon, the only times when the *MXAT's*
stage is not being used for rehearsal of one play or another.

The size of the crew that works a performance varies,
depending upon the heaviness of the production. From
seven to twenty-five carpenters, from six to eight prop
men, and from six to eight electricians form the regular
crew. The "boss carpenter" is in charge after the first
dozen performances which are personally supervised by the
technical director. The stage manager of a play does not
have responsibility for the technical details which the
New York stage manager must assume. His only concern is
with the actors. He has a small booth-like office in a rear
corner of the stage where he can see the entrances from
the dressing-room corridors on to the stage and keep an eye
on his cast. His assistant sits in the prompt box with the
script. The Vakhtangov Theatre, incidentally, has no

prompter and no one at all holds the book during performances.

The routine of running a performance in a Moscow theatre is so similar to that in America that I see no point in describing it. I also see no need for describing the back stage mechanics of other theatres in Moscow, for all those which I saw were more or less modeled on the Art Theatre, though on a smaller scale. The Vakhtangov, for example, has only eighty-four men on its technical staff!

Lighting in the Soviet theatre has little to recommend it to the foreigner. The equipment is poor and clumsy (the Art Theatre has two American spotlights and two German; all the rest are home-made and look like it). The effects achieved are not remarkable. In many theatres footlights have been abolished (not so at the MXAT and Maly), and their place has been taken by front floodlighting which involves wide spilling and a general illumination of everything that lies within a wide circle of the proscenium. Front lighting by spots is customarily effected by the use of arcs or sometimes by incandescent lamps which are operated from side proscenium boxes. Each box may contain two or three spots under the control of one or two operators, usually young apprentices who make distracting movements as they adjust their lamps during the action. These lights are used as "follow spots" and are constantly moving to cover the business of the leading characters. To supplement these side lights from the front, and at the MXAT to replace them, some theatres have a battery of spots on a bar hanging above the proscenium and about twenty feet in front of it. Onstage lights are few and crude, old-fashioned borders with a few spots and floods.

There is little effort to eliminate unnecessary shadows. Very little color is used in lighting acting areas. Clear light predominates, to be varied occasionally by a bright amber, pink or blue. The use of frosting is apparently unknown and many sets are confused by the sharp line of the spotlight's focused circle as it hits the contours of the setting without any softening. I am, of course, aware that many times the sharp beam of a clear spotlight is tremendously effective, and that it is often consciously used, but I think that the Soviet theatre employs that method of lighting to such an excess as to spoil its dramatic quality when it is used properly. Certainly the realistic theatre errs when it practices Meierholdian lighting technique in an otherwise natural setting.

Again I admit that I generalize in leveling this criticism; Meierhold himself and one or two designers (I have mentioned Rabinovich in particular) make fine use of light, but with the exception of their work and of a few excellently lighted performances at the Kamerny Theatre, I saw no play in Moscow which New York could not and would not have lighted better.

At the present time there is no training school for theatre technicians in Moscow. Each theatre has a certain number of young people who serve as apprentices in various departments and after a period of training and experience become full-fledged members of the staff. There is, however, a central school about to be opened by *Narkompros* to which the theatres will send a few of their younger technicians. There they will have a more formal training in engineering, electricity, and various other subjects which will equip them better for work as theatre technicians. As I understand the plan, they will continue to serve as apprentices within their theatre, and while going to school by day will gain practical experience from helping to work the regular evening performances on their home stage.

To conclude, the *décor* of the Moscow stage is brave in conception, weak in execution. The designer is an artist who rarely has to have the particularized knowledge of the New York designer, but who, possibly for that very reason, contrives backgrounds that are bold and sometimes very beautiful. They are executed by the staffs of each theatre which, while amazing us by the number of crafts represented, yet turn out productions which are regularly cruder and sloppier than our own. Again we are up against that characteristic of the Russian people which Western engineers and architects working in the Soviet Union know so well and curse so heartily: the Russians can plan magnificently—dream dreams of surpassing beauty—yet they know not perfection of manual workmanship. But perhaps the theatre needs more dreams and fewer well-built door frames.

CHAPTER SEVEN

Playwrights at Work

IT IS practically impossible to write a chapter on playwrights at work unless one uses it as a springboard
from which to dive off into one's opinions about the playwrights and their finished products, for when it comes to
the actual process of writing a play, that is something
about which dramatists seldom can or are willing to talk,
and the rules of courtesy which may allow an observer to
sit in a darkened corner of a rehearsal hall forbid him
to look over the shoulder of a laboring playwright as he
sits at his desk.

This book is concerned with the theatre and not with
drama—a distinction in terms which I think is clear to all;
I understand drama to be a branch of literature. But I do
find that I have several ideas about playwrighting in
Russia, some of them arising out of a study of method,
and some of them merely desultory comments on the
Soviet theatre and drama which come to my mind when
I think about the playwrights of Moscow and the rôle
they have to play in the creation of a new culture for
the masses. I shall start, however, at the point where the
playwright has finished his play and has emerged from
his study, for my description will be of the rôle he plays
in production. Farther than that into method I cannot
and would not wish to go. But before I begin, let me
deliver myself of one observation.

I seem to have arranged this section of my book in a

series of descending climaxes. The great strength of the Soviet theatre lies in its actors and its régisseurs. Stage design is a weaker allied art, and when we come to playwrighting, we have reached the low point of the Moscow theatre. Of all the artists of the theatre, the dramatists are the least able for their task.

I submit such a statement with the parenthetical warning that it is but my own lay opinion. However, when a Soviet theatre director publishes in a Soviet stage journal a statement like the following, it should strengthen my report. Amaglobely, director of the Maly Theatre, writing in *Theatre and Dramaturgy,* has said, "Soviet dramaturgy, in spite of its tremendous achievements, is as yet a dramaturgy of insignificant forms, of insignificant people. . . . Our demand is that the heroes of our plays must stand abreast with the heroes of the age. The fact that Soviet dramaturgy lags behind the Soviet theatre has been acknowledged by all." He goes on to say that this backwardness is chiefly technical and not at all ideological, but I believe that the dramatist who cannot find satisfactory dramatic expression for his ideas is but a polemist who should be writing tracts, not plays.

With the playwright, as with the designer, is the situation of the individual artist at work with the collective of artists. What is the relationship?

The modern Soviet dramatist has much less authority in the production of his play than the American who writes for the professional theatre and sells his work in New York. The latter—if he is an established playwright, and sometimes even if he is not—has an important voice in the casting of his play; often his contract may allow him to veto a producer's or director's choice of actors. He attends rehearsals regularly where he is sometimes a constant help, sometimes a constant hindrance, to the director. He has an opinion about the settings and costumes which he does not fear to voice. The playwright wields a power in American stage production, a power which is not ended when he lays down his pen.

The Moscow dramatist (poor fellow!) is kept in his place. His contribution to the production is literary and stops at that. When his play is accepted by a theatre, the author entrusts to it all matters pertaining to its production. The theatre casts the play by such methods as its internal organization requires, it chooses what régisseur and designer it pleases, and sets to work to produce the play in whatever manner it sees fit. In the early stages of production the author may be invited by the theatre to attend a series of round-table discussions with the director and cast so that he may elaborate the meaning of passages or lines, but as often as not director and cast may disagree with him about interpretations and choose their own meaning! In any case the theatre is anxious to hear the author's remarks only when they are concerned with the literary side of the production or when they have to do with the psychology of characterization. If he wishes to attend later rehearsals, it will be only so that he may satisfy his own curiosity as to what is happening to his play.

One reason why American playwrights attend rehearsals so constantly is that there are usually many manuscript changes to be made during the period of rehearsing and the author is wanted to supply new lines or scenes or to give his consent to cuts and transpositions. This very rarely takes place in Moscow productions. While the director is at work on the play before rehearsals begin, he may be in close touch with the author and at that time the form of the play is set. A few more changes may take place during the first few weeks of rehearsal at these round-table discussions. Many of these changes may be ordered by the actors who find lines inconsistent with their ideas about the characters, and they may suggest phrasings of their own to substitute. The actor in Moscow has a much louder voice in script revisions than the actor in New York. After this, the script remains unaltered until the last week or so when final cuts may have to be made. These and whatever changes are made during other rehearsals are made by the director at his own discretion and the author is rarely consulted. If, and this seldom happens, a major revision in the script must be made during the period of active rehearsal, the director takes this up with the author, shows him what is wrong, explains what he wants, and asks the author to provide it. It behooves the author to do so, for if he does not, the director will doubtless do it himself!

Naturally the attitude of a theatre and the play's régisseur toward the author will be based upon the author's experience and prominence. Much fewer liberties are taken with the scripts of the better playwrights, and much more weight is given to their opinions, particularly about the literary and psychological problems of their plays, than is the case with unknown and inferior craftsmen. Unfortunately there are many of these latter. The American playwright is a power in production because he knows the theatre and what it can and should do to make his play live most effectively. He understands his medium; the majority of Soviet playwrights do not.

The Moscow dramatist faces another situation which the New York dramatist does not, and it offers a more flattering reason for his slight participation in the actual production of his play. This is the simultaneous production of it in various theatres. When the American dramatist sells the rights of his play to one producer or organization, he knows that no one else will be able to produce it for the time being. The Moscow writer, having no rights to sell, may turn his play over to as many different theatres

as are willing to take it, and it is not an uncommon occurrence for a good play to be in rehearsal at two or three
different theatres in the city at the same time. And con-
currently with the productions of it in preparation in
Moscow, his new play may be in rehearsal in Leningrad
and one or two other places. The author, therefore, would
really have more than he could do if he tried to have an
active hand in all the productions.

Premières, incidentally, have therefore not the same significance in Russia that they have in America. The Moscow critic is as much interested in seeing what a particular
theatre has done with a play as in finding out what the
play itself is. The critics are thus rather theatrical critics
than dramatic critics; the interest shifts from play to performance, much as it might if Gilbert Miller, the Theatre
Guild, Sam Harris and the Theatre Union all announced
that they would produce Sidney Howard's next play in the
same season, each of course with a different cast and different director. This, in turn, has its effect on the theatre's
attitude toward the manuscript, and is one reason for the
small amount of rewriting which takes place. Since no
one producing organization has the exclusive rights to a
play, and since each must stand ready to have its interpretation compared with the performance of it at other
theatres, it is less apt to make changes in the body of the
original text, and is more apt to concentrate on its method
of staging, leaving the script alone.

This attitude does not seem to hold, however, in the production of the classics. Each theatre makes its own arrangement of the text, and this is offered as its original
contribution to the play as much as the style in which it
is done. This is particularly true of classics in other languages than Russian, which have had, at all times in the
Russian theatre, adaptations rather than literal transla-
tions. The adapting process has broadened in recent years

when the Soviet theatre has tried to draw from classics ideas to suit its own dogma—when, for instance, it changes "The Spanish Curate" by John Fletcher from tragedy to comedy by altering the text of its last act.

Meierhold has been the outstanding Soviet producer to change his manuscripts to fit his own ideas. Whether it has been a foreign or a Russian classic or a modern play, Meierhold has rewritten the text with such freedom that he has often claimed, when it was done, that he was the "author of the spectacle" and has so appeared on the program. He has done this for several reasons. First, because temperamentally he is satisfied with nothing which does not bear the mark of his own creation. Just as he must tell the actor how to act, the designer how to devise his backgrounds, the musician what music to compose, so he must tell the author how to write his play, and if the author has been dead a hundred years or so and cannot heed Meierhold's advice, then he must needs take on the task himself.

It is not only to satisfy what appears to be his own egoism that Meierhold revises the plays which he presents. He does so because almost no dramatists exist or have existed who have created both the ideas and in the form of theatre which he wants. Since he has been considered the chief advocate of a drama based on Revolutionary ideology, he would be expected to turn to Revolutionary dramatists for his material. But they are new and inexperienced authors who write in a realistic vein, and he wants something which will be more symbolic or stylized and also more poetic. He has to take then either the writings of the past which in form may suit him, and readapt them to the ideology of the Revolution or the writings of the present (and some writings of the past) and arrange them so that they will suit his own nonrepresentational stylizations. He has done both and he has

been harshly rebuked by foreign critics for his "desecra-
tions." I fail to see what else he could have done under the
circumstances.

This talk of the classics brings me to another point: it is
possible to see in Moscow nowadays a greater number of
productions of classics and a greater proportion of classics
to modern plays than one can find in any other theatrical
capital of the Western world. A study of the official *affiches*
of the Moscow theatres during the season of 1934-35 reveals performances of plays or dramatizations of the works
of Balzac, Beaumarchais, Dickens, Dumas, Fletcher, Goldoni, Gozzi, Hamsun, Molière, Schiller, Scribe, Shakespeare, and the Russians Chekhov, Dostoyevski, Gogol,
Gorki, Griboyedov, Ostrovski, Pushkin, Tolstoy.

Why are the Moscow theatres giving so many classics?
Of all cities in the world, we should expect Moscow to
be the first to turn her back on the past. Certainly Dumas,
Goldoni and their compatriots among the ageless in art
were not Communists and wrote not for a proletarian
audience. I think there are two reasons, the first (which
supports my original contention about modern playwrit-
ing) is that the theatres feel that much of the recent
Soviet dramaturgy is weak, that it does not call forth their
best efforts. They seek something worthy of their stature
and not finding it in the new plays, they turn to the old.
They want significant forms and significant people on
their stage, as Amaglobely says; the classics give them that
and the Soviet writers very often do not.

The second reason is that the theatre in Moscow is aware
of its educational obligation to the people. It considers that
the classic dramas of the world should be known to the
people. Many of its audience have had sketchy educations
and have read very little classic drama. In any case, the
theatre believes that the people should come to know great
plays through seeing them performed and not through

reading them in schools. The American theatre and the other European theatres have no such sense of educational obligation. Perhaps it was shame which prevented the writer from confessing to any Russian in Moscow that two-thirds of the classics of English, French, German, Italian and Scandinavian literature which he saw there he was seeing for the first time.

2

The task which Soviet dramatists have faced during these seventeen years has been a constantly changing one. The Marxian theatre demands that art and the currents of life should never flow in separate channels, that the class struggle must have constant representation in the theatre. The current of life and the nature of this class struggle have changed so radically and so rapidly within Russia that the dramatists have had to be constantly on the run to keep up with it. I think that the continual ideological readjustments which they have had to make are one reason why they have made such little real technical progress. I can best show you what these readjustments have been by reviewing the Revolutionary theatre's history.

In the movement of the Revolution during the past eighteen years, one may observe roughly two great phases. The first was a period of destruction which began with the overthrow of the Tsarist monarchy by the Bolsheviks in 1917, which continued during the period of Civil War when the Communist Party was besieged by opponents, White Russians and Allied Interventionists, and which may be said to have continued further through the years of the New Economic Policy, NEP, instituted by Lenin in 1921 as a temporary concession to capitalism and private ownership in his combat against them both. The second phase, which slightly overlaps the first, is the period of construction, which takes definite form in the First Five Year Plan, inaugurated in 1928, and is continued in the Second Five Year Plan of January, 1933.

The first eight or ten years devoted to the annihilation of tsarism and capitalism were years of bloodshed and civil war, of famine and starvation, of plague, years of internal dissention and sabotage. Physical necessities of life were not available, no food, no fuel, no clothes. Out of this chaos the Communists reared the structure of the Five Year Plan. The famine was over, active resistance had lessened and the government now turned its attention to the long and difficult process of reconstruction. The newly created state must rehabilitate its resources and its industries. The successful accomplishment of this Plan imposed a tremendous responsibility upon the Communist Party. Staggering goals had been set up and the country was pressed to the limit of its capacity and endurance to reach them. Life during the years of the First Five Year Plan was as racking—in a different way—as it had been in the years that had just passed. Factories worked at maximum speed. The tension was great and the tempo of life made for the nervous exhaustion of not only the leaders but all workers, for of all Europeans the Slavs were least used to the rigors of heavy industrialism.

When the Second Five Year Plan, devised to build up the "light industries" and so to raise the personal standard of living of the population, got under way in 1933, life began to relax to some extent. Cultural development and the achievement of certain refinements began to be emphasized. The agrarian problem was on the way toward solution, capitalism was "liquidated," the socialist state seemed assured, and people looked at the future with renewed hope, made stronger by the sight of visible comforts and of the progress appearing around them. They felt that their crisis was behind them; the ideals for which they had fought seemed more tangibly realizable than ever before. There was an impetus for action.

Shortly after the Revolutionary government was established the theatre was brought under its control and made a part of the Commissariat of Education. The Communist Party from the beginning realized the importance of the theatre which in Russia is the closest of all the arts to the people. It appreciated that the theatre could be an invaluable agent in interpreting its purpose to the masses. It realized further that the theatre could serve the masses as well as the Party, and that eventually it could express the masses. To accomplish this, however, the theatre would have to change. Either its imperialistic and bourgeois outlook must be "converted" so that it would cease to be an anachronistic remnant of the abolished society in the new proletarian state, or else the theatre must be wiped away entirely and a new form of dramatic expression created that would harmonize with the new heaven and the new earth.

The history of the theatre since the Revolution is the history of this change in its form and function. The change follows significantly close to the line of progress of the Revolution and it may be divided into three periods which roughly correspond to the three periods of Revolutionary history.[1] First came a period of about ten years marked by the struggle to determine whether the existing theatre should be converted or "liquidated." The radicals demanded its destruction, the conservatives struggled for existence.

That the government did not accede to these demands for destruction is largely due to the influence of the first People's Commissar of Education, Anatol Lunacharski, a

---

[1] I.e., destruction, reconstruction, later reconstruction. For this division of the theatre's history I am indebted to P. I. Novitski of the People's Commissariat of Education, who has suggested it.

wise and discerning leader. While upholding all the principles of Marxism, he yet felt the vital importance of maintaining cultural unity with the past. He insisted that the artistic heritage of Russia should not be destroyed but rather that it should be preserved and made available to the people so that it might thus become a part of their education. In this way the meaning of Marx-Leninism could best be interpreted. He believed that in time these theatres could come to an acceptance of the Marxian interpretation of art. Thus it came to pass that these old theatres were not liquidated, and the task of converting their policies into a form which would not be contradictory to the principles of the proletarian Revolution was begun. This was of course the only wise procedure, for in its academic theatre Russia possessed an inherited artistic treasure the like of which no other nation at that time could boast.

The pursuit of such a policy, however, did not mean that Lunacharski did not encourage the Revolutionaries in the theatre as well. He admitted the need for an immediate response and immediate assistance from the stage, and he saw no reason why a new theatre should not come into existence even if the old were retained. It was this new theatre that Vsevolod Meierhold championed, and for it playwrights were called upon to produce an agitational drama which would enthuse the people to the cause of the Party, would keep that enthusiasm at war-time pitch. It was, in fact, a war-time drama. It was concerned with the military activities of the moment, and it was also concerned with damning the capitalist, both as he remained in Russia and as he was without, and with showing what scoundrels all people in Russia were who for any reason opposed the Revolution. It exaggerated, with much use of the grotesque, the sins of the petit-bourgeois and crudely stirred up as much class hatred as possible. For this sort of task nothing very finished was required of the playwrights. The audience in those early days had little appreciation for the finesses of literary style; anything which agitated the masses was acceptable.

In 1927 began the second period in the history of the Soviet theatre. This coincides with the beginnings of the socialistic reconstruction of the Soviet Union. At a congress held to discuss the problem, Lunacharski presented a plan which had as its two-fold object the acceleration of the development of the socialistic element in the theatre and assistance to the new revolutionary theatres. All the energy of the creative life of the U.S.S.R. was then being devoted to strengthening the basis for the establishment of a new life and the theatre was an essential means of communicating the visions of it. The nature of the theatre, therefore, underwent a change during this period: it ceased to be agitational and turned propagandist. It paid less attention to satirizing and condemning the old and more to depicting the new.

Lunacharski, however, meant more than this by the development of the socialistic element in the theatre; he meant that the theatres themselves must come to a more accurate understanding of the meaning of socialism in order to be able to meet the demands of interpreting its new life. In many cases the artistic temperament had found stimulation in presenting agitational plays and in devising new and revolutionary art forms, but the artistic intelligence had not yet grasped the meaning of the principles involved. The next five years were devoted to solidifying the socialistic doctrine within the theatre.

In appreciating the second aspect of Lunacharski's program it is necessary to understand that a great number of young Revolutionary theatres had sprung up during the preceding decade. It was important to the Party that these new theatres, if they were to continue, should develop along sound doctrinal and artistic lines and should not be

simply the expressions of a period of artistic inflation. A
certain amount of guidance seemed necessary. For the accomplishment of this two-fold program, therefore, the
government, through the agency of its Commissariat of
Education, tightened its authority over the theatre. The
natural result of this was a comparative loss of freedom
and for several years there was imminent danger of standardization. It was during this period that the application
of dialectic materialism in every field became such a fetish.
It was no doubt carried too far.

The subject matter of the plays of this period reflected
the absorption in material progress toward which the
Soviet Union was bending all its energies. Plays were written about collective farming and factory management,
about the construction of railways and farm tractors.
To sit through a play written on one of these subjects is
an exceedingly boring way to spend an evening if one is
not a Bolshevist farmer or factory manager, and foreigners
have come out of Russia with tales about the dull plays
with which the Soviet theatre is beset. With such criticisms of Soviet drama I have no sympathy (mine are
based on other faults which I shall presently point out).
The foreign observer fails to realize that because machinery
and the things created out of it are an old story to him,
they can have romance for anyone else. The Russian saw
a whole new world of experience opening up with the
introduction of the tractor and the expansion of the railroad—a world in which he would share. He found these
new and strange machines and the talk about them fas-
cinating. Machinery and the expansion of industry and
agriculture in their country was a matter of life and death
to the Bolsheviks in the 1920's, and quite naturally their
theatre talked about such things. Grant that Russia from
1925 to 1933 was absorbed in mastering technics, grant
next that the theatre is justifying its existence in a Marxian

state only when it follows the line of life, and you must accept a dramaturgy that is concerned with these same technics.

But the time came, as we have seen, when the drive for industrialization was relaxed a little, and at about the same time, on April 23, 1932, to be exact, the government issued a new decree, with the passage of which the theatre entered upon the most recent stage of its development. This decree was designed to give more freedom to artists, authors and other intellectuals. "The privilege to build socialism must be shared by all creative artists" was the way the Communists put it. There was to be more extensive development of its own set of creative principles within each theatre above and beyond the ABC's of Marx-Leninism. In taking this step the government seemed to have been motivated by the belief that the theatres now understood the required dogma, that the artists themselves were now personally converted to the Marxian principles— an accomplishment for which the preceding five years are significant—that the academic theatres had lost their reactionary character, and that the art of the theatre could be safely trusted to evolve along self-determined lines.

Once again the theatre follows the line of development of the Revolution. The buoyant optimism that succeeded the strain and stress of the First Five Year Plan, and the relaxation of the tempo of life are reflected in the theatre. The theatre can become less propagandistic and can almost entirely cease to be agitational. It can begin a new phase. Now the human element becomes important. The playwrights write about the new man as well as the new machine.

The cultural development of this new man is emphasized. The art of living, now that people have more time for it and more material benefits to assist its florescence, must be cultivated. Their new philosophy and their new ethics which the Bolsheviks have been spreading since the first days of the Revolution, but in crude fashion, must now receive fuller and deeper attention. After fifteen years the Soviet Union has created an intelligentsia of its own prepared to discuss these problems with a public which has after fifteen years arrived at a point where it can understand the discussion. The Russian Revolution has reached a critical period—a time when the masses have passed out of the blind acceptance of childhood's faiths into an inquisitive adolescence. Its guidance is a much more subtle task. The playwrights are among those called upon to assume this guidance.

The theatre in its most primitive stages has always been close to religion. It was out of the Dionysiac rites that Greek drama sprang. The medieval miracle, morality, and mystery plays of the Roman church gave the impetus to secular drama in western Europe. In Soviet Russia a new civilization is being undertaken without religion, and so the theatre is asked, not to interpret a theology to simple folk, but to take religion's place, and not only to teach the socialist doctrines which are to supplant Greek Orthodoxy, but also to admit the problems which its acceptance involves.

The theatre meets this with the new "socialistic realism." Its purpose is to relate the man to the building of the state. This relationship of the individual to society is one of the profound problems of socialism. It requires the maturest kind of thought to undertake an analysis and an explanation of the psychological issues involved. That is why Soviet drama has taken so long to be adequate to the task and has for so long been occupied only with the external aspects of the problem. With the relationship of individual to mass must come the relationship of individual to individual. For a long time this relationship was disregarded as all the emphasis was placed on the new idea of man in society. Now it is beginning to be appreciated that the two may be associated and that a third problem exists as well: the relation of a man to himself. All these relationships it is the duty of a church to unfold and to relate one to another and explain to the people. But where there is no church, other organs must undertake it, and so it comes about that the theatre in Soviet Russia turns philosophical. So it comes about, too, that the theatre makes a swing back toward psychology.

It was thus that Alexander Afinogenov, one of Russia's leading young playwrights, explained to me this recently assumed duty of the Soviet dramatists, and it explains his own attitude toward the art of the theatre. He writes plays about the new man and his inner and his outer conflicts, as well as about the applications of the more philosophical aspects of Communist doctrine. His plays are a little like dramatized sermons, to be sure, but since there is no other pulpit from which sermons may be preached, their presence in the theatre is more pardonable. His writing does show a tremendous advance in thoughtful probing of the problems of the mind and spirit of man in the socialist state than did earlier plays.

3

Now for my accusation that Soviet playwrighting is weak. I have made it plain that my objection is not with the subject matter as such. The theatre may be didactic so long as it is artistic. I do not mind if Soviet dramatists write about collective farmers and factory managers and engineers and their work, if that is what the people need and want—so long as they write with imagination and intelligence and make these men and their problems interesting and convincing. But this the Soviet author fails to do.

His chief fault lies in his play construction and in his characterization.

The Soviet playwright has no idea of unity and concentration of material. His form is usually episodic and there is little inner cohesion among the episodes. He works too diffusely, using a dozen scenes and two dozen characters when his story would be much more forceful if told in a third as many scenes and by a fourth as many characters. And with this diffuseness there comes a good deal of repetition which eventually loses its effectiveness. Plots, also, are at the same time both too complicated and too simple. They are too complicated because as often as not the writer is trying to tell two or three stories at once, which is all very well in itself perhaps, but which requires knowledge of the art of subordination, or at least of how to connect them all together, which the Soviet playwright has not mastered. The plots are too simple because in the great majority of cases one can foretell the outcome of a play by the end of its first act, and that is something which should not be.

In characterization the Soviet dramatist also falls down. His chief trouble is that he tries to paint his people only in black and white, and in maneuvering them around so that one man may seem only virtuous and another only vicious, he has forgotten the truths of psychology. That is one reason why the Moscow Art Theatre has been unable to stage so many of these new plays—there have been only cardboard heroes and villains to enact. Afinogenov, Pogodin, Bulgakov, Gorki of course, and some few other Soviet dramatists are working to give more reality to stage people and the move is away, I am happy to report, from these stereotyped characters. If socialistic realism accomplishes that alone, it will have helped blow Soviet dramaturgy away from the doldrums which threaten it.

As long as this new realistic style and this didacticism

persist to the exclusion of all other dramatic expressions, what becomes of romance in the theatre? Of course, I realize that it is not the mere presence of realism which accounts for the absence of romanticism. The latter has been systematically discouraged from the start because in its search for an escape from the realities of life it is just what the Party disapproves of in art. But paradoxically, I believe, that romanticism *is* perhaps one of the realities of life; at any rate I believe that the U.S.S.R. is in need of just that today. My observation of the people in Moscow leads me to think that they hunger for romanticism (some consciously and many unconsciously), and that they suffer from a prolonged overdose of dialectic materialism. In the Soviet Union, certainly more than in any other country, the people can afford to take a little time for romancing.

It is one of the proudest boasts of the Soviet theatre, and quite justified, that it does not share the bourgeois theatre's mania for the drama of sex psychology. An interest in the theme of romantic love is another matter, however, and I have every reason to believe that Soviet youth is as healthily romantic as the youth of any other country. If I am mistaken and it is not, then I don't see why it should not become so. Let a Moscow theatre produce "Romeo and Juliet" not as a social tract emphasizing the theme of feudal family hate, but for the poetry that is in it and for the exaltation of young romantic passion that is there. Let every Young Communist go to see it, and the Soviet Union would still not crumble away the next day. Romanticism—not to be confused with sloppy sentimentality—should be allowed a place by the side of socialistic realism in the Soviet theatre.

If Soviet playwrighting lags behind the rest of the theatre in finish of technique and in breadth of expression, we must remember that drama in Russia has been a very recently practiced art. There are not the great antecedents stretching back to the sixteenth century which English drama has, nor to the seventeenth century which the French drama has. It has been only within the last hundred years that Russia has had any body of dramatic literature at all. The theatre is one of the earliest of all the arts to be practiced in a young civilization. Dramatic writing is one of the latest and most sophisticated arts. Perhaps that is as good a reason as any why miming and movement are so highly developed in the new proletarian civilization and why dramatic literature is still so crude. He who is willing to allow Soviet Russia time to prove its case must likewise be willing to give its playwrights time to come of age.

CHAPTER EIGHT

The Moscow Scene Expanded

I SHOULD be leading the reader astray if I caused him
to think that the half dozen theatres which I have described in detail were the only fine ones in Moscow. Such
is not at all the case. The necessity to be brief in text and
the physical impossibility of covering with any degree of
thoroughness the work of any larger number of theatres
in the six months I was in Moscow, are the only things
that have prevented me from becoming much more ex-
pansive. In order that the reader may have some idea of
the breadth of activity of the stage in Soviet Russia's
capital, however, I propose to supplement my account of
the history and development of the theatres of Stanislavski
and Meierhold, Tairov, Vakhtangov and Okhlopkov, with
short stories of some of the other great theatres, and with
a description of the rise of several of the newer groups.

Earlier I stated that I found in Moscow some forty professional theatres, all of them composed of permanent
groups of artists performing in repertory. Each of these
forty had its own set of artistic principles consciously codified, and every one seemed to differ from every other.
But careful examination disclosed to me that however their
outward appearances might differ, all of them had an inner
connection and similarity which was the result of both
their heredity and their environment. The further I pro-
ceeded the more it became apparent to me that instead of
finding myself simultaneously at a score of widely di-

vergent ends, I would come upon three or four lowest
common denominators. These denominators I found to be
the theatres of Stanislavski, Meierhold and Vakhtangov.
That is why I have described them first. Now let me extend the picture by discussing briefly the rest of the Moscow scene.

I must take you first of all to the Maly Theatre, which
is really *the* common denominator of all the others, if one
speaks historically, for it is the oldest theatre in Moscow—
its doors having been open over a hundred years. *Maly*
means "little" and *Bolshoi* means "big" or "great." The
Maly and the Bolshoi were the two imperial theatres in
Moscow and they still stand on two sides of the great
Theatre Square in the center of the city; the latter is
the principal opera house of Soviet Russia. In 1917 the
Maly Theatre was considered, as it still is today, to be
the inheritor and upholder of the classic tradition of the
Russian stage. It was therefore looked upon as reactionary.
It had not always been so, however. Lunacharski said of
the Maly: "The struggle for a representative theatre between the feudal bureaucratic autocracy and the surging
liberal public opinion brought victory to the latter and
thus the Maly Theatre was the offspring of the progressive
part of the Russian intelligentsia in her warfare with all
the crusty attributes of the feudal order, and even to some
extent with capitalism."

Lunacharski was describing the situation in the middle
of the nineteenth century. At that time the Maly was
the chief proponent of realistic domestic drama of which
Ostrovski was the Russian master. Ostrovski and the Maly
are inseparably connected in the minds of all who know
the history of Russian drama. Ostrovski was the great
dramatic social critic of his time, and his writing reveals
the contradictions and weaknesses of the Russian middle
class. With deep psychological insight he drew his charac-

ters, people from every-day life, which the Maly seemed able to incarnate with rare understanding.

In addition to this strain of contemporary criticism, the Maly found itself attracted to heroic romanticism, perhaps chiefly because it possessed artists of sufficient power to portray with the necessary breadth the heroes of classical romantic tragedy; so to its realistic strain was added the romanticism of Shakespeare, Schiller, Goethe, Hugo. Satire it also made use of and we find on its stage works of Gogol, Griboyedov, Lope de Vega and Molière—a ponderous repertoire, but a grand one.

The Maly Theatre was always a theatre built around great acting. The actor was its strongest bulwark to which all the other instruments of theatrical creation were subordinated. The names of Shchepkin, of Mochalov, master of the tragic rôle, of Lenski, Ermolova, Samarin, are those of actors who, if tradition speaks truly, were as great as any western Europe knew at any period of her dramatic history. It was they, and particularly Shchepkin, who gave to Russian acting its characteristic qualities. Theodore Komisarjevsky, writing about the latter in *The Theatre*, says that although a realist, he "did not aim, like the first French adepts of this school who came after, at the 'exact, complete, sincere and simple reproduction of the social *milieu* of the period which one is living in.' The Russians felt the presence of eternity and God in actual life both in its depths and ugliness as well as in its heights and beauty. To Shchepkin realistic forms and characters served as means to express [his] feelings and ideas, and [he] condensed and adapted them to suit [his] artistic and philosophic purposes.

"Shchepkin's acting was the condensed imaginative acting of life-like characters. Although Shchepkin held that a close observation of people was a necessity for an actor, he called imitative acting 'actoring.' He considered it necessary that a player should not only 'live through' his part on the stage, but transform himself into a character and be an 'embodiment' of it."

In his description of this great actor, Komisarjevsky has set forth the foundations of Russian realistic acting which the Maly Theatre created. In his work one can observe the roots of Stanislavski's system. By the end of the nineteenth century, however, and during the years before the War, the Maly began to lose strength. After Ostrovski it could seem to find no contemporaneous dramatist who fulfilled its demands or drew out its full strength in realism or heroic romanticism. "The romantic tendency degenerated into stiltedness, affectation and pseudo-classical pathos; the realistic inclinations became fixed upon an empirical approach to the portrayal of every-day life," says Amaglobely, its present director. Moreover, the great geniuses had passed from its acting company and those who followed used their talents in an effort to imitate the masters who had preceded them. The Maly thus weakened both its progressive tone and its artistic resonance.

The course of the Maly Theatre since 1917 follows the general evolution of the theatres during that time. An "academic" theatre, tied by taste and tradition to the past, it was slow to accept all the implications of the new system. It wisely preferred to preserve its inheritance until such time as it could be of use to the new theatre of the Revolution. Gradually as it came to understand the Communist ideology it undertook to restage its classic repertoire in conformity with Marxian principles. Ostrovski retained his position as leading dramatist on its stage, and the plays of several Soviet writers were included when their writing suited the Maly's realistic style. We find such plays as "Skutarevski," "The Fighters," "Lyubov Yarovaya," playing side by side with "Don Carlos" and "Wolves and Sheep" and "Mad Money" by Ostrovski.

Down to the present time this theatre has brought its traditional style of acting, its emphasis upon the importance of the actor's art. Little influenced by the new forms of staging which have sprung up around it, it continues to pass on from generation to generation of its artists the body of acting traditions which began a hundred years ago with Shchepkin. Its great actors work by intuition, its lesser actors imitate as best they can the results of the intuitive process of their superiors. The Maly has developed no system, it has had no guiding genius in recent years. Consequently, within the general bounds set up by its traditional demand for truth to life, a certain eclecticism of style is apparent which has resulted from the diverse talents of its individual actors and the various directors whom it has invited to stage its performances. The Maly, nevertheless, remains to this day the symbol of the great Russian theatrical past, and it is loved and revered by all cultured Muscovites. It is even rumored that this fortress of conservatism is Stalin's favorite.

It is the Moscow Art Theatre, however, and not the Maly, which has played the chief rôle in setting the style of Russian acting. This is principally due to the work of Stanislavski in assembling the best things out of the Maly's tradition, and with careful analysis creating a system of acting based on them which could be passed on in some tangible and conscious form to other workers in the Russian theatre.

Even before 1917 Stanislavski had begun this work by creating what was afterwards known as the First Studio of the Moscow Art Theatre. For a number of years he had been devoting a great deal of thought to the formulation of his conceptions of the art of acting based on the work of Shchepkin and other masters of every country as well as upon his own observation. He had finally worked out his system whose aim, he says, "was to give practical and conscious methods for the awakening of superconscious creativeness." The First Studio was formed to provide an opportunity for young actors and even for some of the more experienced actors of the Art Theatre to try out the system. It was created largely as an experiment with Sulerzhitski at its head, for Stanislavski could not personally devote his entire time to it. After a long ripening process, during which the Studio spent a summer living communally on the shores of the Black Sea—a scheme devised to bring the actors into closer understanding of each other as individuals—their first performance, a dramatization of "The Cricket on the Hearth," was presented, and the Studio started on its creative career.

Stanislavski had intended that this studio should be a training school for actors who would eventually be received into the company of the Art Theatre. Such, however, did not turn out to be the case. The Great War and the Revolution intervened and fashioned out of this younger generation a group which developed ideas and theories of its own and which found the principles of the Art Theatre not entirely to its satisfaction. Its founder wisely did not bind the group to himself but, feeling that it possessed sufficient artistic strength, let it go free to pursue its own way. The First Studio eventually became a theatre in its own name and right, but in its title it proclaimed its distinguished parentage and acknowledged its tie to the past, for it called itself the Second Moscow Art Theatre.

To understand wherein the Second Art differed from the First Art Theatre we must return to a part of what is the difference between Stanislavski and Vakhtangov. The latter, together with Michael Chekhov, was the guiding spirit in the development of the Second Art Theatre's principles of acting. In its search for realism and truth, the Moscow Art Theatre had come to believe that the artist must study the character he portrays until he understands its psychological nature so completely that when he is called upon to play the part, he ceases to be himself and fuses his spirit with the spirit of the rôle. "I *am* the person whom I represent," he must say and believe. The Second Art Theatre did not entirely accept this. They wished to add an outward theatrical effectiveness to this psychological truth. "Let us suppose," they would say, "that the play we are presenting to the audience is a chicken. The First Art Theatre will serve you the chicken: it will be a real chicken and it will be well-cooked; you can eat it and be nourished and know that you ate a real chicken. That is true. We also shall serve you a chicken, but we shall add a few garnishings and a sauce. It will be no less a chicken than the one which the First Art will have given you, but it will have a little added flavor. It is true that our chicken itself will be no better or more nourishing than theirs, but perhaps you will think so because its taste has been heightened a little."

In reply to this their forbears would make answer, "You err. In the process of preparation you have substituted, perhaps without knowing it yourselves, veal for chicken. It looks, when cut fine, very like chicken; it is probably just as nourishing, it tastes much the same, particularly when you have added your sauces and garnishings. But you mustn't tell the public that it is chicken because it isn't."

"But after all, isn't it the taste and the nourishment which count, whether they come from a cow or a fowl?"

In the process, it is true, the actors of the Second Art Theatre did make a subtle change. They believed that psychological truth was an essential element in their portrayal—in this they were true children of the First Art; but in order to add that extra theatrical effectiveness which they wished, they found it necessary that the actor in creating his rôle should approach the image of the character without ever entirely losing his own identity. He must fall in love with the character, as it were, and bring himself as close to it as he can, but he must never *become* the character, for in doing so he would give up his objective perception of the rôle.

This problem of differentiation is an exceedingly subtle one, particularly here in its first stage where the dividing line is thin, but the Second Art Theatre has accomplished the graduation of technique with skill. Its leading régisseurs, Bersenyev and Birman, have a keen understanding of the actor's approach to his rôle; they know how close he must come to it without losing himself in it. It was the former who suggested to me the example of the chicken and the sauce.

The Second Moscow Art Theatre is today characterized by a strong, bright style, by a certain buoyancy and love of color to which witness is borne in their recent productions of "Twelfth Night" and John Fletcher's "Spanish Curate." Problems of setting and costume fascinate the Second Art and it offers as decorative a stage as any in Moscow. In line with its principal desire for theatrical effectiveness, a heightened realism, its backgrounds are real without ever becoming natural, decorative without being abstract. Always they are colorful, seldom monumental. The Second Art seems most fitted of all theatres to serve this last phase of the Revolution which calls for light-hearted relaxation and amusing entertainment.

Many people in Moscow consider that the Second Art Theatre has no face of its own. Lacking an individual genius to give form to the whole theatre, it is true that it possesses a less codified system of aesthetics than some of the other theatres. Its work, however, seems to me no less satisfactory than that of many theatres of more specific artistic character. What the Second Art Theatre loses in the lack of one guiding hand, it has made up for in the closely knit group consciousness which is present. I know of no theatre in Moscow which is so completely collective as this one. It has been said, also, that the Second Art Theatre today more clearly portrays the spirit of Vakhtangov than the Vakhtangov Theatre itself, and this is very possible, since his contemporaries, the people with whom he worked longest, were at the Second Art, and his disciples at the Vakhtangov, knowing his influence over a shorter time, may have less successfully grasped his meanings. At any rate, there is a close similarity between what Vakhtangov wanted and what the Second Art Theatre offers today.

After the First Studio had been well established, Stanislavski founded a second studio to continue his work of training actors under the Stanislavski system. This studio, instead of becoming a separate theatre like the First, was absorbed back into the parent organization then in need of new blood, and so its members became the second generation of the Art Theatre. With "The Marriage of Figaro" in 1927 this younger group began to come into prominence, for in that production the older actors played the small rôles and the newer ones assumed the leads. In "The Days of the Turbins" the whole cast was composed of the young group. It is this membership drawn from the Second Studio which has probably largely effected the Art Theatre's acceptance of the Revolution. But the process of fusing the two generations into unity has not been easy. Here were the grandfathers and grandsons, as it were, but the sons were in the Second Art Theatre, and the loss of that intervening generation made the alliance harder. I suspect that there is still a tragic break between the elder generation and the younger within the Moscow Art, a break which could not have been avoided when we consider the speed with which Russian ideology has changed.

Both Stanislavski and Nemirovich-Danchenko in the early years of the Revolution not only turned their attention to the perpetuation of their theories through the establishment of acting studios, but sought to express themselves through a new medium, that of opera. In this they abandoned their old collaboration and each worked in music toward his own end. Today, therefore, although both perform in the same building, the Stanislavski Opera Theatre and the Nemirovich-Danchenko Musical Studio exist as separate organizations.

For Stanislavski this was not a new interest. In his youth he had hoped to be an opera singer and had always had certain ideas about the production of opera. Other theories developed out of his work with the spoken drama. Chief of these was the importance which he became more and more convinced derived from rhythm. Not only the outward rhythm of movement and action but "the inner rhythm of that unseen energy which calls out movement and action." This inner feeling seemed to him more easily summoned through the medium of music where the composer could come to the poet's aid.

The Opera Studio was founded, like the Art Theatre before it, as a protest against the truthless, empty and elaborate conventions of the day—this time in opera. Stanislavski sought simplicity, adherence to the truth of inner feeling, in order to bring out the rhythms of the music in their full meaning. Attention to the psychology in their rôles and the application of the Stanislavski system in their work had its effect on opera stars who no longer advanced to the footlights and addressed their passionate hopes and fears full blast to the audience; they sang and acted naturally. The slow, measured tempo of movement which we call "operatic" was abandoned to be replaced by tempi which the scene demanded. A singer might run or skip if the mood required; striding and pacing with advanced chest and head thrown back were proved to be not entirely necessary adjuncts of the operatic art. A prima donna might sing an aria perched on a window sill or while lying on her stomach looking down over the edge of a cliff, as I saw one do in a rehearsal of "Carmen"!

Nemirovich-Danchenko has created a "musical studio," not an opera theatre, the difference being that his is a theatre where actors can sing, rather than a theatre where singers can act. He is working for a new synthesis of action, word and music, and toward the production of a new kind of "musical theatrical realism." He has found that certain modern artists, notably Shostakovich, who gave him "Katerina Ismailova" (known to America as "Lady Macbeth of Mzensk"), are seeking this same synthesis, and so he has made excursions into the field of contemporary music.

His studio has also felt the social demands of the Revolution more strongly than Stanislavski's opera theatre; it has been more influenced by new techniques in stagecraft. Its presentation of "Lysistrata" in America showed audiences here toward what forms of expression this studio was working. In the 1935 production of "Traviata" by Nemirovich both trends are apparent. Great liberties were taken with the libretto in order to emphasize the social contradictions of the world which produced the situation depicted in "Traviata." The chorus ceased to be decorative vocal appendages to be brought onstage and taken off without rhyme or reason; they sat in boxes surrounding the stage where they became commentators upon and not participators in the drama. In other ways the form of the production is a far departure from the conventional operatic pattern. The front curtain and footlights have been banished, the stage extended beyond the proscenium on both sides. Actors enter from the orchestra pit before the act begins, await their cues on this fore-stage in full view of the audience, the chorus marches in and seats itself in the semicircular tier of boxes that backs the acting area. A curtain opens *behind* the actors at the beginning of each act to reveal impressionistically painted backdrops which set the location of the action. Properties are changed in front of the audience. Perhaps to a certain extent the performance appears to be a *tour de force*. But at the same time, is it not possible to suggest that it may be the forerunner of a new day or at least a new way on the operatic stage?

2

In the early days of the Revolution when Meierhold was hailed by his many disciples as the savior of the theatre from that certain decay toward which its bourgeois affiliations were leading it, he established a theatre which is now called the Theatre of the Revolution. It was composed in large part of actors who had responded more quickly than their fellows to the call of Revolutionary art and who ran from the academic theatres to the Meierhold standard. With these artists he conducted a sort of experimental laboratory where he worked on his more radical theories of staging. Here he developed the application of constructivism to the theatre and produced such plays as Ernst Toller's "Masse-Mensch" and a new version of the old "Snug Place" of Ostrovski. However, the force of Meierhold's personality requires that his acting material be completely flexible. The performers of this theatre, many of them having gone to school to Stanislavski, were too fixed in their methods of work to be able to go all the way with him in his radical experimentation, and so he withdrew from the Theatre of the Revolution and went on to the creation of the theatre which bears his name and with which he is now identified.

The Theatre of the Revolution nevertheless continued to grow. It naturally continued to practice many of Meierhold's principles—productions like Zarkhi's "Joy Street" are full of the movement and the "bio-mechanics" of their former leader—and this has given the theatre much of its dynamic force and has influenced its scenic backgrounds very strongly. To the Meierhold principles the succeeding directors have added much from the system of Stanislavski. It is this realistic strain in the method of presentation, no doubt, which has made it possible for the Theatre of the Revolution to incorporate so many of the new realistic plays about Soviet life of the last five years into its repertoire. The new socialistic realism is definitely the burden of its song and its chief choristers, Pogodin, who gave his "My Friend" to that theatre, and Zarkhi, Faiko, Vishnevski, all are performed there.

Aside from its importance as chief champion of most of the recent plays, it is also an interesting theatre because of its methodological aim to weld the theories of Stanislavski with those of Meierhold into a satisfying harmony. Through an elimination of the outworn in the Moscow Art Theatre and of the impractical in Meierhold, and through a combination of what is left of the inner feeling of the former and the outward form of the latter, this theatre hopes to create something which can have the greatness of both. To a certain extent the Second Moscow Art Theatre has in mind some such fusion, although the name of Meierhold is left out of its councils, for that was what Vakhtangov while he lived was working toward. Okhlopkov and Vakhtangov's disciples seek this too. But it is not easy to serve two masters. Vakhtangov might have succeeded, although he would have ended by being servant to neither and a master himself. Lesser souls have smaller chances, but that is what they want to do.

With the so-called Studio Theatres, small and intimate, all of them comparatively young, the path toward the future continues. The two which seem to be most important at this time are the studios of Zavadski and of Simonov. Both of them were pupils of Vakhtangov, both are actors of excellence themselves and both are trying to combine the Stanislavski and Meierhold ideas of theatre in line with Vakhtangov's approach, but sifted through their own personal temperaments. Zavadski is probably more interested in the chicken; Simonov's taste runs to the sauces. But Zavadski's theatre has added to soundness of psychological portrayal a heightening of style and an intensification of pictorial values which makes its performances of "The Devil's Disciple" and "Wolves and Sheep," for example, brilliantly theatrical. Zavadski works toward the irony which Vakhtangov loved so well, but like his it is gentler than Meierhold's. His laugh is as hearty but his lip is less curled. He uses the grotesque and caricature to fine advantage—in this he has learned a lesson from Meierhold. He has also learned the use of dynamic movement. Everything about his stage seems in action. He has a fine ear for the theatrical value of music and his productions have a running orchestral commentary which strengthens and elucidates his thoughts.

Simonov is also a master of movement—faster and less lyrical than Zavadski—and he is also a musician. His productions are a series of scherzos and rhapsodies. Never has he reached symphonic heights, but his performances are *chef d'œuvres* of rhythmic composition in a light and amusing key. Throughout his performances also music plays intermittently, not with the desultory sentimentality of our "incidental off-stage music," but to give point to a situation, to help bring a laugh, to intensify suspense, to deepen a mood. The actors as well as the audience seem to hear the music and to respond to it. It is thus integrated with the performance. Some Russians say there is much of the music hall in Simonov, and this they mean as no compliment, for the Russian has no high regard for music halls. If by that they mean that he possesses no great philosophical profundity, that his skill is chiefly comic and that his comedy is surface, they are right. Were he to portray a president it would not be with the brush of Sargent but with the pen of Peggy Bacon. But like her he often surprises one by the accuracy of his seemingly superficially and lightly drawn lines. His characters may not be three-dimensional, flesh and blood, weighty, and his plays may not have the power and sweep of greatness, but his comedy is apt and intelligent, his tragedy, while not perhaps real tragedy at all in his hands, has sharp poignancy; one is more deeply moved over the plight of Ellen Jones in his version of "Machinal" than one is over the more tragic Ellen of Alice Koonen at the Kamerny Theatre.

There are a dozen other stages in Moscow which should be reviewed. They are interesting for various reasons, more perhaps because of the individual circumstances under which they work or because of the need which they were designed to satisfy, than because of any great artistic contributions which they have to make. The ones which I have in mind are the more definitely workers' theatres, the theatres for young people and for children, for the Red Army, those for the so-called National Minorities. All of these theatres, excepting the latter, have as their basic artistic principle the teachings of Stanislavski, most of them are directed by various artists who once went to school to him, and so they are all creatively akin to the Art Theatre. The Stanislavski system is practiced on these stages with varying degrees of orthodoxy and according to the style and ability of the individual director and his company.

The MOSPS or Moscow Trade Unions Theatre was founded some ten or twelve years ago for the purpose of producing exclusively Soviet plays with a direct message to the organized industrial worker audience. They were realistic in theme and required a realistic treatment. Factory management, collective farm organization, labor and industrial problems, and in the last few years plays a bit more psychological dealing with the life of the "new man" in work and play, are the themes of the work of dramatists like Bill-Byelotserkovski, Kirshon, Finn, and others which MOSPS has presented with a very fair degree of artistry.

The VTSPS Theatre, also a workingman's stage, developed out of the old Prolet-Cult, which found its origin in the factory and had such distinguished leaders in its early days as film director Sergei Eisenstein and dramatist Alexander Afinogenov. At that time it was much influenced by Meierhold, but recently under the direction of Diki, a régisseur of great talent, it is working toward a creative path of its own which carries it away from the spectacular Meierholdian experiments of Eisenstein.[1]

The TRAM, or Theatre for Young Workers, also developed out of the factory dramatic work and is a direct expression of the young proletariat. It too occupies itself chiefly with the output of the modern Soviet authors and chooses those plays which will most appeal to an audience composed of young workers in their late teens and early twenties. The actors themselves are of about the same age as their audience and were all formerly industrial laborers who have proved themselves more able on the boards than in the mill.

To appeal to an audience still younger, Moscow has two outstanding stages, the Theatre for the Young Spectator and the Moscow Theatre for Children. Their performances

---

[1] Huntly Carter in *The New Spirit in the Russian Theatre* has much to say about this Prolet-Cult Theatre.

are *for* children, not by them, and the adult artists who create the dramas, ballets, pantomimes and operas which entertain and enlighten their young audience, work along very scientifically developed lines combined with a high order of artistry. Natalie Satz, not so old herself, but the founder of the Theatre for Children, is the originator of the movement in Moscow.

If we pass by the doors of the Satire Theatre, the Dramatic Theatre, the Historico-Revolutionary Theatre, the Workers' Art Theatre, the Studios of Ermolov and of Khmilyov, the Len-Soviet Theatre, and half a dozen others, we shall end our tour with the stages on which Russian is not spoken—the theatres of the National Minorities, the two outstanding of which are the State Jewish and the Gypsy Theatre. The former has the more highly cultivated art, finding expression in rhythm, vivid color, dynamic movement, albeit a little harsh and strident to unfamiliar ears and eyes. A peculiar form of the grotesque seems to attract the Jewish actor, who plays in a highly stylized and oddly musical monotone. I must frankly admit that I do not care for this theatre, although many people do. Shortly after I left Moscow, however, this theatre presented for the first time a production of "King Lear" which has been considered by all critics as one of the finest performances to be seen in the Soviet Union today. Gordon Craig, who saw it in the spring of 1935, even went so far as to tell me that it was one of the finest performances he had seen at any time in any country. The earlier plays in the Jewish Theatre's repertoire were drawn from old Yiddish material —"200,000," "The Travels of Benjamin III," "The Tenth Commandment"—treated modernistically. Later, contemporary subjects found their way onto its stage. S. M. Mikhoels, its present director, is also its leading actor and possesses a rare and unique talent. The Gypsy Theatre is more primitive but equally vivid and picturesque. Plastics and color are richly used; music is highly important. In plays like their version of "Carmen," or in "Life on Wheels," the Gypsies give their audience a glowing, moving and primitive picture of not only their life but their art.

CHAPTER NINE

Across the Footlights

"THE RUSSIAN, more than anyone else, is infected with
the passion for spectacles," writes Stanislavski. "The
more the spectacle excites and captivates the soul, the more
it attracts him. The simple Russian spectator loves a drama
at which one can weep a little, philosophize about life,
listen to words of wisdom, more than any noisy vaudeville act after which nothing is left to feed the soul."

Stanislavski knows his fellow countrymen. One night I
went to the Music Hall in Moscow. It is a poor imitation
of the London music hall. Half the seats were empty, the
audience was apathetic. Another night I went to see Tolstoy's five-act tragedy "Resurrection." The house was sold
out, there was cheering at the end of the performance.
The Russians had found something "to feed the soul."

A study of the Russian theatre which stopped at the
footlights would fail to consider what is to my mind its
most vital element—the audience. In England and America
there is talk about a "people's theatre." One can have no
idea what that means unless one has been to Russia. For
America has no conception of a theatre which exists for
the audience, and that is what the Soviet theatre does. It
has served many functions during these strenuous years.
It has allowed hungry men and women to forget for a
little that they had nothing to eat; it has given them
glimpses of future happiness; it has encouraged and excited them; it has relaxed them and made them laugh; it

has given them brightness and color when all about was drab and bleak; it has talked to them about their problems of work, has shown an interest in what they were doing at the factory or on the farm; it has given them self-confidence and hope; it has helped to give them an education, has opened up the host of art treasures which the world holds as its common heritage. Always the theatre has done all this *for its audience;* it has done it because the people want it—it is fulfilling a demand. The audience, therefore, is not a contribution to the theatre at all, it is the end and purpose of its existence.

In Moscow one cannot use the term "theatre-going public" as we do to define a certain part of the populace. The whole populace is the theatre-going public. The servant girl in the house where I lived in Moscow, who washed the dishes and cleaned and hauled the firewood, went to the opera more than I did—she doubtless sat in a better seat.

Come with me to a Moscow theatre and let us take another look at this audience together. It is so different from a house full of spectators in New York or Chicago or London or Paris or Prague or Berlin that if the play bores you, you can spend the four hours watching those around you and be well repaid.

The appearance of the Moscow audience is the first thing that interests one. The Second Five Year Plan has done a great deal toward raising the standard of dress, but a crowd in Moscow still puts forth a pretty drab appearance. There are no evening clothes in the audience, only simple cotton frocks, the inevitable beret, heavier dresses of old-fashioned cut when the cold nights come, shawls, fur in abundance, for fur in Russia is a necessity and not a luxury; many men still wear the Russian blouse, white on warm evenings, gray, khaki or dark blue in winter, their trousers may be stuffed into high boots; those who attempt Western dress look uncomfortable, many of their ill-fitting shirts are worn without ties. These people appear to have come to the theatre as though it were an every-day occurrence which required no gala raiment (if they have it). They look as though they had just come from work, as no doubt many of them have.

We get the feeling that here theatre-going is a habit. These people come to the theatre as though they belonged there. They appear to feel perfectly at home. In America theatre-going is something of a rite. We put on our good clothes, slick down our hair, enter the place with a certain awed and slightly ill-at-ease manner. I strongly suspect that the average American who enters the theatre (not including that hardened species known as the New York First-Nighter), seldom feels that he really belongs there at all, even though he has paid for his ticket. You can tell it in the way he moves restlessly and self-consciously in his seat, his forced conversation, the surreptitious way in which he examines the drapery behind the boxes as though trying to discover a quick way out if it should all prove too much for him in the end. Now at the movies it is different. The "Average American" feels at home there. It is all a question of habit. In America we have the movie-going habit. In Russia they have the theatre-going habit and the opera-going habit and the ballet-going habit.

When the Russians enter the theatre they give themselves over to it completely. They are required to check their hats and coats in the *garde-robe*. Therefore they cannot give the impression as they wander through the foyer, top hat on head and wrap drawn around shoulders, that they are on the point of leaping forth at any moment into the night. They have surrendered themselves into the theatre's custody and they make themselves as much at home there as possible. Before the performance they read the evening newspaper. In the intermissions they buy sausage sandwiches and apples and rich cream pastries from the buffets and drink tea or a deadly looking but insipid pink beverage called *"kvas."* Every theatre has a large buffet and there are many little tables each with its bunch of flowers or pot of chrysanthemums. Bolsheviks love to eat and to look at flowers. The Russians have the European custom of the promenade, and boys and girls, men together, old couples, go arm in arm round and round in a sober circle. Then three bells ring and back to their seats they go.

The easy manner of the Russian audience when the lights are on is lost as soon as the curtain rises. These folk may make a habit of theatre-going, but never does it lose its excitement for them. Many times they remind one of a football crowd in America. They sit forward on the edges of their seats, sometimes almost fall off them in their excitement; they laugh loudly, they weep copiously, they applaud vigorously. "How well he is playing," you hear someone behind you whisper to her companion, a spontaneous comment often heard in our grandstands but seldom while our plays are in progress. When the performance is over, they run down to the footlights to applaud exuberantly and cheer their favorites by name. No hired claque here and no need for it.

When the audience in America and England goes to the theatre, it sits back with a sort of an "all right, you show me" attitude, waiting to be amused, waiting for the actor to come to it. Not so in Moscow. There the audience reaches out to the stage, it goes more than halfway to meet the actor; the artist comes more than halfway to meet the audience, and in that something-more-than-one-hundred-per-cent which is engendered lies the greatness of the Soviet theatre.

The fact that the theatres of Moscow are permanent has much to do with the organization of the audience and makes it possible for the different theatres to cater to different elements of the people, just as no doubt in my descriptions of these Moscow theatres, certain ones have sounded more interesting and congenial to the reader than others. One of the most erroneous impressions entertained in the West is that all Bolsheviks are alike, that under Communism a great regimentation of personality has been effected so that the proletariat looks alike, thinks alike, feels alike, and acts and reacts alike. While it is perhaps true that more solidarity and unity of purpose has been created among these people, perhaps even thrust upon them, than is true in other places, individuals continue to respond in ways as different as their personalities continue to be.

The Moscow Art Theatre and the Maly Theatre are the most universally popular (after the Bolshoi Opera) in Moscow today, if one is to judge from the demand for seats. They seem to be perpetually sold out and one sees all kinds of people there. This is particularly interesting in view of the fact that both are "academic" theatres. The audiences seem more quiet and refined, and you see more better dressed people at the Art Theatre than elsewhere in Moscow. The traditions associated with this theatre have probably had something to do with this. Stanislavski once wrote an interesting account of the conversion of the early proletarian audience into this civilized gathering of citizenry one sees today:

But yesterday our Theatre had been filled by the old public which we had educated through many decades, and today we were faced by an altogether new audience which we did not know how to approach. Neither did the audience know how to approach us, and how to live with us in the theatre. We were forced to begin at the very beginning, to teach this new spectator how to sit quietly, how not to talk, how to come into the theatre at the proper time, not to smoke, not to eat nuts in public, not to bring food into the theatre and eat it there, to dress in his best so as to fit more into the atmosphere of beauty that was worshiped in the theatre. At first this was very hard to do, and two or three times after the end of an act the atmosphere of which was spoiled by the crowd of still uneducated spectators, I was forced to come before the curtain with a plea in the name of the actors who were placed in an impasse.

On one occasion I could not restrain myself, and spoke more sharply than I should have spoken. The crowd was silent and listened to me very attentively. Until the present day I cannot imagine how these two or three audiences managed to tell of what had happened to all the other visitors in our Theatre. Nothing was written about it in the papers, no new decrees were issued on the score of what had happened. Why did a complete change in the behavior of the audience take place after what had happened? They came to the theatre fifteen minutes before the curtain, they stopped smoking and cracking nuts, they brought no food with them, and when I, unoccupied in the performance, passed through the corridors of the Theatre which were filled with our new spectators, boys would rush to all corners of the foyers, warning those present:

"He is coming."

To be sure, in other theatres than the MXAT, in fact, everywhere in Moscow, audiences are in these days perfectly behaved; nut-cracking seems to have universally disappeared, and the differentiations which I make are subtle and apparent only to one who has gone often to many theatres and sought grounds for comparisons. But one is aware in every theatre that one could only be in the Soviet Union.

The Meierhold Theatre draws young radical students but nowadays few workers. There are many empty seats

there except when "La Dame aux Camélias" is being performed. Then the theatre is crowded and I was amused to
note that at this production, which Meierhold claims that
he has produced in order to show the degeneracy of the
nineteenth-century bourgeois morals, the audience weeps
copiously! The Kamerny Theatre appeals more to the white
collar workers and a few of the more conservative intelligentsia than to the factory laborers. The many foreign
plays and the musical productions of Tairov attract a limited public, but "The Optimistic Tragedy" always fills
the house and with a different kind of audience altogether,
many soldiers.

Many of the smaller theatres cater particularly to the
workers' districts in which they happen to be located. At
the Krasnaya Presnaya, MOSPS, Zavadski Studio, the now
defunct New Theatre, and several of the smaller studios,
the audiences are largely composed of factory workers living in the neighborhood, and they give a more obviously
proletarian appearance to the house. Outstanding productions, like Okhlopkov's "Aristocrats" or Zavadski's "The
Devil's Disciple" or "Wolves and Sheep" draw people from
all over town, but as a rule one feels a difference between
the type of people at these theatres and at the larger and
more centrally located state theatres.

The Jewish, Gypsy and German theatres play to much
more specialized audiences, since they perform in their native tongue. The Theatre of the Red Army is supposed to
play principally to the soldiers and its repertoire is designed to appeal to such a public. Outsiders, however, may
attend this theatre—a beautiful hall in the handsome
House of the Red Army, and of course the army may and
does go to plays in other theatres than their own. Its presence elsewhere is, as I have said, one of the characteristic
features of the Moscow audiences.

The most specialized theatres are those for children, of

which the Moscow Theatre for Children, founded and directed by Natalie Satz, is the finest. It has been in existence for sixteen years and in that time has presented about 4,500 performances to 3,500,000 children. This theatre's relationship to its young audience is the most significant thing about the whole undertaking, so an account of it comes more appropriately in this chapter than elsewhere.

When Natalie Satz began her work she found that she was virtually a pioneer in the field. Plays written for children were very few, and were usually merely dramatizations of children's fairy stories and not really plays at all. Satz found that she had to create children's drama for her theatre either by herself or with the help of writers who would create the kind of plays she felt should be given to children, for she wished her theatre to be a social as well as a cultural factor in the development of youth. Her theatre could best be of service if it was an auxiliary to education. "Education Through Art" is a slogan of the U.S.S.R. and nowhere more appropriately applied than in this work. This gave it a realistic and a purposeful existence and took it out of the class of Saturday morning, dramatized-nursery-rhyme, play-time children's theatres.

"It was once argued," writes Satz, "that all a child seeks in a performance is food for the eye; that the fairy style is the best kind of performance for children. The forms of our plays are various, but we are in fundamental disagreement with this assertion. A child wants above all to understand what is happening on the stage, to follow the sequence of the action, to live through the events of the play together with the characters. Food for the heart and for the mind—that is what a play for children must be above all else. While we take into consideration the educational significance of merry laughter and of artistic impressions, we do not at all aspire toward bare amusement;

our main aim is that the performance should be imbued with ideas, with content."

If the theatre was to be a constructively educational project, it would have to be carefully and scientifically carried on. The study which Satz and her staff of research assistants under the direction of Professor E. A. Arkin, have made of their audience and the way they have worked out their productions accordingly, is one of the interesting stories of the Soviet theatre.

The audiences of the Children's Theatre are carefully organized. Most of the children come in groups or classes from school. Certain plays are for certain aged audiences, and boys and girls are admitted only to those performances which are designed for their age. They may not attend a play which is intended to appeal to and be understood by older children, and they are not encouraged to go to a play for their juniors. Thus there are plays for the younger ones, from six to eight years old, then those for children from about eight to ten, and on into the plays for high-school age, although there are fewer of these at present in the theatre's repertoire.

"The main principle in all the work of our theatre," says Satz, "is to 'activize' the audience, not only during the performances but also after them. The whole idea is that the children should be able to switch on to real life the 'electric charge' they have received in the theatre." (Incidentally, that is an excellent statement of the mainspring of the Marxian attitude toward the theatre.) "Only by taking into account the peculiarities of different ages is it possible to give the content in the correct dose; to give a content which the spectator will assimilate not superficially, but deeply, which will infect him emotionally. If the spectator has to make no effort whatsoever for the perception and digestion of the performance, then this theatrical food does not give the necessary 'activizing' result. The per-

formance plus the independent work of the spectator—
that is what we want."

It is in conferences among the régisseurs, authors, psychologists and child specialists, where many carefully prepared charts and diagrams are used for illustration, that
this work is carried on. Here there is talk of age evolution, of the rôle of social factors in the development of
children's personalities, of the relationship of games and
organized children's activities to the theatre, of the children's speech and their creations. The theatre workers have
borne in mind, to paraphrase a report of Professor Arkin,
that the child is not a reacting apparatus but an active
personality. They have considered it important to study
not only his particular reaction during the performance of
the play but his subsequent reactions in life. For sometimes a child who appears at the time to be getting little
from the play, will later, by some chance act or remark,
reveal what a profound impression has been made upon
him.

Study is made of individual types and of group reactions by unseen observers during the performances. The
most successful research has been made with individual
types, which is done by selecting "polar pairs." Two children, chosen with the advice of their teacher, who seem to
be alike except in the one respect noted below, are watched
by the theatre's specialist and note is made of all their reactions throughout the play. A child with vividly expressed emotions will be paired with a child with dully
expressed emotions, an introverted, introspective child
with an extravert, a child who is an organizer with a strong
resisting nervous system with a child who is disorganized,
a child with highly developed intellect with one of an
underdeveloped intellect. The "after acts" of these polar
pairs continue to be observed after the performance is
over. Notes are made by the teacher of what these par-

ticular children do in school during the two or three days
after the performance. The theatre's own worker revisits
the school to collect the information, and sometimes makes
another visit even three weeks or more afterwards. The
families are sometimes asked to coöperate in the study and
furnish the theatre worker with observations about the
child's behavior at home which may have been affected by
the play. The child's own creative work and conversation
often contribute the most to the study: the drawings or
the remarks he makes, the games he invents, the stories he
tells—these sometimes done voluntarily, sometimes provoked by suggestion.

Group observation is less effective because it is more
subject to chance, the theatre's psychologists believe. However, groups of five boys and girls have been studied. Children of the same age, social sphere (an interesting phrase to
find in a Communist report), and of normal ability, have
been grouped together, boys with boys, and girls with girls.
If three of the five children had the same reaction it was
counted as the group's reaction. From these studies it was
found that the girls were more conservative, reserved and
unified in their reactions than the boys. Therefore, their
reactions were more actually group reactions. Little else
was concluded.

A further source of observation of the reaction of plays
upon children, an indirect one, has been an analysis of the
letters which the children are urged to write to the theatre.
Most of them are addressed to Natalie Satz, but some are
addressed to various characters in the plays which the children have seen. From these letters may be drawn information about the peculiarities of the children's perceptions
and their interpretations of the various aspects of the performances. The degree of subjectiveness of the audience
may be judged in this way, as well as their opinions upon

contents and ideology, designs of scenery, and a dozen different things.

This work has a two-fold value. It is of much use to the schools and even to parents in their relationship with the child, for it often brings to light things about him which had been unknown or passed unnoticed before. Usually, of course, the children of the "polar pairs" react as one would expect, but sometimes there are upsets: children who were considered highly emotional seem phlegmatic beside duller children who turn out to be very excitable when subjected to the conditions of the theatre. Children previously thought dull catch things in dramatic representation which the brighter ones miss. Thus the schools profit by the research that is carried on by the theatre.

The theatre itself is directly benefited, for through watching the reactions of its young audience, it discovers many of its own mistakes. If children laugh at lines or incidents which were not intended to be funny, or if they fail to laugh where it was expected that they would, if their interest regularly seems to flag at certain points, then there is something wrong. If they cry when it was not intended that they should be so moved, or become more excited than is good for them, then those passages must be calmed down; if the duller and average ones fail to respond in certain parts and only the brighter-than-average react, then simplification or clarification will be ordered.

A visitor to the Theatre for Children, even though he were ignorant of this scientific work which is being carried on, could not help being interested in this most unique of Moscow's audiences. The children arrive some time before the play is to begin and assemble in a large downstairs room. Here they play group games and learn songs. Then they go upstairs to the auditorium. There are no programs. Instead Satz or one of her assistants comes before the curtain and talks to the children, telling them what they are to see, what to look out for, urging them to write their letters, asking a question or two. Then in the intermissions one of the staff stands in a front corner of the auditorium under a sign which invites any of the audience who have questions to ask to come to her. The children do not hesitate to do so. For those who have no questions, there are more group games downstairs.

The Theatre for Children is one of Moscow's most spectacular examples of the theatre dedicated to its audience, and one of the most absorbing places to study the Bolshevist public—this time a public in the making. With such mature and carefully considered plays offered to the Russians from the age of eight, what wonder that the theatre-going habit and an appreciation for good work in the art of the theatre is common to the adult population and will continue to grow as the youth grows.

2

, One of the most widely publicized features of the early Revolutionary theatre was its custom of admitting workers free, and I am frequently asked whether this is still practiced. It is not. The Moscow theatres still do, however, provide facilities for group theatre-going and for reduced rates to workers. This is effected through what are known as "closed performances." These are performances which are bought out—all the seats in the house—by some one factory or institution at a slightly reduced rate offered by the theatre. The factory then sells the seats to its employees at a further reduction which makes it possible for the workers to buy the seats at about fifty per cent of the original cost. The difference is divided between the theatre and the patronizing factory or organization.

The choice of play and theatre is made by the factory, and the popularity of a theatre and its plays is exhibited by the number of "closed performances" it is requested to give. Factories also have certain boxes and permanently reserved seats at the opera and a few dramatic theatres for most performances. These are given to *"udarniki,"* or special workers, as rewards for outstanding accomplishment. The government also has a box in all state theatres to which certain high Communist leaders and their friends may have access without pay. The theatres themselves set aside a certain number of free tickets for all open performances which are allotted to Red Army men and to a few others. The members of any theatre are supposed to be allowed admission to any other theatre as its guests, providing the "complimentary" list has room for them. But with the demand for tickets at the box office as great as it is, theatre managers give few passes.

There are certain theatres which have subscription series open to individuals, but the majority of people buy their seats for open performances at whatever time they find convenient and as often as finances will allow. The cost of tickets in Moscow varies in the different theatres. The Bolshoi Opera is most expensive, its best seats costing thirty roubles. Of the dramatic theatres, the Art Theatre and the Maly are the most costly, the smaller theatres are less. In no theatre are there unreserved seats, no "pit," and there is a range of price extending in the average theatre down to about four roubles for a gallery seat. This price range means little, insofar as its figures are concerned, for no doubt costs of seats will have changed by the time this book appears, or, if not, then the buying power of the rouble will have fluctuated. Because of the peculiar monetary situation in Russia it is impossible for me to tell you how much a man is paying in dollars and cents for his ticket. But if the worker who gets an average of three hundred roubles a month spends eight roubles for a theatre ticket which would cost $1.50 in New York, he is ob-

viously spending a larger per cent of his income than a
worker in New York who earns one hundred dollars a
month. But one of the most interesting facts of all is that
it is not the theatres with the cheapest rate for seats which
draw the biggest crowds, but theatres with the most expensive tickets.

The theatres have another tie with their audiences
through a system of theatrical patronage to various organizations. The Moscow theatres have certain detachments of
the Red Army and certain factories or collective farms to
which they serve as artistic counselors, and for the cultural life of whose members they are responsible. The theatre sends artists to help this affiliated organization with
the building and maintenance of its dramatic circle and
amateur art work. Other artists make periodic excursions
to the factory or barracks or farm to present dramatic
programs, "concerts," there. And often when a new production is presented at a Moscow theatre, the affiliated factory will be invited to a special dress rehearsal and the
audience will be asked for its opinion about the ideological
and artistic content of the play. The factory workers, soldiers, or farmers, as the case may be, flattered by this contact with a big Moscow theatre, are encouraged to culti-
vate their opinion and taste in dramatic affairs, guided and
sponsored through their association with the members of
the patronizing artistic collective.

CHAPTER TEN

Artists' Life

IF IT can be said that an aristocracy exists in the class-less society of the Soviet Union, then the artists of the theatre are a part of it. As Russia advances, a certain dif-ferentiation of types—I will not say classes—is develop-ing. In proportion to the contribution which each man makes to the collective enterprise, privileges and remunera-tions are allowed him. The old misconception of the bour-geois world that the Communists insist that every man is in every way the equal of every other and that all must share and share alike, has been gradually dissolved by the consistent reports of observers of the U.S.S.R. who see quite a different situation working out, more in line with the Communist slogan, "From every man according to his ability, to every man according to his needs." The other belief, that in a workers' state all men are reduced to the status of day laborers, which actually led one of my in-telligent friends to ask me to try to find out when I got to Moscow if it were true that all professional actors had to work in factories by day and could act only in the eve-nings, is equally preposterous.

The artists of the theatre straight through the years of the Revolution have been the darlings of the government. When others were starving the artists were given subsist-ence—poor, of course, but still all that was possible. For the Soviet government does not, and never has, subscribed to the romantic notion that genius flourishes best in a gar-

236

ret. Now that living conditions have improved, provisions for the material welfare of the artistic world have expanded, and it lives in as great comfort as any of the inhabitants of Moscow.

The Soviet government has paid a great deal of attention to honors for its citizenry. It has created the Order of Lenin, the Order of the Red Banner, of the Red Star, and half a dozen other Communistic investitures as rewards for distinguished services chiefly in technological work. For the artists also it has a system of honors which involves not only titles but privileges. The Council of People's Commissars, an organization vaguely comparable to the Cabinet, but with more collective power, is authorized to confer upon worthy artists the title of "Honored Artist of the Republic," "Honored Worker of Art," "People's Artist of the Republic." There are about five hundred Honored Artists, the least honor of the three, and but a select handful of People's Artists. Recommendations are made to the Council of People's Commissars by the directorates of the theatres who judge the artistic talent of their candidates, by the party representatives in the theatres who subscribe to the candidates' political orthodoxy, and by the *Narkompros* which reviews the citations.

"Honored Artist" is a rank to which almost every good actor may be raised after he has proved his ability and sincerity over a certain number of years. "Honored Worker of Art" is a higher position which comes to artists as a reward for distinguished service to the profession over a long period of time. It does not, however, stamp the artist as really great. Only People's Artists are that: Stanislavski, Kachalov, Moskvin, Meierhold, just this year Tairov, and others of their preëminent ability. It is an honor which comes late in life. There are no young People's Artists, but the young Honored Artists may look forward to becoming one day People's Artists, for the system is progressive.

These honors are not empty ones. They bring with them certain privileges. In Moscow, because of the terrific over-crowding, a limit has been placed upon the household space which any one individual may occupy. A short time ago it was nine feet square. But this maximum may be exceeded by certain privileged citizens, among whom are numbered the creative artists. The right to have one's own apartment is granted to honored artists some of whom occupy alone or with their families apartments of four or five rooms. A few of the great People's Artists have an entire house. They all may have one or two servants.

The medical aid which artists may receive is superior to the average citizen's. They need not stand in line at the free clinics but may receive more personal attention. I was told of the time when one of the finest actresses of the Vakhtangov Theatre developed serious complications after childbirth and whose life was in grave danger. The only specialists able to save her were attending a medical conference in Kiev hundreds of miles away. The director of the theatre telephoned the Kremlin at once, talked to the Secretary of the Central Executive Committee and explained that the life of his artist was at stake. The Kremlin ordered a fast military plane at once into service to fly the doctor back to Moscow. He arrived in a few hours and the actress's life was saved.

Vacations for all members of the theatrical profession are provided with pay, and well-equipped rest homes and sanitoria are available. Some of the greater artists are even allowed freedom to travel abroad, a privilege which is extended to few citizens; and not only is the freedom to travel granted, but an allowance of a certain amount of *valuta* is made for the artist's foreign expenses, since his own roubles are valueless outside of the country. Honored artists of all ranks enjoy the same internal privileges as the highest members of the Communist Party, although few of them are members of it.[1]

Honored artists are also privileged to perform less often than the regular members of the profession. Certain People's Artists may appear only once in several weeks and yet receive steady salary. On the question of salary specific information is hard to acquire. The great artists possibly receive several thousand roubles a month, an income which allows them to live as comfortably as life can be lived in Moscow. A young playwright whose play was performed a year or so ago in a hundred theatres throughout the Union, from all of which he was receiving royalty, is rumored to be the richest man in Moscow today. He literally has more money than he knows what to do with!

It is of little use, however, to talk much about salary because, in the first place, the figures of one's income are little indication of one's advantages or disadvantages, since the taxations on the one hand and exemptions of one kind and another on the other, alter the meaning of them. The exemptions and privileges often amount to more, in the long run, than the actual monetary remuneration a man receives. In the second place, a large salary has little meaning because it is of little use. There are still so few niceties of life which can be acquired in Moscow that prominent artists continue to live simply. There are few fine automobiles—a handful of old Rolls-Royces and some shiny Lincolns convey high government officials; a two-thousand-rouble-a-week prima donna arrives at the opera's stage door in a Ford or on foot. Leading men have no elegantly tailored suits, for there are no elegant tailors in Moscow to

[1] It is interesting that Sudakov, régisseur of the Moscow Art Theatre and an Honored Artist, was the first member of the acting company of three hundred in that theatre to be elected to membership in the Party, and that took place seventeen years after the October Revolution. (There are a number of Party members on the technical staff of the theatre.)

do their work. Saving money for the future is unnecessary and is disapproved of.

The chief reason, however, why it is of little use to talk about salary is because the artists are not working for it. Acting is an art to which they have dedicated themselves for its own sake and for the service of the people. In New York an actor regularly talks about his "job." I have never heard an actor in Moscow so refer to his occupation, for he does not regard it in this way. There has been a good deal of talk about the possibility of eliminating the desire for private profit from man, and the effect of the acquisitive urge upon the success of the Soviet "Experiment." I can only say that among the artists of the Soviet Union this motive seems to me to have been completely sublimated. No one in the theatre is working for the sake of the privileges he may be granted therefor, nor for the salary he may receive. To be sure, the usefulness of money is not denied and the advantages of comfortable material environment are not scorned, but the lust for wealth is absent. Devotion to art takes its place.

Privileges are allowed and remunerations offered in Soviet Russia in return for service and in proportion to earning capacity. All artists therefore have not the advantages which the honored artists enjoy. It is true that many of the beginners in the theatre receive only a hundred or two roubles instead of a thousand, that the living conditions of the average young actor, not an honored artist, are hard and inferior to those of the average young actor in New York. But he has one great advantage: he is sure of employment. His income is certain; he has not that fearful feeling of insecurity which all young actors in New York know before they become established, and which some feel even thereafter. There are no unemployed actors in Moscow.

2

Noblesse oblige—sagesse oblige.

If the artists are members of an intellectual aristocracy in Soviet Russia with privileges and position, they have tremendous obligations to fulfill in return.

Everyone in Russia is working incessantly. The greater the contribution a man can make, the more are the demands which are put upon him. Therefore, this intelligentsia is among the hardest worked of all the laboring masses of Russia; the artists of the Moscow theatres are busy from morning to night. Their lives are so different from the lives of American professional theatre people that apart from the significance of the implied commentary on the system which is there, the contrast is interesting for its own sake. In the first place, Moscow artists spend much more time on themselves than Americans. In the second place, Moscow artists spend much more time serving others than Americans. In the third place, there are no cocktail parties in Moscow.

Let me expand. The Russian actor devotes much of his day to keeping in training, just as great concert artists spend hours a day practicing. Most American actors spend no time at all. During the few weeks when they are in rehearsal, our actors will work on a part; once the show has opened, there is nothing more to do until it has closed and they have found another "job," when their work will begin again. I do some actors an injustice. The influence of the Russian theatre has already been felt by some in New York and there are artists who "study" with Ouspenskaya or Daykarhanova or who used to work with Richard Boleslavski; others who go to certain voice specialists and learn things about the use of the spoken word which the rest never bother about. They are a small minority.

I am inclined to agree with those critics who say that

when success comes in America, it comes too easily, too suddenly and too soon, that it stops the normal and measured development of the individuals' talent. It is for this reason more than for any other that so few American artists spend time working on themselves and the art that is in them. Young actors come too soon to thinking that they are good, that they "know all about it." It is true, too, I think, that the older generation of artists works more on itself than the younger, and that in itself is a disturbing sign. Too many young actors have the idea that education for a profession or an art is a specializing process that is to occupy those two to four years which center around twenty, that when it is concluded education is acquired and nothing more need be done about it.

The Russians believe that education and training must continue to be acquired for as long as one wishes to make use of them. Several hours a day are spent at their theatres by young and old actors alike in exercises which are designed to keep them flexible in body and mind. There are fencing and gymnastic and dancing classes, there are lessons in the Stanislavski system or in the principles of bio-mechanics. There are reading exercises and small dramatic problems at which they work.

I have already discussed the amount of time which actors spend each day in rehearsal for a new production. In addition to these rehearsals there are understudy rehearsals and general rehearsals of many of the plays already in the repertoire, and these they must attend also. The fact that the Moscow theatres perform in repertory does not make easier days for the artists.

A long time ago, for six years is a long time in the Soviet chronology, Maurice Hindus wrote, "Social service under the banner of the Revolution, insist the Bolshevists, will bring to man new interests and new raptures. . . . Social service is to be the great method and the great goal,

the great motive and the great fact. . . . It is such enter-
prises [social tasks], they never cease to emphasize, that
will give man a fuller sense of dignity, of personal worth,
than any form of worship, for they will inculcate in him
a sense of mastery instead of submission, of triumph instead of fear."

This Bolshevist prophecy seems to have been realized in
the theatre. In addition to their regular work in the theatre which is, as I have suggested, but part of the greater
service to which that art is at all times dedicated for the
people, the individual artists have work outside the walls
of their theatres. Some of the actors and régisseurs are
teaching in the State Theatre Technicum and Institute;
others are instructing the students of their own technicum
(not strictly speaking extra-mural activity, but still not
part of the regular rehearsal schedule). Many of the régisseurs and actors of the large theatres are directing productions in other and smaller theatres. Sudakov has more or
less taken over the TRAM and is assisted there by several
other MXAT régisseurs. Zavadski, besides being managing
director of his own studio theatre, also acts occasionally at
the Moscow Art Theatre and sometimes directs plays for
the Red Army Theatre. Still other régisseurs and actors
spend many hours each week at the clubs where they are
in charge of dramatic circles. Some even journey out to
collective farms to carry on the same kind of work there.
I once asked for an interview with a prominent régisseur
on a special day and was told that she would not be at
home until after eleven o'clock at night as she was rehearsing three different productions in three different places
from ten in the morning until eleven at night.

The "concert" is an institution which is important in
the social life of the urban people and a constant occupation for theatre workers. These concerts are really variety
programs which are the entertainment at the big collective

parties given by institutions and factories for their employees, and the performers are largely drawn from the opera and the professional dramatic theatres who go to give readings, a form of entertainment very popular in Russia, and to present sketches, to sing, to dance.

These concerts are private affairs open only to the members of the factory or organization, but there are concerts of the same description, though a bit more pretentious, to which the public is admitted by ticket. 1935 was the year of the seventy-fifth anniversary of the birth of Chekhov, and his widow and other actors of the Art Theatre were in constant demand to talk of him and to give readings of his works at these public concerts. All these things are part of the cultural education of the masses and the artists recognize it as their duty (and perhaps their pleasure, if the spirit of social service is as triumphant as the Bolsheviks announce) to accept all requests for appearances outside their own theatres.

Many Moscow actors top off all this labor with cinema engagements which must be fulfilled at the same time as their regular theatre work, for, unlike the American actors who seldom perform and rehearse in both media at once, the Muscovite star shines half the day and night on the stage of his theatre, to which he has permanent obligations, and the other half of the time blends his glitter with the Klieg lights of the film studios.

I do not know whether I should say that there are no cocktail parties in Moscow because the people are working so hard all the time, or that the people work so hard because there are no cocktail parties. At any rate the hours which the New York professional theatre spends meeting social obligations the Moscow world knows not of. To a certain extent the social activities of the New York theatre people are part of their business; it is one important way to sell themselves to their public and their services to each other. Nobody in Moscow has to do that, therefore he doesn't. Not that there are no parties at all there, but there is not the same perpetual round of gayeties to weary the spirit and soften the brain. When parties take place, they are events.

Social life in the Soviet Union is tied up with the economic collectives. The collective works together and it plays together. The common forms of entertainment among actors are banquets or parties given by the theatres for all its members who share the expenses and are joint hosts. They may invite a few outside guests but the party retains its homogeneous character. At such parties, which usually take place at the theatre after a performance and which last the better part of the night, there will be a supper first which will last until two o'clock or so, then a long program of entertainment. At one of these, I heard the composer Prokofiev play, Kachalov read, one of the leading prima donnas of the Bolshoi Opera sing, Otto Schmidt, the Soviet polar hero, speak of his adventures. After this there will be dancing, but since it has only recently been looked upon with favor in Moscow, more people are on the sidelines than on the floor.

Private parties are not unheard of, even though collective amusement is the order of the day. More and more, small groups and couples seek entertainment according to their individual tastes. But time is scarce and many of the young theatre people would prefer to spend their leisure on the hockey rink than in the restaurant—a most understandable choice to anyone who has made the rounds of Moscow restaurants.

3

There is in Moscow an institution which New York sadly lacks—a central meeting place for members of the theatrical profession. The Actors' Dinner Club, the Lambs'

and the Players', the Actors' Equity Association, divide
among them some of the functions of the Moscow Club
of Masters of Art, but that organization has them all
beaten on breadth of its activities. The year book of the
Club states that it was organized to promulgate Party
work and to improve artists' knowledge (of that work),
to carry on organized endeavor, to improve artistic
quality, to further the exchange of experiences, the critical
analysis of artistic production, to cater to the cultural life
and the leisure hours of its members, to offer concrete assistance in productional work, to connect artists with manual laborers and farmers—people outside the theatre, in
other words—to recruit art workers to the study of the
fundamental principles of political life and of the reports
of Joseph Stalin, to take care of the publication of activities, conferences, debates, and so on, of its members.

The members of the Club are creative workers of the
Moscow theatres—i.e., actors, régisseurs, designers, musicians—painters, dramatists, historians of art, critics, com-
posers, cinema workers. There are in the neighborhood of
four thousand of them. They pay dues appropriate to their
incomes; those whose salaries are one hundred roubles a
month or less pay fifty kopeks, and so on up to those who
receive over 350 roubles and pay three roubles a month.
Honored and People's Artists pay no fees.

Two buildings house the Club's activities, one quite near
the center of town, the other not far from the old Her-
mitage. To enter the main one, we descend the stairs, for
the Club is in a basement. Here there are attractive lounges
with muraled ceilings of Tony Sarg-like caricatures of
various "Masters of Art." The walls of one room are devoted to exhibitions of recent paintings by members, walls
of others are covered with photographs of prominent artist
members. There is a small but excellent auditorium with a
little stage, there are special rooms for meetings of the dif-

ferent artist groups, there is a restaurant, a library. The branch club house has its auditorium also, and its library, a small ballroom, a dining room, billiard rooms, card rooms, several small rooms for group meetings, a barber shop.

The work is carried on under the Presidium of the Moscow District Committee of the Union of Theatrical Workers, by a board—of which the Club's director is a member—elected by the membership. This board arranges the program of activities. There are series of meetings at which prominent men of letters discuss the great masters of art—a series about Pushkin, another dedicated to Chekhov, were held during my stay. There are meetings at which the work of the different creative collectives and of individual artists is reviewed; for instance, a series of evenings dedicated to the Maly Theatre, when representatives from it talk of its past and its present, and when outside critics analyze its work. There was an evening when Meierhold talked about Pushkin and Chaikovski and what he was trying to do with their "Queen of Spades"; another when Tairov talked about Shaw, Shakespeare and Pushkin, and explained his ideas for the production of "Egyptian Nights."

There are evenings when the members may hear special reports—a lecture by Natalie Satz on her trip to Prague and of theatre work there, one by Tairov and Amaglobely on the International Theatre Congress in Rome at which they represented the Soviet theatre. The artists are eager to hear news of the outside world. There are special conferences arranged between the painters and the theatre workers when they discuss their problems with each other. There are social evenings, dances in the branch club house on the evenings before free-day, and very popular they are. There is an institute for instruction open to young members under the direction of a special bureau, where special courses are offered in Marx-Leninism and where round-table discussions on various trade union subjects are held. There are recitals and "concerts" for and by the members; one evening I attended a dance recital by a visiting foreign artist there. Once a week free law consultations are available for members.

The combined libraries in the two buildings contain about 35,000 volumes in fields of sociology and politics, history of art, literature, drama, art, children's books, encyclopedias, periodicals—there are thirty foreign magazines available. The library has a traveling fund to send these books around Moscow to the various factory and trade union clubs with which the Theatrical Club is in constant contact. The library organizes children's exhibitions, it arranges meetings between writers and readers, it helps in the selection of literature of use in play production, particularly for the amateur circles.

One night before free-day I found myself in a company of young artists at this Club of Masters of Art. None of them were famous, all of them were regular members of good theatres in Moscow, young men and women in their twenties. There were about a hundred others dancing there to the small and inferior jazz orchestra that the Club had provided. I looked about me, curious to make comparisons with similar groups of my friends of the same age at home. They presented no very prepossessing appearance externally, and they could not fox-trot very well, but there were qualities which I liked. The young Soviet artists have none of the superficiality, none of the self-consciousness of young artists elsewhere. They lack their sophistication but they have sincerity. There is no striving for effect, no artificial "personalities," only simplicity, earnestness, eagerness. The artists of the Soviet Union are a healthy lot; they present a much more normal and "average" appearance

than a like group of artists elsewhere. Abnormality of
every sort seems to be absent. There is complete absorption in work. Long discussions about the art of the theatre
were in progress at tables around me, and they knew what
they were talking about. Their earnestness, however, has
room for humor. There was laughter enough that evening.

All these young artists possess personal dignity. Is it the
innate dignity which the peasant and the common man
have but which the bourgeoisie, as a class, lack? Or is it
that "fuller sense of dignity, of personal worth" that Hindus says the Bolsheviks assert will attend an awakened
social consciousness? Is it dignity which arises from pride in
their art, in their own work, in their position in Soviet society, in the consciousness of a mission? I think so. Artists
of the theatre in the Western world have difficulty in for-
getting the very near past when acting was a hardly re-
spectable occupation. They still feel, perhaps ever so
slightly, that they are jesters to the public. If they feel that
their art is a high and great calling, they are confused by a
surrounding society which disagrees with them, and, in an
effort to rid themselves of what they feel to be an unright-
fully imposed social inferiority, fall back on conduct and
an attitude of mind which robs them of dignity. The artists
of Moscow are not jesters to the public, they are its leaders,
its teachers, its servants; they are Russia's respected citizens, its great men.

CHAPTER ELEVEN

Whither America?

BOOKS about Russia customarily end with a chapter
entitled "Whither Russia?" I do not wish to seem
to strain for originality when I substitute for that a chapter called "Whither America?" I do so because my chief
concern is with tomorrow in our own country. The future
of the Soviet theatre is, after all, in the hands of the Bolsheviks. The problem is theirs, not ours. The line the future
will take there is as unpredictable as manifestations of the
creative urge always are. However, before I left Moscow
I had been developing a theory of my own, that in the
work of the last very few seasons, perhaps only two, all
the theatres of Moscow were becoming more alike. The
Moscow Art Theatre, in productions like its recent and
popular "Pickwick Club," or its earlier "Dead Souls,"
while not working from quite the same point of view as
the externalists, yet was moving toward a realism that
was beyond its old quasi-naturalism and which had some
Meierholdian elements in it. Its latest theory of physical
action was a clue. Nemirovich-Danchenko in his musical
studio was himself resorting to some of Meierhold's inventions to help him express his new musical synthetic realism.
    In the Meierhold camp, on the other hand, there was a
gradual falling back to more realistic elements, and the
retreat (or advance if you prefer to consider it so) would
have been farther if Meierhold had listened to the demands
of the day. But, as it was, constructivism was well on the

way out, wilder experiments were over; foreigners found
"La Dame aux Camélias" of 1934, in outward appearance
at least, much more realistic than they had expected. Tairov's "Optimistic Tragedy" revealed how far he had moved
away from the formalisms of "Salomé" and "Phèdre" toward a common neo-realistic meeting ground with the
other great schools; and the various studios and theatres
under the influence of Vakhtangov were all in one way
or another working toward a sort of halfway point between Meierhold and Stanislavski.

In examining each theatre's individual development, I
have shown how the trend has been toward the new
"socialistic realism." It seems to me that it is this which
is the common denominator of the immediate future. It
is coming about already. For to get rid of its naturalism,
the Art Theatre has sought elements from the other extreme, and Tairov and Meierhold, to replace their formalisms, have done the same. None has done more than bor-
row a few externals, but that has seemed to do the trick
and they are all already able to offer up their interpretations of socialistic realism. That the theatres are still quite
different is because as yet none of them is quite sure what
this new style is, and because each is still strongly bound
to its past forms. But it would seem that they may become more and more similar as they pass in time from
the assumption of new external forms to a grasp of internal meaning.

Will this then mean that eventually, because of the
exigencies of the new phase of the Revolution, a standardization of method and style will take place, that when
the first shock of the upheaval of everything in Russia
has been stabilized and life becomes calmer, the theatre
will lose the vitality of its individual expressions which
has made it so varied and so vivid? Were three New
York producers presenting the same play at once, it might

be very possible to see the first act in one theatre, the second in another, and the third in a third and still receive a fairly unified impression of the play, for the idiom of the New York theatres is on the whole a common one. In Moscow ten years ago this would have been impossible, for there were as many completely different vehicles for the expression of an idea as there were theatres. What will the situation be there five years hence?

If realism is the art of a materialistic society (and it does seem true that a mind preoccupied with *things* and material progress will create realistically in art; the triumph of realism in late nineteenth-century Europe and in America today points to such a conclusion), then so long as the Soviet Union remains in its present materialistic mind, realism will be its most satisfactory medium. But as materialism is not an end but a means in the Communist state, and since Stalin's most recent pronouncement has been that the elevation of man above the machine must now be the aim of Russia, perhaps it will have its effect on the doctrine of socialistic realism in art. Perhaps the inherent mysticism of the Russian will reassert itself in romanticism and poetry. These may not, it is true, replace realism, but may instead give to it new vitality; on the other hand, there may be a return to a dozen different styles.

But after all, as I have said, the future of the Soviet theatre is in the hands of the Russians and we can only look on curiously as they work out their salvation. The future of the American theatre, however, is in the hands of ourselves. My constant desire throughout my year of observation of the theatre in Europe, and particularly during the six months in Russia, has been to discover things which I could relate to our own stage.

I have throughout this book suggested comparisons between Moscow and New York in which our theatre stood to lose thereby. But when we come right down to it, many of those things which I wish our theatre were also doing are not feasible—at least not now. Take the matter of rehearsals, for instance. One of the outstanding differences between the Moscow theatre and the New York theatre is that the former takes about four times as long to produce a play as does the latter. The result is not four times better, but it is quite a little better. If we rehearsed in New York four times as long as we do, would our productions be any better than they are? I doubt it. In fact, they might be far worse. For our casts would go stale. Used to an intensive rehearsal schedule and accustomed to going not much beyond the surface in their study of a play, our artists would grow restive and become muddled if a director led them through four months' preparation of a performance. The American mind is perhaps more intuitive than the Russian and less analytic. This I must and do bear in mind. But at the same time I believe that we would have even better productions if we followed the Russian rule, "Never present a play to the public until it is ready." Perhaps sometimes it would only take a month, and all very well; but sometimes six weeks' or two months' or even possibly three months' work would improve it. I have seen many good actors take three of the four week rehearsal period hunting for the character they were to play. When they found it, there were but four or five days left to rehearse the part. By the end of the first month of performances they were good and had got into the stride of it, a stride which should have been reached before the play ever opened.

A long-time system of rehearsal is, however, obviously impossible on Broadway in the present state of affairs. Actors would not trust themselves, nor would they be allowed to by Actors' Equity Association, to a manager who said, "Your services will be required in rehearsal over an indefinite period—perhaps one month, perhaps three; at least, until we are satisfied that the play is in condition to present." The only circumstance under which they would agree would be if the manager were willing to give them full pay during rehearsals. The manager cannot afford to do this, for there is always the chance that the play will fail and he may never get his money back from it.

The conclusion that we reach, therefore, is that New York would not find it feasible to emulate Moscow in making perfection a goal in art because it cannot afford to. It cannot take the time to make a good thing better. It cannot take the time because time means money, and money is the most important stake in the eyes of all.

Thus we come to the major problem of our theatre: the degenerating and deadening effect of commercialism in it. The American theatre is a selfish and a money-making enterprise, not an art. I said in a previous chapter that America does not know what a theatre that exists for its audience is. The theatre in America exists for every-one *but* the audience. It exists, first and foremost, for the real estate men who own the buildings that house these products of our spirit; for the big business men and the wealthy fellows who back shows for the gamble and for the money they hope to get out of it; for the theatrical magnates of the show business, who know their trade— and that is what it is—and are in it, too, for the money they can make. The theatre exists next for a set of highly egotistical, selfish, shrewdly ambitious men and women so that they may flaunt their egos and parade themselves and their charms before a gullible crowd, fill their pockets with dollars, see their names in lights and their faces smil-ing back at them from the expensive fashion magazines. They submit themselves to the commercially minded mag-nates because they are commercially minded too.

Unionism in the theatre is the twin evil of commercialism and is its child. Because of the exploitation of the capitalist producers, labor organized for defense and offense, and now is as great a menace to independent artistic creation in the theatre as commercialism. A dozen of the things that contribute to the Moscow theatre's excellence: the masterful use of musical effects in drama, the creation of certain complicated scenic effects, the long period of rehearsal with all props and with full sets and lights, to mention but a few, are all impossible in New York because the Unions' rules regarding regular and overtime wages make their practice prohibitively expensive. "Beating the Unions" has become a popular game with certain producers and the struggle between them is disgusting to artists who hate to see the stage turned into a petty battlefield.

The trouble is that there are not enough people—producers, artists, or union men—who are willing to make sacrifices for the theatre. Do not call it sacrifices if you'd rather not; say rather that there are too few people who are willing to put the theatre before their individual desires and demands. There is nothing to be sneered at in making a living from an art. The Russians are doing it, for that matter, and I am not crying out against material reward for artistic enterprise. I do not approve of artists going hungry for their art, but I do say that if the glorification of the box office and of the pay check continues much longer, it will bring about the destruction of our theatrical art. If the films are to kill the legitimate stage, it is much more likely to be done through the effect of Hollywood money-mania on our artists' psychology than by any triumph of one artistic medium over another.

A few years ago the hope of the American theatre was seen by some to lie in the non-commercial Little Theatre movement throughout the country. Time has lessened the optimism of that report, not because the movement has turned commercial, but because many people now feel that, as Broadway is the feeding post of the money-minded, over-egoed, professional artists, so the Little Theatre is the parade ground for equally ego-stricken dilettantes hungering for "self-expression." A young friend of mine, the director of an average Little Theatre, writes me justifying his recent resignation by saying, "The trouble with little theatres lies in the fact that they are essentially affectations. The people who sponsor them are rarely quite sure what they are all about; they just seem like a good thing and the people, straining and striving just a little, get self-conscious about them. If there was ever an indigenous impulse toward dramatic art in this state, it has been shamed out of existence by the elegance and sophistication of the movies." [1]

Is the theatre in our country then to fall prey either to commercialism or to "artiness"? I purport to be neither a Jeremiah nor a John the Baptist. The cry I voice is a familiar and an old one, I know that. But I have seen the theatre regarded as an art and a very high one where I have been, its artists selfless, not selfish. Of course, I can recommend certain parts of the Stanislavski system to the attention of our actors, I can point out the value of the *maquette* to the designer and show new uses for the revolving stage to the technician; but these things would not improve the New York theatre. Many of our actors act quite well as it is, most of our designers design quite well, and our stage mechanics are far superior to Moscow. It isn't these things, anyway, which really make the Moscow theatre fine. It is the belief and its practice that the theatre is ennobling, that it is not a quick and flashy way to make money and gain publicity, that its participants must serve with humility the needs of their fellow men, whether those needs be to laugh or to cry, to be edified or to be inspired.

---

[1] Exception must be made to acknowledge the excellent accomplishments of the Pasadena Community Playhouse, the Cleveland Playhouse and a few others.

I do not say, even, that the Revolution alone accomplished this in Russia, for I remember that the Moscow Art Theatre considered itself a non-commercial idealistic group of true artists long before 1917. The good Russian artist seems always to have been actuated by some force outside himself. Before the Revolution, it was devotion to art, afterwards to this was added devotion to fellow man —to the Mass, as proletarian theorists would call it. The Revolution was responsible for this latter motivation and for giving it expression on a large scale.

Furthermore, I do not say that there must be a revolution to accomplish this in America. In part it can come from within the theatre. As the leavening forces, I look at two heartening presences. One is the arrival on Broadway in ever-increasing numbers over the last five or ten years of what I might call "intelligentsia." Many well-educated, university-trained young people with a knowledge of the history of art and of the social and economic problems of the day, coming from colleges where theatre practice is well taught, have decided to make the art of the theatre their profession (not their business), and have accepted the system of Broadway for the time being, although they despise its commercialism and dislike its pettiness, because it seems the only way of learning more about its practice. The other is the arrival in the last less than five years of an increasing number of artists with a class consciousness who are anxious to create a theatre which will exist for its audience and not for the box office. These artists are interested in the social and political propaganda drama and disdain the Broadway "success" type of play. The success of "Peace on Earth," "Stevedore," "Waiting for Lefty," has heartened them and quite justifiably.

There are dangers in store for both elements. The former may easily fall into the stream of commercialism through its attendant lures; their education has been a capitalistic one—the golden calf, although hazy in outline, looms in the background. The latter may become so absorbed in a future state of society that it will lose its realistic value in the expression of contemporary American problems. The United States is not now a socialist state and the proletarian theatre must not forget this. The Left theatre in America must not imitate the Left theatre of Communist Russia until its environment is more comparable. And it must remember that even in the Left theatre of Communist Russia, it is not only what you say but how you say it that counts. The Soviet theatre has been great, not because it was a propaganda theatre, but because it used propaganda and converted it into art. Most Soviet dramaturgy has been bad because it has not done so. Propaganda can serve art by giving it renewed meaning and purpose and a new virility. But art cannot serve propaganda.

Casting about for a constructive idea instead of more warnings, to offer to these two hopes of mine, I return to the Moscow theatres and find the structural organization which both groups, and any other artists working for creative excellence in the theatre need—the collective permanent theatre. This is, to be sure, no new suggestion. A not inconsiderable amount of talk about group theatres and the creation of several have taken place in the last few years. In one or two instances some of the most significant work being done in New York is in these collectives, particularly the Group Theatre. However, wide expansion of this idea for the organization of the professional theatre is attended by many difficulties.

In the first place, under the present commercial organization of the profession, or indeed under any system, to finance a collective theatre over long periods of non-productivity when a sizeable company of artists must be supported, requires a tremendous outlay of money with no immediate return in sight. In the second place, a group of

artists must be assembled who will be willing to turn their
backs to tempting offers from the outside because of devotion to a collective enterprise which may be less remunera-
tive financially; who will be willing to subordinate their
individual ideas of creation to group creativeness; who
will be willing to forego stardom and its luster to become
pieces in a mosaic. This group must be so united in common knowledge of what it wants to say and how it wants
to say it that it will be willing to make these sacrifices
(for they would be looked upon as such, I am sure) in
order to accomplish it. The most difficult thing about the
whole procedure would be this last—to find fifty or a
hundred artists in America who could agree to a common
aim.

Nevertheless, such a collectivization seems to me essential
to the development of higher art in the theatre of our
country. No one denies that a great symphony orchestra
must be a collective of artists who will assemble together
for constant practice and performance for a year or many
years. Orchestras are not "cast" a few weeks before a concert, hastily rehearsed and disbanded afterwards. If the
performance of plays is to be simply a collection of solos
rendered simultaneously in as many different keys as performers find suitable to their vocal registers, then perhaps
the comparison with an orchestra is unjustified; but if it
is to be an orchestrated ensemble (the very use of the
word seems to be necessary) in which every player com-
plements every other, in which ideas and emotions are to
be expressed in a flow of vocal and visual harmony, then
the production is as difficult as the performance of a symphony and needs the same long and studied synchroniza-
tion of its participating interpreters.

In the group theatre there can be more time for rehearsal,
more development of a style or a system of acting and production, deeper mutual understanding among the artists of

their common artistic principles, a definitely defined line toward advancement of the art of the theatre, to replace the helter-skelter molecular movement of the present system. In the group theatre many of the contributing elements to the final superiority of form of the Moscow theatres can be explored, elements which I need not resummarize now, for they have appeared throughout this book.

The collective theatre composed of a group of artists has been the unit of dramatic production throughout the history of the theatre in the seventeenth and eighteenth centuries when the theatre was at its high point in Germany, France and England. The breakup of the collective was caused by the growth of individualism and the beginning of the "star system" in the last century, and it resulted in the exploitation of the individual artist which ended in commercialism. It is only if the individual will once again submit himself to the permanent theatre organization and accept economic protection as well as artistic inspiration therefrom, that these artists can assist the "liquidation" of commercialism, as the Bolsheviks would put it.

I am well aware, however, that the collective theatre in itself is no insurance against commercialism. It is easy to imagine a Broadway composed of a number of collective theatres, all giving beautiful ensemble performances, but each of whose aim would simply be the making of more money through its collective strength than could be acquired by every artist working individually. Group theatres which became theatrical "trusts" would be the final step in destroying whatever artistic integrity is left to the New York theatre.

I am obliged to admit, therefore, that the collective theatre idea is no panacea. It is, again in the end, as in the beginning, a question of motive—what our workers in the theatre are willing to put into it; what they wish to get out of it; what they want to make of it, an art or a business. If there are artists who believe in the theatre as a stimulating force in society and as a medium for the creation of beauty, then banded together in groups, and only so, can they carry the theatre on to the accomplishment of those ends.

Some readers may have expected that the returned student from Moscow, if he did not demand that the American theatre become at once proletarian, would at least urge state control of the theatre. The elimination of commercialism has been effected by government ownership in Russia, and would be effected by the adoption of the same arrangement in the United States. I have not, however, demanded the former, nor do I urge the latter.

I make no plea for the expansion of the proletarian theatre in America which will be in advance of the expansion of the proletariat itself. The United States is a bourgeois country; there continues, for better or worse, to be a great and powerful middle class in America. The theatre there must continue to address itself to that class, not exclusively to be sure, for it is imperative that the theatre admit the existence of other classes in our country and serve them as well; it must admit, too, the struggle between classes. But the theatre must follow life, express it, interpret it, move with it and change with it. If it cannot, it dies. That lesson from the Marxists it may be well to ponder. If our society is a capitalist one, then our theatre owes—not allegiance to capitalism at all—but owes to that society the exploration of its problems. If its major problem is a life and death struggle for existence against a rising proletariat, then the theatre must not close its eyes to that; and if the proletariat ever wins in the struggle and a new system begins, then—and no sooner—is the time when the theatre must turn proletarian.

There has been desultory talk of a state theatre, a "national theatre" in the United States. To this I am likewise opposed for two reasons. One objection, and the one most commonly advanced, is that the theatre stands to lose its freedom of expression if it were subsidized by the government. This is very possibly true, although I believe that influences just as powerful can be brought to bear on unorthodox dramatic expression under the present organization of the theatre by those very forces which dictate the policies of the government itself. Limitations to freedom of expression have been as flagrant in privately endowed institutions of learning in America as in the state-supported ones. However, any move which would curtail the freedom of our playwrights to face whatever problems of our life they wish, as they wish, would be unfortunate.

It is very possible that the boundaries which the Communist régime has set up for thought in the Soviet Union have had their effect upon the drama of Russia which, as I have pointed out, does most surely lag behind the other arts of the theatre. The dramatists are, it is true, the first artists of the theatre to be affected by loss of intellectual freedom. However, I believe that the battle cry for freedom-in-art has been shrieked a little more loudly than is necessary, particularly in respect to the Soviet theatre. Freedom in art really means only one of two things, either the unrestricted right of the artist to comment upon life as he sees it, or else his right to withdraw from life altogether and to escape into his art.

The restriction to keep within the tenets of Marx-Leninism seems to me no sharper than the restriction by which the sculptors and glass-makers of Chartres were bound to keep within the theology of the equally strict and equally narrow medieval church. They seem to have managed to create something living and beautiful and, what is more, universal, despite the fact that there is no window illustrating the Koran, no porch dedicated to Buddha, and no piece of sculpture which seems to suggest a representation of a pre-incarnated Mary Baker Eddy. (Incidentally, let those who decry the very presence of propaganda in art remember, the whole of Chartres cathedral was, and still is, a glorious piece of simple and direct propaganda.)

What the mourners for the lost freedom of expression in Soviet Russia fail to realize is that life as the Soviet artist sees it, *is* the realistic life of the Communist state. He sees it with Bolshevik eyes, not from the nostalgic bourgeois point of view. And seeing it thus, he has no desire to make use of the second privilege which freedom must grant: the right to escape. Art as an escape is impossible in a state where people have nothing from which to escape. People who glory in the triumph of socialism have no desire to escape into an art which pays no attention to it. Art has been escapist only when society has lost its self-confidence. When it has been sure, as, in the Middle Ages, society was sure of the Church, or hopeful, as in the Renaissance, when men looked to a newly opening future, art and life have been one. Only when society has been confused and upset, as in the dawn of industrialism and the early days of the new scientific materialism when its confidence in accepted truths and customs has been broken, has art fled from life into artificial creations of its own imagination. Insofar as the liveliness of its art is concerned, the Soviet theatre is neither better nor worse for its government control.

My chief objection to the state subsidies for our theatre is that there is no demand for it. America has no right to a national theatre until the nation calls for it. The movement for a state theatre must not come from artists who believe that they could work more easily if the pressure of commercialism were removed, or that they would have a broader scope for proselytizing their art. The movement must come from the taxpayers who would have to support the state subsidy. When and if the people of our country really want and feel the need for a national theatre, as the Viennese, for instance have wanted and needed their music and opera, then it should be brought into being. Otherwise our state theatre would be as empty and as purposeless as the Comédie Française is today.

But as a matter of fact, our country is not dramatically minded, it does not care two hangs about the "great art of the theatre." It does not hunger for spectacles to feed its soul, as Stanislavski claims the Russian nation does. State subsidies for major league ball teams would be more highly acclaimed by our citizenry than the patronage of Washington on Broadway. If the government were to enter into the motion picture industry and bring an end to the commercialism of Hollywood by creating a state cinema, it would be infinitely more justified. The movies are a *popular* art in America, the theatre is not, seldom has been, and I doubt if it ever will be. Supply will not create demand. There is no demand for a state theatre.

The people of Moscow want the theatre, they need it, it is part of their souls. The people of New York do not need the theatre. A show, yes; an amusement to escape from monotony and routine and worry, yes; but a fine art, not yet. If they did, they themselves would demand no more of the clap-trap circus tricks which they see at every turn. They would order an art to come out of the mess and feed them, and I think it could and would come (just as it sometimes does). America has fine playwrights, a larger aggregation of them than any other country can boast of today. It has good directors and actors and designers. The theatre could be a tremendous power in our world if the people wanted it to be. The Soviet theatre has risen to a peak because the people of Russia have pushed it there.

The future of the American theatre rests with America,

and Moscow-bred missionaries who have envisioned the Soviet theatrical apocalypse can do little. Not they or anyone else can make the people want the theatre, but they, with the help of everyone else, can make the theatre fine for the public which does want it.

APPENDIX

I

RÉGISSEUR'S REPORT ON "ARISTOCRATS" TO THE AR-
TISTIC COUNCIL OF THE VAKHTANGOV THEATRE,
JANUARY 17, 1935

by B. E. Zakhava

Comrades: As there is very little time I shall try to be
as brief as possible in explaining my basic views. The
theme of this play is extraordinarily simple. You needn't
think profoundly about the lines; the idea is obvious: the
socialist method of educating people—conditions of work
organized on a socialist basis—reforges, remakes everyone,
even hardened criminals. But it does not follow that this
inevitable rule applies to everyone. Not all who were sent
to the White Sea Canal were made over. There are many
instances of failures. Often men have been heroic, and
completely conscious of what they were doing and yet in
the end relapsed into their old way of life. Nevertheless,
the fact remains that an enormous number of people have
turned to the true, human way of living. How that happens, it is up to us to show in this play.

It is all simple, clear and intelligible. That should be the
point of departure in explaining the idea of the production. I believe that the form of the play should be simple,
clear and intelligible. The directors would make a great
mistake by being too figurative. In parenthesis, let me say
that several days ago R. N. Simonov, K. J. Mironov and
I went to an interrogation in a criminal proceeding. We
watched a very moving scene between a bandit and his
mother. He was threatened with being shot. This he was
aware of and yet when the prosecutor said, "You will be

shot," he retorted, "Go ahead and shoot. Why play around with me?"

Afterwards we compared our impressions. Before his mother was to come in to the room, we were all much excited because we were to be witnesses of a great event. It was a little embarrassing because there we were studying real human beings just as we study animals. But the most remarkable impression that I carried away was that nothing happened in the way I expected it to. The whole scene was striking in its unexpected and extraordinary simplicity. Simonov, in our conversation after this visit, also remarked that there was no similarity between what happened there and what takes place in the theatre. Therefore when I speak about simplicity of the forms that must be put into this play, I am speaking about a simplicity which is difficult to achieve, difficult to find—I mean the simplicity of living truth.

I do not want to have any theatricality in this play. To a certain extent there must be some, that we are agreed on—on that the Vakhtangov Theatre is based. But I would like to concentrate the attention of the actors in this production on a deep comprehension of simple truths. I feel that I am giving you a great and difficult task. To give this play, we can use the lines in various ways. It will draw; there will be applause; it will make an impression. But that is not what I am after. I want more than that. To achieve this greater objective I have tried to arrange our work to run smoothly. I have talked with many people. I have heard the tales of real witnesses. I want to see movement put into this production. There must be action in everything—in the psychological development of the images, in the external conception of the play, in the scenery, the costumes and finally in the music. Everything must have movement in it. Of what does this consist?

I shan't go into detail about the music or the external

form of the production but shall try to speak of it as a whole. How does the play begin? It begins with a musical introduction, which is very loud, played behind the drawn curtain. After the first few bars the curtain rises. In the overture there should be strains of ancient folk songs from the Karelian North. In these you will sense the struggle with nature, the struggle of the people who find themselves in its grip. Therefore our point of departure is the characteristics of the Karelian North: pines, stone, dampness, rain, a heavy sky. This is what the audience sees when the curtain rises.

The curtain goes up. It is raining, a wet red flag flaps limply in the wind. This is the only indication that the play is in our time. There is pantomime to the music. A crowd gathers, some with umbrellas, some with knapsacks; those worst off have no overcoats. They stop, wait for some others to catch up with them, then they go on by. Everything is very quiet; only occasionally you hear the voice of a guard yelling, "Get a move on!" When the curtain rises again, we see the place these people have come to, a government office, where they are to be checked in. First of all, the impression must be made that they have come to a concentration camp, not a holiday resort. They are dejected, morose, feeling intense resentment. They have come here and do not know what awaits. They have come to hard labor, to terribly hard labor, and they haven't the slightest conception of what is to become of them. Therefore the point of departure for each actor who is playing one of these people who are to be transformed, should be to be as vivid as possible in order to create an immediate impression that under no circumstances can anything be done with them. This will heighten the effect made later on. Therefore, too, it would be a great mistake for any actors to show any faith in what is going to happen. They must not know what is in store for them.

They must expect hard labor, acting like wild animals who will bite, protecting and defending themselves. Suddenly they will find that they are not to be treated as they thought. It seems to me that here in this place to which these people have come, we do not want the usual type of heroes in the theatre. Everything must be done with precision, in silence, glumly and naturally. From this images will proceed. There will be development in the external shaping of the play and in the music.

What is this development? We have before us chaos, overwhelming nature. Gradually the preponderating forces will be severity, clearness, precision, intelligence. This must be part of the external form of the production and it must be in the soul of everyone participating in it. The music should be made up of these elements: folk melodies from Karelia, street tunes, and church music. The composer's job is to see that all this sounds integrated. I see the scene as follows: a barracks. As Kostya Kapitan comes in and says, "Howdy, Urki," and the orchestra plays snatches of street music, perhaps in a gay strain, the people are lying around and thinking about their past. The music should play an important rôle. When Kostya produces extraordinary variations on his harmonica it would be hopeless to reproduce these variations just on a harmonica. One person couldn't possibly do that. The orchestra must do it. Just as in "Egor Bulichev" the impression would have been totally different if one man had blown his horn, so here the orchestra must play the harmonica. The music must rise to the heights of "pathétique." Out of this music, the folk melodies of Karelia and street tunes, we should have a welding together of moments out of which should grow "pathétique" music to sound like the third movement in Beethoven's Ninth Symphony. At least it should approach that in some measure. It will be an ode, a contemporary ode like Schiller's "Ode to Joy." That is what I wish to have happen.

This note should carry into the costumes as well. I imagine that a year goes by. We shall start the play in the autumn and end it under a spring sky, because it is necessary for us to show the hardness of work in winter. We must show how difficult it is for people to live in these parts, and to work under the conditions which surround them. We must find colors in which to paint this difficult picture, these hard conditions of work, and therefore it must be winter. They come to this place in highly individual clothing. All these clothes are worn out, are all shabby. A tie sticks out or a scarf, but in general in this scene all these bandits look alike. Then in the end (this I look upon as the third stage) individual costumes will come into the picture again. And here, comrades, it will be necessary to put certain demands up to every one of you, as this is a most important point. Each production calls for a certain accent or emphasis. That is to say, in every production there must be everything that an actor's inner technique requires. But in different productions the accent is struck at different times. Remember how we worked on Gorki. We said that we must learn to think on the stage and to reproduce that image as truly as possible. We didn't need to "act" in that production but we had to learn to live with those feelings. We all succeeded in being earnest and therefore there was life in our lines. That question is the one I always put to myself at the beginning of a piece of work and I put it now. This play is based on the fact that certain people are in strange circumstances. They appear from an entirely other world. Now they have come out into the fresh air. These people are unusual, the conditions are unusual; life is extraordinary, everything here is extraordinary. This creates a great difficulty—the difficulty that we cannot appreciate, evaluate the facts. Imagine people going into a concentration camp. They have passed the gates, beyond those gates is their life, their country, and now the gates have been closed with barbed wire and there is no possibility of getting out.

I went down to the Volga Canal Camp. At the gate stood the guard to check us all so that no extra people came out. At that moment my feelings were unpleasant and fearful. Think of the far north and of those people who have come to stay ten years. What must they experience as they pass those gates, how must they carry themselves, how must they feel, what must their inner emotions be? Just this presents a vast difficulty. The play is made up of episodes; there is no regular unfolding of action, no sequence of acts. You have an event and the actor is immediately galvanized into complete tension; he is instantly required to be in action, he has the spotlight on him. He reaches a point of tension that obliges him to mobilize his capacity to do what we call evaluate, to sense circumstances, and as these circumstances are extraordinary, the rôles in this play present great difficulties. Consequently, what should an actor be thinking about, what should he mobilize? He should remember how he prepared sketches during his first year in training.

Suppose that I come into the room. I open the door, I go in. Everything which I have has been stolen. I must experience and weigh that fact. Or suppose that I am sitting reading a newspaper. I hear a bell; I receive a telegram. I open it and read that my father has died. We know very well that that is a most difficult thing to accept. To receive the unexpected and to weigh it truthfully from the point of view of the exactions I have already mentioned—that is what I want.

It is difficult to say anything about the external form of the production, the scenery. I have asked V. F. Ryndin, our designer, to create an external form which will sug-

gest harshness, severity, logic and simplicity, and with this
in mind, I invite you to look at his model.

Another point about this harshness and about people
who live under harsh conditions: they find themselves becoming harsh, apathetic; they lose all interest in life—and
that is what really happened.

Now if you put together these monumental demands
on you with what I said about the third movement of
Beethoven's Ninth Symphony, and about the simplicity of
living truth, then, it seems to me, you should get a conception of the production as I dream it and as I wish to
create it.

That, comrades, is the exposition of my idea in general
terms. There are many questions that could be put about
the breadth of the performance. There are comic parts,
melodramatic and dramatic parts and there are even places
which rise to the tragic, to "pathétique" heights, but it is
not worth while to take up here the justification of what
the fundamental type of this play is. It may be necessary
to discuss individual images, but I think that we can talk
about that in rehearsals, otherwise it would take up too
much time.

II

AT THE REHEARSALS OF "THE INSPECTOR-GENERAL"

A Stenographic Report of Meierhold's Work with the Actors [1]

MEIERHOLD (*to the actor playing the part of the Mayor*): The whole entrance is effected before you come to the lines. Once we have agreed to carry the rôle through at a certain tempo, it is up to me, as a technical expert, to do what I can to lighten the work of the actor and to think of putting him in circumstances that will be easy for him. The actor must be freed from everything that creates weight on him. Forget about talking like an old man. Let the make-up show a man of fifty, but in speech, be young. We shall discuss the reason for this too. It seems to me that among this museum piece collection of idiots—even the superintendent of schools is an idiot, and Luke Lukich, and the judge are idiots, the postmaster is an idiot—among all these completely stick-in-the-mud and the-devil-knows-what kind of creatures, the Mayor stands out in relief. He is more clever and more intelligent and is a man with a certain polish. It is possible that this mayor was yesterday in some other town. Not in the capital, of course, but if this is a district town, he was in the chief city of a province. He has come here after having been elsewhere. All the directions indicate that he is head and shoulders above all the others. In the Mayor you see traces of some sort of external polish, it would be difficult to call it education. You see it in what he says about teachers, in that he knows something about history, and in his orders—to put up a monument of some sort—in all this there is a quasi-culture;

[1] Acknowledgment of permission to reprint this report in translation should be made to the Soviet journal *"Theatre and Dramaturgy."*

of course, what kind of culture! But when he talks, he controls his tongue, he knows how to form phrases a great deal better than Bobchinski or Dobchinski. Their brains work hard but he has a kind of adaptability which makes it possible for him to find his way around as soon as he is on good terms with people. He is an orator, *sui generis,* he can recite a monologue. It is necessary to give him a youthful aspect. To have a characteristic mode of speech would not be of advantage, it would be difficult. It would be better to forget it. It would be better for him to have a mobile diction. Why is it that up to now he has always been played by old actors with great ponderousness? Maksheyev, for instance, and Vladimir Nikolayevich Davydov played him when they were getting on in years, and when younger actors took the rôle they played under Davydov and imitated him. I don't know how Vladimir Nikolayevich played the Mayor when he was young, when he was still at the Korsh in Moscow, but it is possible, according to tradition, that even he played him as an old man. That is why all these gestures and intonations have accumulated and waxed strong, because they were used by people who played according to the example of older men with big names.

Inasmuch as you are young—because you must be twenty, or at least fifteen years younger than I am—forget all about talking like an old man. Fire away with completely free, clear-cut diction. Don't try any groans for the present, not until later when we have straightened out things a bit. Perhaps we shall give you, even during rehearsals, a big easy chair—to sit in, to think, to get ready, to begin. Until he puts on his uniform the Mayor is always in his dressing gown. Perhaps he takes a nap after midday dinner, then he receives the letter before he has gotten up and gives orders to send for all the heads of departments, and then is taken ill himself. Give him that easy chair out of "The Forest." Let him sit there, like an invalid. Give him a glass of boiled water.

THE MAYOR: Perhaps he would read the letter with spectacles on?

MEIERHOLD: No. No use making him heavy. Read the letter without spectacles. They will hold a candle in front of him.

QUESTION: That means that the action takes place in the evening?

MEIERHOLD: Yes, in the evening. We want to make it evening.

DOBCHINSKI: After dinner, Bobchinski and Dobchinski will have been running around town the entire day.

MEIERHOLD (*to Hibner*): This is what the doctor has to do. (*Is that clean water?* ANSWER: *Yes.*) Interfere with him; give him some water from time to time in a teaspoon. You bother him, but he is obliged to take it. He takes it, sometimes he pushes it aside, sometimes he drinks it, then he takes the glass in his hands and takes several swallows, finds it is something one can drink by the tumblerful. You should say your lines in German so that your lines will get mixed up with his. This will help him slightly to get rid of his difficulty. You will set the pace. This will be the first obstacle, and you will help him to increase the pace. In direct proportion to the obstacles will arise the desire and the necessity to get rid of them. You can even speak loudly, never mind if the public hears. Keep talking constantly. He's a kind of *perpetuum mobile*. You speak in German. You see, you come from Germany. Has anyone a handkerchief or a shawl? (*He binds up the Mayor's head.*) There. You must keep near him. Tap his chest, put mustard plasters on the soles of his feet to draw the blood away from his head. Can you manage some German? Keep repeating any old sentences.

All in the foreground—over there. All are seated. The

Mayor comes in. But we shall begin quietly, after he has settled himself in his easy chair. He groans. You (*Hibner*) get ready his glass of medicine and all sorts of things. As soon as he has spoken a few lines, begin to make him drink. When they all say, "What, an Inspector-General?" they must do it all alike. Some must stagger the syllables— In-spec-tor. There should be a variety of logical accents, and also some should pronounce it briefly while others drawl it out.

"Well, for God's sake!" etc., very quick. The reaction must be quick and they do not say this in character. The public won't know anyhow who is saying what. They all sit in a crowd on the sofa, perhaps ten of them. You must soft pedal characteristics. The public won't know which is Amos Fyodorovich, or Artemus Philipovich or Luke Lukich—they all talk at once. They must blow off steam. Avdotya takes part in this. She is on her knees wiping her soles. Mishka holds a candle and the letter. Perhaps the Mayor has told him to bring him a candle and the letter.

(TO THE MAYOR): Groan. Groaning will help to heighten the tone, and immediately after you groan, say, "So that's the situation." The Mayor is in the armchair. Mishka, Avdotya, Hibner, are standing around him. This will give him the air of a generalissimo. He is a sort of tsar in this town.

(TO AMOS FYODOROVICH): "I think, Anton Antonovich, that there is some fine . . ." You should give more intonation to the expression "in your ear." I don't know how this will be on the stage. But we should have a more confidential tone, more of a word-in-your-ear effect. Nothing pensive about it, but confidential. Then you can set the tempo.

(TO HIBNER): Each time excitement affects the doctor. He calms the Mayor by saying, "Seien Sie ruhig!" and he makes gestures to restrain the persons talking. Excitement is bad for a sick man. I don't know what you will say, but say something to them and to him. This annoys the Mayor and his irritation toward the doctor gives him a chance to set the pace. The doctor has a word of admonition to each one of them and continues to fuss over the Mayor. Here we have a complication. An instructor must be called in. "Warum sprechen sie so?" or something of the sort. Hibner has a tremendous rôle. It is even bigger than the Mayor's.

(TO THE MAYOR): Make your remarks to the judge with a great deal of irritability; that will bring up the tempo. "Moreover, I just mention this . . . God will protect him" we will cut. It holds back the tempo. It's good but it's too literary. We'll do it this way. We will place you (*the Mayor*) so that you will be half-turned toward the others. Whenever you can free yourself from the ministrations of Hibner, you can be turning to someone: "And now you, Luke Lukich"—"Especially with regard to the teachers. . . ." You raise yourself up, you get up on your knees in the chair. You are all set up and on fire with expression. The fine shadings will come along by themselves here. While you are sitting up, Hibner takes advantage of your position to unfasten your trousers and apply a mustard plaster. I give you all this to help jack up the tempo.

"One of them . . ." to be said not too loud, quickly so that it will be light, and more transparent. Luke Lukich responds to the tempo. The Mayor talks but Luke Lukich does not keep silent; he says, "But what am I to do," or something of the sort. As to the inspector of schools: station yourself so that we can see the Mayor. The Mayor speaks irritably. He is annoyed that they have gone wrong. Instead of standing up in the face of what's happened, they laugh. They have become, as it were, disorganized. The Mayor not only takes the Postmaster aside but he raises himself up or leans on him and on the doctor. He talks confidentially, but quickly and loudly, so that he can be heard. You understand, he speaks confidentially but terribly hurriedly.

(To THE MAYOR): You take hold of him (*the Postmaster*) and choke him. Then it will be easier for him to struggle out of your grasp, and all the while the doctor will be grumbling, "Dieser Postmeister" . . . "Gott!"

(To THE POSTMASTER): "Now then, wait a minute, wait a minute!" He digs in his pockets. There are letters in every one. He is a walking cupboard.

Why are you lagging in tempo? Keep moving, keep moving. Let him have quantities of letters at rehearsal so that he can keep taking them out, keep rummaging around in them, sorting them, until he finds the one.

(To THE MAYOR): For the surprise it is better to stand on your feet; you go out, leaning on the doctor, and then later you appear on the stage without compresses. The doctor will help enormously and make it possible to sustain the tempo. That's much better. That's perfectly clear.

(The end of the rehearsal)

INDEX

INDEX

285